MANAH WARS
Glimmer in the Darkness

D.A. Di Muro

Manah Wars - Glimmer in the Darkness

Manah Wars, Volume 1

D.A. Di Muro

Published by BigNose Publishing & Retail, 2022.

MANAH WARS - GLIMMER IN THE DARKNESS

First edition. March 20, 2022.

ISBN: 979-8201700027

Written by D.A. Di Muro.

Table of Contents

For Selin and Selda.

Cover Illustration by Rory Fallis.

Instagram: @thebeardwheel

Etsy store: @bellwheelvintage

Darkness Rises

There is a place, deep in space, beyond the vastness of what we will ever come to know. This place is called Alteria. A planet not much bigger than our own, tidally locked to the giant star Usil and host to four moons: Lum, Lumbra, Aura and Annah. The side of the planet facing the star is scorched, and the other side is frozen, with deserts, archipelagos, oceans, and continents scattered between the two extremes. Life saturates the surface in all its forms and various sentient beings, including Humans, who steer the future of this cosmic home.

On this planet, there is a powerful source of energy known as manah. Long ago, during the Great Manah Wars, nearly all the manah on Alteria was ravaged from Nai, the giver of life. Then, according to legend, the free people of Concordia, under the leadership of Mhan, rallied the other nations of the world to help overthrow the forces of Akh, the destroyer, and his army of monsters and men. Together, they defeated Akh and Alteria entered a golden age of peace and prosperity.

But peace does not last forever. It has been a hundred years, and darkness rises in Concordia once again.

THEY CAME IN THE NIGHT. Things that had not been seen in over a hundred years crested the hill beyond Fort Bosk on the edge of Sylvinar forest. Multi-limbed creatures of ancient design, sullied by decay and pestilence, lumbered forward, hungry for living flesh. Their blight putrefied the land as they slithered over it. Rotten webs of flesh hung onto bones as maggots and weevils feasted on the funk of their hosts. Tortured voices traversed the night through the psychic aether terrifying the minds of sentient creatures.

A SOLDIER SLAMMED A fistful of cash onto a table.

"There you go. To hell with this game," said Salei, a footman no more than eighteen years old, who had enough of drinking and gambling for one night. "I want some real action for once!" he yelled as he stumbled back to the barracks.

A bellow of laughter burst out from the rotund soldiers in the foreyard.

"The young boy wants a fight!" mocked fat Yorgu. Who looked like a ball of cheese trying to squeeze out through the gaps in his hauberk.

Salei stopped in his tracks and turned around. He drew his sword.

"Aye! Put that away, or I'll gut'ya fo'real," blurted Yorgu. He stood up and fumbled for the hilt of his dagger.

"Shut up and listen," Salei yelled with his index finger to his lips, "Can you hear that noise? What is that sound? Maybe it's an attack?"

Another round of bellowed laughter roared up from the soldiers.

"The boy is so drunk he thinks me an army!" Yorgu quipped as he propped himself against the fractured wall, almost losing his footing as one of the bricks gave way under his bulk.

A pack of wild Kuns barged in through the many gaping holes around the dilapidated fort. The soldiers who sat in the foreyard gambling, eating and drinking ale, were caught off guard and torn apart by the bull sized wolves. Their screams alerted their companions in the surrounding alcoves, who took up arms in an instant.

Captain Zanzar, a Hardened Blade of the Mhan Royal Army, was well past retirement. His countenance was of a man who loved to live the manly life of testing one's resolve in combat. He was weathered and tanned, with silver hair scratched off one side of his head by the talons of a beast. He always wore his leather brigandine armour with the capital 'M' emblem for Mhan emblazoned on his chest and the silver trimming on his shoulder pads indicating his rank as Hardened. His brown eyes coursed with energy and courage as he let out a roar ordering his soldiers into formation, ready to absorb the onslaught.

Many of the soldiers were experienced veterans, familiar with bloody-thirsty combat; but, not since the Great Manah Wars had any of them fought or trained. They had become portly, lazy and rusty with their blade, spear or bow. Captain Zanzar had excused his soldiers' apathy because he felt the war was won and they deserved to relax. Unfortunately for them, they would get no respite on this night.

The Kuns continued their rampage. Their black fur camouflaged them in the dark of the night. The soldiers hacked at the beasts' leather hides as they stormed past while trying to avoid the creatures' powerful jaws. A female fighter was snatched and shaken to death by one of the damned animals.

The beasts attacked without rest, testing the soldiers' resolve; but, even after so many years of laziness, the soldiers were still strong enough to hold their ground. They kept their backs to the perimeter wall, their shields in a united front, and their spears jutting out like a barricade of gigantic thorns.

A sea of reinforcements poured out of the barracks and flanked the Kuns. Together, the fighters were able to annihilate the Kuns in a barrage of coordinated attacks, but it had little effect on the beasts' vitality. The Kuns would not die.

A Kun leapt over the barricade of shields and spears. The soldiers were flattened beneath the animal's bulk, but an up-roaring command from Captain Zanzar rallied the soldiers into a unified effort to shove off the beast. It was at this moment when the Kun was bearing down on them the soldiers noticed it was already dead. Its flesh was torn from its hide, its gums were bloody, its rotten teeth falling out, its eyes vacant, and its breath stunk of decay.

It was reanimated. It was undead.

Shiba, a young female fighter, screamed through her grimace, "What are these beasts?"

"They are your enemy. Focus and fight them!" Zanzar yelled at the woman but also wondered the same thing.

Captain Zanzar had never seen an animal that was dead yet still alive. Only in ghost stories told to scare children had he heard of such abominations. He raced through his memories, trying to remember if any of those stories spoke of how to defeat the undead.

The soldier on the eastern watch tower was frozen with terror. Her eyes transfixed on a black cloud flying through the air. The black morass of airborne terror consumed the woman. Her agonising screams saturated the air. Within seconds the swarm dissipated, leaving behind a skeleton devoid of any flesh. The cloud of death swept through the fort, feasting on the soldiers. The ground army of beasts blasted through the fort gates, tearing everything in their path to shreds. Scream, after scream, after scream, each soldier succumbed to a horrid death.

The fort was drenched in chaos and blood. The savagery shook stone blocks off the perimeter wall as if it were a bookshelf of bricks. The fort's rusty iron gate collapsed under the tsunami of the undead. The sounds of destruction reverberated across the peaceful savannah. The villagers in a nearby hamlet trembled in their beds at the frightening imaginations they conjured from what they could hear. Soon, they would be next.

Had the soldiers been in shape and fighting spirit, it may have delayed their doom long enough; they could have lit the distress beacon and warned the garrison in the City of Mhan. But alas, their deaths were swift; dealt with ruthless efficiency. No one was left alive.

In his final moments, Captain Zanzar thought of all the things he wished he had done with his life: to have travelled the Great Ocean; to have visited the beautiful city of Uro; to have married a wonderful woman; to have fathered charming children; to have grown old, and wise. It was too late to retire now. Had he not been so addicted to meat, ale and gambling, he may have left sooner and have avoided his death and lived out his dreams. Instead, his last thoughts as the jaws of a Kun crushed his skull were those of regret.

In ten days, it would be The Ritual. It would signal the end of all living things was nigh. It was only a matter of time before everyone and everything would die.

On the horizon, a tall, shadowy figure draped in a rustic, brown tunic, who held an ancient, gnarly staff, vanished into the darkness of Sylvinar Forest.

THE UNDULATING CANOPY of Sylvinar forest was iridescent green. It underlined the vibrant, purple horizon which bled golden hues as Lumbra eclipsed Lum, ushering in the darkness of night. The soft sound of pattering raindrops filled the air murmuring in ancient, rhythmic tongues. The golden moon Aura was visible in the cloudless sky. Her soft light textured and rendered the landscape of Concordia with a beautiful warmth. This vision of colours and light signalled the transitioning cusp of the month of Kria to Shinar.

The massive Mhan river flowed out of the western edge of Sylvinar forest. The river commenced its journey from the natural geyser Agwa'den at the southern end of the woods. The river cut its way north by north-west through the forest, turned west at Sylvinar city, then flowed through the savannah towards the high mountain range where Castle Mhan's mountainous presence thrust out of the ground with regal authority.

Aedan's crimson eyes glowed like burning coals in the darkness of the impenetrable night, absorbing the sight from his vantage point. He was perched at the peak of his massive home tree in the city of Sylvinar. The rain trickled down his earthen skin, moistening his tunic with each cordial drop. He pulled on the cuffs of his fibrous boots because he enjoyed the feeling of the rope-weaved soles on his feet. He loved the period following the life-giving month of Kria when Nai's waters melted away from the mountain tops under the scorching heat of Lum. Shinar ushered in a new generation of critters and creatures in the forest. Aedan would be filled with joy witnessing the fauna grow over the following cycles. But tonight, Aedan's mind was deep in thought, for tomorrow, his life would change forever.

Aedan's people, the Sa'ami, were considered one of the most traditional races on Alteria. A tribal civilisation with a patriarchal society and a close affinity for nature. Boys grew up to either be warriors, priests or tradesmen. To be a warrior you had to pass The Trial of The Depths. Afterwards, you earned the title of Campesino: the official title for a Sa'ami warrior. The Trials, as the Sa'ami called it, was the coming-of-age ritual for all Sa'ami boys. Those who failed The Trials, or chose not to attempt it, would become priests of Nai or specialise in a trade. Being a warrior was the highest honour.

Aedan was eighteen years old. Old enough to attempt The Trials. He would no longer be a boy if he passed the trials. He would be a man of the people.

Aedan was alerted to a presence. Someone was coming up behind him. He knew who. He turned and smiled at Ferni. She was trying to sneak up on him but made too much noise shaking the foliage on the branch she was climbing.

Ferni quipped, "You're like a wild Kun. I can never sneak up on you. Just once, I'd like to surprise you." She smiled, sat down next to Aedan, and rested her head on his shoulder.

"I'm worried about tomorrow," Aedan thought out loud.

"Don't be. I know you can do it," Ferni comforted him, "I am so sure of it that I am going to be a Maiden of the Festival."

Aedan startled and turned to Ferni, "What? You can't do that. What if Kainan completes the trial and I don't?" His mind raced at the possibility, and his heart pounded against his chest. Finally, he pleaded, "I am not sure I can complete the trial. I am too tall and lanky. Please, Ferni, wait until after the trial, and we will get bonded in private."

"No," Ferni opposed, "I want to be a Maiden of The Festival. I've always wanted to be one. It has been a dream of mine since I was two years old." Ferni leaned towards Aedan's lips. Her body pressed against his. Her long, golden hair fell over her shoulders. She stared into his soul with her crystal-clear, blue eyes. He could not control himself. Aedan gulped and leaned in to kiss her. Ferni pulled back. Aedan looked at her with burning desire and confusion.

"If you want me, then make sure you finish the trials before anyone else picks me," Ferni whispered in his ear, "I'm off to bed." She stood up and walked away. As she climbed down from the canopy onto the lower branches, she gave Aedan a wink and a perfect smile. At that point, Aedan had no doubt in his mind he would pass the trials, for he loved Ferni with all his heart.

Just below, on a branch in the tree across from where Aedan sat, Kainan watched seething. Kainan would never let Aedan have Ferni. He would rather die than come second to his younger brother.

SYLVINAR CITY LOOKED like an enormous spider's web weaved amongst the majestic trees of the forest. Rope bridges and makeshift, wooden walkways co-joined each cyclopean tree to the next. The city was an organic, crafted patchwork of wood, rope and vine. Sylvinar was an earthen city full of carts, tables, chairs, huts, alcoves, houses, stables, farmyards and schools embedded into the environment, melding the metropolis and the forest together. Sylvinar spanned an area greater than most cities in Alteria, not just across but also in vertical stature. But, unlike the crammed footprint of more affluent cities, Sylvinar was not crowded.

The trees stood like massive, monumental pillars that held up the sky, so tall they vanished into the air above. The gigantic tress provided thousands of homes for the totality of the populace. Some of the homes were wooden extensions propped up against the gargantuan trunks with complex cantilevers. Other homes were carved into the trees, with each enormous branch serving as a room for the inhabitants. Younger families tended to be housed in extensions, whereas older generations were allocated the more sensible inner dwellings.

Every single citizen of Sylvinar was a Sa'ami. An adult Sa'ami resembled a human adolescent in height and build. They remained teenage in appearance for their entire lives, with wrinkles and grey hair providing the only indication they had aged. Other races referred to them as baby humans, which the Sa'ami found quite offensive as they were neither humans nor babies. The Sa'ami lived stress-free lives with an affinity for nature. They were most happy with homemade bread, cheese and tea in their bellies. They loved to sit around a warm fire in the company of family and friends. Outside of Sylvinar, the Sa'ami were far and few between, with only a handful having ventured east and settled in Antillia.

Sylvinar city was alive on this first day of Shinar, the first month of new life and rebirth. The entire population of Sylvinar was on the move. They were all heading towards the Great Amphitheatre, built on the cusp between Sylvinar city and The Depths. The Great Amphitheatre was so large it could host the entire population of Sylvinar.

Aedan slept. He tossed and turned at the persistent rumbling that kept rousing him from his sleep. Then he was slapped! The stinging strike on his right cheek awakened him with a shock. It was his diminutive father, Eldoran, in his royal white cape, hobbled over his artisan-crafted walking stick, peering through his thick glasses, which made his eyes look like black beads suspended in a crystal ball. His face looked like someone was squeezing it from the sides forcing his skin to have wrinkles upon wrinkles.

"You moron. Wake up! All you could talk about was The Festival of the Ages, and now that it is here, you want to sleep through it!?" Eldoran blurted as he pointed his index finger right at Aedan's face.

"Just leave him dad. He does not deserve to participate in the games. Why embarrass yourself by letting him enter?" snorted Kainan, Aedan's fraternal twin brother, who was born two minutes before Aedan.

"Shut up. I'm not talking to you. You better focus on today lest Aedan beat you at every game there is. I've seen your form slipping. Now get out of here!" Eldoran snapped at Kainan and shoved him away.

Kainan strutted around for a while with his chest puffed out, running his fingers through his short blond hair. Then, finally, he exited the room, grumbling, "Whatever you wish, father."

Aedan mumbled, "For Nai's sake. Is it morning already? When's breakfast?"

"I'll breakfast you in a second if you don't get dressed in your formal Campesino garb and present yourself for the games. I think you sometimes forget I rule Sylvinar and don't have the time to be chasing you around like a child anymore. Now get ready and present yourself on time." Eldoran kicked Aedan and knocked him off the bed.

Aedan howled when he landed on the floor. "Alright. I'm coming. What about Ferni? Is she coming too?"

Eldoran stopped at the door with a troubled look on his face. He responded in a soft voice. "Yes she is, but your mind should be on the games, and more importantly, The Trial," as he closed the oak door behind him.

Aedan picked himself off the ground and started to get dressed in his traditional clothes, just like all the other Sa'ami boys participating in the festival. He wore a tight, white, sleeveless shirt; a pair of dark greenie brown pants; a matching, hooded tunic; a couple of knee-high, brown boots with many buckled straps; and an ornate, thin, leather belt riddled in ancient runes. He hooked his hunting axe through the left side of his belt, placed his hunting knife behind his waist in its scabbard, fastened his quiver and bow on his back, and looped his climbing rope through a latch on the right side of his belt.

Aedan checked himself in the mirror to make sure everything was in place. He wanted to present well for the games. He could not bear to have to listen to Eldoran complaining again. Even though he loved Eldoran, the old Sa'ami got on his nerves sometimes.

Aedan darted out the door, flung himself over the balustrade, slid down the stairway railing to the bottom of his home tree, and vanished into the crowd making their way to the Great Amphitheatre.

Festival of the Ages

Eldoran stood before the entirety of the Sylvinarian tribespeople who had amassed in the Great Amphitheatre. He cleared his throat and projected his voice, like a thunderclap, across the vast ocean of people above him, below him, and all around him.

"Welcome to The Festival of the Ages!" Eldoran boomed.

The audience cheered, whistled and clapped. The excitement in the air was palpable. Little Sylvinarians, only a year old, looked around in awe as this was their first festival. They had never seen such a massive congregation and so much excitement before. Some of the little ones joined in the cheering, others were scared, but most went bonkers. Finally, after a few minutes of unbridled celebration, the crowd settled.

Eldoran elucidated, "Over the next five days, we will celebrate the arrival of Shinar and the wondrous life that flows forth from the beauty of our beloved Nai. We remember, with each and every second, we live because Nai gives us life. So, we celebrate with fun, festivities and games. Tomorrow, those who wish to join the ranks of men, and become great Campesino warriors, will embark upon The Trial of the Depths. It will be a long and perilous journey, taking a grand total of four days. One day down. One day to retrieve a scale from a Traxy. And two days to ascend back up to Sylvinar city. Only the smartest, bravest and most resourceful Sa'ami will return victorious!" Eldoran punctuated the final word with emphasis, eliciting another great applause from the kaleidoscope of people before him.

Eldoran continued to talk over the applause, which subsided with each syllable he spoke. “Tomorrow at sunrise, we will begin The Trial in this very amphitheatre, but until then, today, near the amphitheatre, many of the contestants will be versing one another in various games of skill in a demonstration of respect and sportsmanship. So, let the games begin!”

The crowd responded with a final, conclusive cheer as Eldoran walked backstage to his quarters where Kainan was waiting for him.

Kainan approached his father with his arms spread wide and a broad smile on his face, “Great speech father. You really know how to rally the masses.”

Eldoran threw off his formal cape. “Don’t call them masses you nincompoop. They are your fellow Sa’ami and you must never look down upon them.”

“Sorry father. I just meant you are a great leader. They don’t deserve you,” said Kainan as he waved his hands towards the stadium entrance.

Eldoran grumbled in response to Kainan’s sycophantic behaviour. “Yes, well, you need to think before you speak, lest you offend an entire nation with your blabber-hole. As heir apparent, you need to learn how to lead and learn quickly, for I will not be around forever.” Eldoran then realised Aedan had not yet arrived and lambasted, “Where in the blazes is Aedan?”

As if on cue, Aedan burst in through the door, slid across the polished floor, and skidded to a stop. He huffed and puffed, “Whoa, there’s lots of people out there. I’m really sorry I missed your speech, but....”

Eldoran snorted, “I don’t want to hear it.”

“But...” Aedan pleaded.

“Shut up,” Eldoran barked, pointing at Aedan, “Enough of this whinging and whining from you. Sorry this and sorry that. I haven’t spent my entire life raising you, not to know you are capable of so much more. Listen, the both of you. I know you don't get along, but you are brothers, and I expect you to help each other during The Trial. We Sa'ami find our strength in our unity with one another, not in our competition."

Aedan and Kainan looked at each other in reflex and then back at their father.

Eldoran demanded, "Promise me you will not let anything petty stand between you two, and you will support one another?"

Aedan and Kainan both nodded in agreement.

Eldoran continued talking. "Now go get ready for the first game which starts in less than twenty minutes. Otherwise, I don't care how old you are; I will bend you over my knee and spank you in front of everyone. Now get out of here!"

Aedan and Kainan bolted out the door while shoving each other out of the way.

Eldoran shook his head and spoke to himself. "What am I going to do with these two idiots? Oh Nai, give me strength." He then hobbled over to his desk and picked up a note which lay there. He read it:

> *Urgent. I must see you before tomorrow. It cannot wait. Refusal to listen will have grave consequences. Meet me at fourteen o'clock, just before the archery event. Grandor.*

Eldoran folded up the note and tucked it into his robe. He looked out the window, deep in thought, his mind full of worry.

AEDAN RAN AHEAD OF Kainan. Kainan grabbed one of Aedan's legs and tripped him. Aedan fell face down in the dirt. Kainan jumped on top of Aedan and grabbed him by the collar.

Kainan menaced Aedan. "I saw you and Ferni last night. Don't think I'm an idiot. I know what you're doing."

Aedan pleaded, "What's it to you what me and Ferni do?"

Kainan raised his voice and tightened his grip on Aedan's collar, "You know I want her. You are not the eldest. You are not the heir. Show some respect and back off!"

Passers-by stopped and started to surround them. Everyone in Sylvinar knew who they were. The potential gossip was far too juicy for the citizens to ignore.

"I'm sorry brother, but Ferni loves me, and I her. That is all there is to it," said Aedan, his eyes full of passion.

Kainan yelled back, and he shoved Aedan into the dirt, "Don't lie you wretch. Ever since you knew I wanted her, you have been making moves on her. You just want to ruin my life!"

Kainan raised his right fist to punch Aedan.

Aedan thrust his hands between Kainan's arms and rolled him over onto his back. They started to wrestle. The spectators murmured to one another. Some of the citizens laughed and pointed.

Aedan blurted. "You fool, I'm not competing with you. She loves me and I love her. That is all."

Kainan used all of his available strength to manoeuvre himself behind Aedan and started choking him.

Kainan blurted through clenched teeth, "I will finish the trial first, and I will pick her as a soulmate. Not you."

Kainan was kicked in the face, and he fell off Aedan.

Ferni stood over him and yelled, "Get off him!"

Kainan was shocked back into reality. He looked around at the sea of glaring faces.

Kainan pleaded. "No, we were just playing a game. Tell her, brother."

Aedan, gasping, nodded and replied. "That's right. It's nothing. It's part of a play we are working on."

"Oh, shut up Aedan. You don't need to defend him. He thinks I am a trophy to be won and to be owned," said Ferni.

Ferni walked over to Aedan, knelt next to him and stroked his face. Then, she looked over at Kainan and said, "You will never have me, Kainan, and with your attitude, you will never have anyone."

Kainan stood up in a huff. He yelled at the crowd, "What are you all looking at?" and stormed off.

"I swear, we were just rehearsing a play," Aedan quipped, with a smirk on his face.

There was a slight chuckle from the crowd as it dissipated. Some of the people murmured, "What a spoiled brat. It's a shame Aedan wasn't born before Kainan."

Ferni helped Aedan stand up. "Why do you defend him? He is a fool, and one day he will kill you in a fit of rage."

Aedan laughed. "He won't kill me. Besides, he is very upset. I understand. He is jealous, but he is my brother, and I will never turn on him even if he turns on me."

Ferni leaned into Aedan. She touched Aedan on the cheek. Her hand felt as gentle as a butterfly landing on a flower. "Be careful, my sweetheart. Now get going; you have a game on in five minutes."

"Oh, Nai! See ya!" Aedan stole a kiss on her cheek and ran off. He looked back at her for a split second and gave her a wink.

Ferni blew him a kiss.

The Race

Twelve ropes made of vine dangled, equidistant from each other, around a large tree. They vanished upwards into the canopy—twelve ropes for twelve contestants. The ropes were made from the robust and fibrous vines of the Dredloq tree. The Sa'ami thanked Nai for this gift of nature, for without it, their entire way of life would not exist.

Aedan presented himself to the game official with only a few seconds to spare before registration closed.

"Aedan's the name. Climbing's my game," he joked.

The official, a senior Sa'ami who'd seen it all before, peered over his sap-framed, reading spectacles, snorted in derision, and said, "Very well, you made it, position Number 12 next to Kainan over there." The official smirked, knowing the rivalry between the two. Really, who didn't?

Aedan took his place next to Kainan. They stood within the hollow tree trunk, facing outwards. In front of each of them was a curtain made from large leaves. Aedan snuck a glance at his brother, who ignored him and glared ahead.

"Good luck," Aedan said, offering his hand to Kainan.

Kainan did not respond.

The official entered and addressed the contestants. "Soon, the curtains will be pulled back, and each of you will be announced to the crowd. Please step forward, wave your hand and smile at the crowd when your name is called. Then take your place behind your starting line. We will call ready, set and drop a petardo. When the petardo bangs, run to the rope in front of you and climb as fast as you can. Retrieve the coloured cloth from the canopy and return it to the bottom as fast as possible. The first one to touch the ground with any part of their body while holding onto the cloth will be declared the winner. You may not use the tree or any other object except for the rope to climb, and on the way down, you must always be in contact with the rope." The official paused to add emphasis to his final point. "Falling to the ground is not considered a legal descent. Does everyone understand?"

Everyone nodded except for Kainan.

The official asked Kainan. "How about you, sir, do you understand?"

Kainan barked back. "Just do your job, fool."

The official was unperturbed by the animosity and continued with the ceremony.

Aedan said to Kainan, "You don't need to be so rude brother."

Kainan gave him a death stare.

Trumpets blared, and the curtains in front of them rose. The official called each of their names in turn. Each one stepped forward, smiled and waved. Different sections of the crowd cheered for each participant representing their borough in Sylvinar city.

When Kainan's name was called out, he stood there without moving, not even bothering to acknowledge anyone. The cheering subsided. The crowd went quiet.

The official continued. "In the Number 12 position, we have the second son of Eldoran. Aedan."

The crowd went bonkers. Even those who had cheered for other participants joined in to show their love and support for Aedan. Aedan waved and smiled. He soaked it all up.

He spotted Ferni jumping up and down, cheering for him. He scanned the crowd looking for his father. He spotted Eldoran, who was shaking his head in disapproval. Aedan gesticulated at him, mouthing, "What?" Eldoran walked away, out of the viewing platform. Aedan's spirit sank.

"I wouldn't worry too much. It's better he doesn't see your lame attempt. With your lanky body, I will be surprised if you even finish," said Kainan.

Aedan was affected by the words. He lowered his head.

"On your marks," called the official.

Each contestant took their place.

The official continued, "Ready... set... and...."

He dropped a petardo: a tiny, white flake from the Poppinore shrub. It floated down to the ground, dancing through the air, its little mass swaying to and fro. When it touched the ground, it made a deafening bang!

Kainan shoved Aedan as he bolted forward. The shove was enough to throw Aedan off balance, so he was the last one to reach his rope. The contestants climbed up their ropes like hyperactive caterpillars. The very short contestants seemed to be having a fit. Their bodies stretched and compressed at a blinding pace. Kainan was leading the race with two other contestants.

Aedan was last and struggling to keep up. He was too tall to be as quick as the rest of his colleagues. He kept cursing his own body as he climbed. How he wished he was shorter, like a normal Sa'ami. *I am such a freak*, he thought to himself. He could feel Ferni's disappointment from across the crowd. *Why does she love me?* He thought. Maybe it was all a ruse to make Kainan jealous, and at the end of The Trial, she would choose Kainan? Then, he remembered how Ferni kicked Kainan in the head, and it cheered him up. He shook off his sadness and focused on what was going on around him. He thought to himself, *Climb! Climb, you idiot!*

Aedan focused his efforts. Rather than trying to climb faster, which he could not do as well as the rest, he climbed stronger. With each heave, he pulled his body up as far as possible, latching his feet around the rope. He then used his height to leap upwards, propelling himself farther than any other contestants could. With each movement, he climbed twice as high as his competitors. Aedan was galloping into the lead as everyone else struggled to keep up.

Kainan was halfway up the enormous rope with the end in sight. He looked down to laugh at everyone else but, instead, saw Aedan gaining on him. This shocked Kainan into overdrive. He pushed his body to the limit. He had never climbed this fast in his entire life.

Aedan was at Kainan's heels. All the other competitors had fallen far behind. As Aedan and Kainan approached the top, two officials perched above the canopy, watching hawk-eyed, ensuring neither Aedan nor Kainan broke any rules.

Aedan made a final push with more strength than he was able to muster before. He launched himself towards the green cloth at the top of his rope. His leap was so powerful he grabbed his cloth just before Kainan grabbed his one. Aedan began to drop but managed to wrap his left arm around the rope to control his descent. Kainan opted to hook his legs around the rope, hurtling, facedown, towards the bottom.

Kainan thought he would rather have all his teeth pulled out one by one than lose to Aedan. Climbing was Kainan's strength, and he was not about to let some lanky loser, let alone Aedan, take that away from him.

Aedan and Kainan were eye to eye as they shot past the other contestants. Then, Kainan spat in Aedan's face. Aedan wiped the saliva out of his eyes and, when he cleared his vision, he saw Kainan at the bottom. Kainan had won.

Kainan held his cloth up high. Few in the audience cheered, then the crowd went wild! Kainan smirked until he saw Aedan walk ahead of him, holding up his cloth. The crowd was cheering for Aedan's second place, not for Kainan's victory. A young official ushered them to the podium and told them to hold their place until their names were called. Kainan exchanged some private words with the official.

One by one, the remaining contestants arrived.

"You're a cheater!" Aedan snapped at Kainan.

"Really? You must be dreaming. I beat you because I am better than you. I am pretty sure you are the one who cheated Aedan," Kainan said with a smug look on his face.

One of the two officials at the summit approached Aedan and said, "I'm sorry, son, you have been disqualified."

"What? Why?" Aedan asked.

"According to the rules, you must always be in contact with the rope on your way down. But, unfortunately, as Kainan pointed out, you did leap upwards and drop a couple of metres downwards before engaging with the rope. As such, by definition, you were not always in contact with the rope on your way down. I'm sorry, son. Please step away from the podium and come with me to the waiting room," said the official.

Aedan followed the official without further questions. He was not going to give Kainan any pleasure by showing emotion.

"Look, Ferni. Your hero is a cheater!" hollered Kainan at Ferni from behind the podium.

Ferni was unsure what was happening, so she ran down to meet with Aedan in the waiting room. As the awards ceremony took place outside, Ferni and Aedan spoke in the waiting room.

Aedan explained to Ferni. "He tripped me at the start, and then on the way down, he spat in my face. I was going to win, no doubt about it."

Ferni was puzzled and asked. "So why did you get disqualified? I don't understand."

"They didn't see what he did but, apparently, I fell from the top a couple of metres which is against the rules of contact with the rope,"

Aedan said, waving his hands in frustration. "That may be true, but it feels like I am the one who has been robbed. I am not a cheater."

"I believe you," said Ferni with a reassuring smile on her face.

Eldoran burst through the door dragging Kainan by the ear. Eldoran grabbed Aedan's ear as well, twisting it with an almighty heave. Ferni smirked at the sight of these two soon-to-be-men being treated like insolent children by their father.

"What did I do!?" yelled Aedan.

"Stop embarrassing me!" demanded Kainan.

Eldoran exploded into an uncharacteristic fit of anger, throwing them both down onto the floor and yelling at them. "I should have you both banished and never to return. You disgraceful twits! Didn't you think your idiotic fight would get back to my ears?" Eldoran pointed at Kainan. "You tell me to stop embarrassing you? You have made a mockery of yourself and this family with your behaviour. People are saying you were choking your brother in public. Trying to kill him!"

"That's not true," pleaded Kainan.

"Shut up! I am talking now." Eldoran continued ranting. "And you, Aedan. I expect more from you. How could you stoop to his level?"

"What?" said Kainan and escalated his voice. "Expect more from him? Stoop to my level? What is that supposed to mean? Oh, I get it. He's better than me. Am I that worthless father? You have always hated me and have always loved him more. Well, I hate you, father. I hate you with all my heart." He turned to Ferni. "And you, how can you want to be with him? He's not the heir. I am the heir! He doesn't care for you. I care for you!" Then, with a final whimper, he said, "I hate all of you," and stormed out of the room.

Eldoran mumbled, "What have I done?"

Aedan comforted his father. "Nothing, father. You just spoke your mind, and he became angry. He does it to me all the time."

"You be quiet," Eldoran snapped back. "It all came out wrong. He is my son, and I didn't mean what I said. I meant. Oh, I don't know what I meant. I was angry." Eldoran paused for a bit. "Listen, Aedan, one day you will understand. Things will not turn out the way you expect them to or want them to. There are too many things wrong that I need to make right." Eldoran left the room with his head low.

Aedan asked Ferni, "What do you think he means by that?"

"I don't know," Ferni said with a furrowed brow.

AEDAN COULD SEE ELDORAN in the official's tent through a slight opening in the entry flap. Aedan wanted to walk in and ask his father what he meant when he spoke earlier. Aedan wasn't sure if it would be rude to pry; after all, he remembered what happened when he asked Eldoran if he missed mother since she had passed away; and, Eldoran smacked him that day. Eldoran was a sensitive father. It was always difficult to know what to say, how to say it, and when to say it.

A dark figure crossed Aedan's line of sight. It startled him. He leapt back while making nary a sound, took a moment to calm down, and peeked in again. The dark figure stood in the tent talking with his father. The figure was tall, wore a long, brown tunic with a hood. Who was this? They were not a Sa'ami because they towered over Eldoran. The gnarly staff in their hand was taken from a sacred Karkeha tree. That meant it was most likely a druid underneath the tunic. Sure enough, the brown leather satchel they carried bore the leaf symbol of the druidic grove from Agwa'den. The grove was located in the deep south of Sylvinar Forest. What was a druid from Agwa'den doing here?

Aedan crept into the tent until he was within earshot. The druid and his father were arguing.

"We will not abandon the city. There is nothing you say which frightens us," Eldoran said with a fist to his chest.

"You do not understand. No one will be left alive. When evil descends upon this place, it will consume every living soul. So for once in your life, do not be so stubborn and heed good advice when it is given to you, old Sa'ami." The hooded figure spoke with a deep, masculine voice.

"Yes, I understand. I understand perfectly. I also understand this is our forest, and no one knows its secrets as well as we do. We will resist any threat which impedes our sovereignty. I am certain Mhan will send reinforcements if we need them. There is nothing you say which will dissuade me." Eldoran stepped closer to the druid who towered over him.

"You are foolish to believe you completely understand the situation," added the mysterious man.

Aedan had to lean forward to hear better.

The druid continued, "I have come here to give you the opportunity to save your entire people before the end arrives." The man turned his head and spotted Aedan.

Aedan froze in fear. His eyes locked with the man's eyes. The druid had a weathered face, which looked like it had lived a thousand lifetimes yet was lively and youthful. The man pretended he had not seen Aedan and walked out of the room with his head held high.

As he exited, the druid said to Eldoran, "You *know* why this is happening. You are unable to keep the boy a secret forever. You must tell him. You must evacuate now, or we all die," then he was gone.

Eldoran sat down with his back to where Aedan was hiding. Eldoran mumbled incomprehensible profanities regarding the druid's fearmongering.

Aedan was scared by the druid's threats and thought if he should reveal himself and ask his father what was going on. But, if he did reveal himself, Aedan considered how much trouble he would be in and decided, best, to sneak out and ask after the festival.

Eldoran turned around and saw the tent flap swinging. He shot up out of his chair, darted over to the flap, stuck his head outside, but saw nothing.

Eldoran spoke to himself. “Now I’m also going mad. Just what I need.”

Champion of the People

Eldoran peered over the cascading crowd in front of him. The audience's attire was a kaleidoscope of flowers and forest flora. The Sa'ami always wore colourful garb for events like this. The officials' box Eldoran sat in was constructed a little too low for his tastes. He always had to stand on tiptoe to see the line of archers at the base of the stadium.

Eldoran was looking forward to the archery game because it was Aedan's forte. He could see Ferni, a few rows down, clutching onto her father's hand in excitement. Eldoran liked Ferni. She was from his favourite family. Her father was good friends with him. He knew her personality was a perfect match for Aedan; yet, once the truth came out, he doubted very much even Ferni would go against her father's wishes. Maybe it would all work out some way, maybe it wouldn't, and maybe he should just evacuate the city back to Mhan. Everything was weighing on his mind.

"Dad, are you ok?" Aedan whispered as he sat next to his father, placing a hand on his shoulder.

Eldoran was shocked back to reality by his son's voice and replied with a croak. "Oh, son, what are you doing here? Shouldn't you be registering for the event?"

"I already have. I just wanted to see if everything was ok." Aedan asked with a gentle breath.

Putting on a stoic face, Eldoran replied. "Of course. What makes you say that?"

"Nothing, father. I am just worried something is wrong," said Aedan.

Blast! How does he know what I am thinking? Eldoran thought to himself but then replied. "No everything is fine. You just go and win this game. I want to see you win." Eldoran smiled with pursed lips and waved Aedan to go away.

Aedan complied and headed down to the archery field.

At the base of the stadium stood twelve contestants at the end of their respective archery ranges. There was a target, twenty metres in front of each contestant. The contestants held their bows ready, with quivers on their backs replete with arrows.

An official addressed the crowd through her trunket: a trumpet-like device made from a tree trunk. "Each contestant has five seconds, from the sound of each horn, to shoot their arrow. Let us begin."

Each contestant placed one of their hands on an arrow in their quiver, tense with anticipation. All were focused on the bullseye in front of them. It was an easy shot. No one was expected to miss, but every contestant treated the moment as if their lives depended on it.

Aedan stole a glance to his left and saw Kainan grimacing as if some deep-driven anger was fuelling his competitive spirit.

I wonder if he'll ever stop being such a grumpy-bum, Aedan thought to himself.

As if hearing Aedan's thoughts, Kainan glanced to his right and caught Aedan's gaze. Aedan smiled at Kainan.

Blaaaah! The horn sounded.

Without missing a beat, Aedan drew an arrow and released it. It travelled straight and true, hitting the bullseye.

Kainan was not ready for the start of the competition. He fumbled for an arrow and took an awkward shot. It wobbled in the air as it traversed the very short distance to the target, landing just outside the bullseye. An official approached Kainan and tapped him on the shoulder. He was out of the competition.

Kainan argued with the official, making hand gestures indicating he believed the arrow was on the line and therefore hit the bullseye. The official waved off the protests and signalled for Kainan to exit.

Aedan was watching the commotion as the second horn sounded.

Blaaaah!

The target was now at thirty metres. Again, without much thought, Aedan fired an arrow. He did not even bother to look if it would hit the bullseye. He knew it would. He turned his attention back to Kainan, who was being herded away by a group of officials. Kainan made a beheading gesture with his right hand and pointed at Aedan.

Blaaaah! The third horn sounded.

The target was now at forty metres. Aedan took a quick shot and looked up to see if he could spot Eldoran. He made eye contact with his father and waved. Eldoran gesticulated at Aedan to focus on the competition and stop mucking around.

Blaaaah! The fourth horn sounded.

The target was now at fifty metres. Aedan took an extra tick of time to align his shot and let the arrow go. It travelled a slight, parabolic trajectory finishing its arc in the dead centre of the target. Aedan looked up at Ferni, who waved back in excitement. Aedan mimed an exaggerated firing motion, then struck a hero pose with his hands on his hips. Ferni cracked up laughing.

Aedan cut a very animated, jovial presence amongst all the other competitors who were serious and focused on the task at hand. To him, it was all fun and games. Because, as a small boy, he always loved archery, and it was natural to him, he never felt it challenged him that much. As a result, he never took it seriously like the other Sa'ami, who treated it like a religion.

Blaaaah! The fifth horn sounded.

The target was now at sixty metres. Aedan focused and fired his arrow. A couple of the other competitors were eliminated and ushered off the pitch. Aedan stood tall to see who they were. Fat Frango, as everyone called him, waddled away with a big smile on his face. Frango was never upset. His big brown eyes and huge smile always radiated from underneath his long, black, curly locks. He was a good kid. He would never become a warrior but could focus on the arcane or religious texts. Silvian looked unhappy; he was an excellent archer with strong back muscles, short blond hair, piercing brown eyes and an open countenance. Aedan was expecting him to reach the seventh horn in the competition.

Blaaaah! The sixth horn sounded.

The target was now at seventy metres. Few of the contestants would make this shot. Aedan aimed and cleared his mind. He was thinking of nothing, just the arrow and the target. He sensed what it would feel like to release the arrow; to see it travel through the air; to curve, and land in the dead-centre of the target. Aedan released the arrow just as he finished visualising what would happen. Sure enough, it did.

All the competitors were knocked out, bar Aedan and two others. Miriam was a squat Sa'ami girl, with green eyes, brown hair in a ponytail and freckled face, who practised day and night. She had earned her skill through hard work and dedication. Aedan felt sorry, knowing he would beat her. Jonin looked just like Aedan but a tad shorter with blue eyes. He was also a gifted archer who seemed never to miss a shot. But, unlike Aedan, Jonin doubted himself. He was worried Aedan would win. Deep down, Jonin believed Aedan was the best archer in all of Sylvinar.

Blaaaah! The seventh horn sounded.

The target was now at eighty metres. Aedan pulled the arrow back, taking a deep breath into his lungs. As his hand reached the end of its backward motion, he held his breath and, within a moment, took aim; his visualisation complete, he released the arrow. He tracked it with his eyes as it travelled through the air. It seemed to correct itself in mid-flight. So was his skill that his shots defied logic. The arrow landed smack-bang in the middle of the bullseye.

Miriam's shot landed just outside the bullseye. The pressure got the better of her. She received a standing ovation from the crowd as she was ushered off the pitch.

Jonin hit the bullseye. Just. He was sweaty and nervous, having just made the shot. He took a deep breath and tried to calm himself. He looked at Aedan and nodded. Aedan returned the gesture.

Miriam crossed her fingers, hoping they would both misfire. No one ever did. Contestants would miss the bullseye, but no one ever misfired. But she hoped today would be an exception to history.

"On your marks," boomed the announcer.

Jonin and Aedan both drew an arrow and placed it against their bows. Aedan studied the air in front of him as if he could see undulations in its viscosity no one else could see.

Kainan had made his way, under the stadium, towards the front row of seats. He aimed a mouth dart at Aedan's neck.

The announcer continued, "Draw your bows and...."

The announcer's voice trailed off as time slowed down for Aedan. He drew his arrow back, flush against his cheek. Without a doubt in his mind, he knew, when the horn sounded, he would hit the target.

Blaaaah! On the horn, Kainan struck Aedan's neck with a tiny, sharp pebble.

Aedan shrugged his shoulders at the slight distraction. He released the arrow right on the horn. The arrow was off-target, but as it travelled further along its trajectory, it went on-target. It landed in the pinpoint middle of the bullseye.

Jonin's arrow landed a centimetre off-centre. His head dropped in disappointment.

The crowd went wild!

Aedan jumped up in excitement. Even though he felt all along he would win, he still could not believe it happened. Then, he remembered something had struck his neck. He rubbed his hand where he felt the sting. He checked his hand. There was a trace amount of blood on his fingers. He figured it must have been a tabano, stinging fly and gave it no more thought. Ferni, who had run down from the stadium, leapt onto him and hugged him.

"I knew you would win! I think everyone in the crowd just knew it!" squealed Ferni.

Aedan was led away by an official. Ferni blew him a kiss.

Eldoran smiled to himself and then spoke to one of the officials nearby. "Where's Kainan gone too? That damn fool is surely brooding over this. Tell him to come here and speak with me at once."

The official hesitated.

Eldoran barked. "Well, don't just stand there like a bombadded dune-goat. Hurry up and find him now!"

The official sprinted off one way, then another, unsure of what direction he should be going.

Kainan sat beneath the stadium crying. His fists were clenched, white with rage. Not only had he been humiliated in front of everyone he knew, but Aedan had also won Ferni's heart.

Aedan tricked me into looking at him. Aedan distracted me so I would miss the first shot. The easiest shot. He made me the laughingstock of Sylvinar!

Kainan felt he would never live this down. He hated Aedan so much he would do anything, anything at all, to make sure Aedan did not complete The Trial.

The medals for the archery event were awarded with much pomp and celebration. Horns blared, petal-confetti dropped, and vine-streamers shot out of petardo cones. Aedan revelled in the adulation and was happy to see Ferni so excited for him.

Eldoran greeted Aedan when he stepped down from the podium. Eldoran, for a moment, had forgotten about all the burdens he carried and was able to offer a warm smile to his second son. "Aedan, you are a little rascal. Only you can win without even trying and, at the same time, win the support of the entire populace. Well done, my son. I am proud of you."

Aedan replied, "it is because of your love father that I do what I do."

"Don't take me for a fool, son. I know who's love really drives you." Eldoran mused while glancing over at Ferni. At that point, he remembered Aedan and Ferni would never be together, so he mumbled to Aedan. "But we must grow, and we must learn. Some things are just simply not exactly how we hoped they would be. And even though that may be the case, well, there is a reason and a purpose to our existence which may lead to a future which, if we are open to it, could be more satisfying than the one we have imagined for ourselves."

Aedan was confused by his father's rambling, so he queried, "I'm sorry, dad, I have no idea what you just said. Can you repeat it?"

"This is not the time or the place. But, I promise, I will tell you after The Trial. You are exceptional, and I am sure you will embrace your gifts," said Eldoran.

Aedan's interest was piqued at this point. "Oh, come on, dad, tell me. What is it? Did you get me a present or something? Is Kainan adopted?"

"Cut that out! He is your brother, no matter what happens. So don't make fun of him," Eldoran ordered, back to his usual, stern self, adding more orders. "Now clean yourself up, and I will see you tonight at home. Don't waste too much time daydreaming, or I will make you hand-wash all of our clothes for the next hundred years!"

"Yes, dad!" Replied Aedan as he scurried off with Ferni.

Family & Tradition

Eldoran sat on his family heirloom rocking chair by the fireplace in his quaint home. The room was tinted a deep red hue from the radiating fireplace. Old parchments, books, and a few candles at different burn heights adorned the room, with family paintings hanging on the walls. Adornments made from stone and wood dangled from the ceiling and clinked together as a slight draft came in from under the door.

Eldoran was rummaging through old manuscripts and sketches of his family from many years ago. His eyes welled up with tears as he admired a drawing of his wife, Jasi, holding baby Kainan and Aedan in her arms. Jasi had black, curly hair, fair skin and green eyes. He flicked through a few more sketches, letters, and curiosities, which were in a wooden box adorned with carvings of trees and emblazoned with an image of an ice dragon representing Nai. Finally, he pulled out an old letter.

The letter read:

It is incredible to think how my life has turned out. I would never have imagined it being this way, and now I cannot imagine it being any different. Everything that has passed has been by Nai's design, and I thank her for each and every gift she has bestowed upon me. I love you dearly, my Eldoran. I foresee our son Kainan will grow up to be a great leader. Just don't be too stern with him. Show him love and support. He is like you when you were young: hot-headed, short-tempered, and single-minded. Don't forget it took you many years of discipline before you learnt to manage your temper. Which, might I add, is still your defining personality trait, my grumpy little husband. As for Aedan, I do not know what to do with him. We won't be able to keep him forever. Eventually, his height and size will surpass his brother, and it will become apparent he is not one of us. Who will guide him then? That gruff druid? I do not trust him. Promise me you will find a safe home for him. I worry so much for his safety. What if what the druid says is true? It may bring much danger to Sylvinar and anyone else who is near him. But I love him as my own, and I want him to be safe. I am sure you will find a way. You always do. Yours now and forever, Jasi.

Eldoran folded up the letter and tucked it away. He realised someone was standing behind him. He turned around and saw Aedan.

Eldoran asked, "Where is your brother?"

Aedan ignored the question and replied, "Dad, why are you crying?"

Eldoran said, "Just thinking of your mother. Nothing to worry about. Now, tell me, where is your brother?"

Aedan shrugged his shoulders and sat down. "I'm not sure. I haven't seen him since the archery tournament when he was ushered away."

"I am really worried for him," Eldoran confided. "I love him, and I think what I said today was out of line. I only want the best for him, and I wish you two to be true brothers. You understand what that means?"

Aedan nodded.

Eldoran leaned into Aedan. "I hope so. Because there will be a time when things will get very complicated, and I need to know you two will be able to help one another, support one another, and love one another. At the end of the day, he will be the tribal leader, and I want him to know he is loved. So, he may lead with pride. But after today, I am worried his pride is too far gone."

Kainan stepped into the room. He had been listening to everything. Tears streamed down his face. "I'm sorry, father, I am a failure. Your words mean so much to me."

"Come here, my boy!" Eldoran cried out.

Kainan ran to his father and hugged him with all his might. After a few moments, Kainan and Eldoran broke their embrace. Eldoran asked both Aedan and Kainan to sit down as he needed to talk to them.

Eldoran shook his head as if trying to shake away a feeling and said, "I wish your mother were here. She always had a way of making me feel in control. She provided me with the inspiration I needed to make the right choices. Ever since she passed away, though, I have been unsure of what to do. So now that you both embark on The Trial tomorrow, I must ask something of each of you."

Aedan and Kainan looked at each other and then back at their father.

"Aedan, I need you to accept your older brother as your leader. He will lead Sylvinar in the not-too-distant future, and you must be able to support his decisions and follow his lead. Eventually, it won't matter too much to you, and I have other plans for you, which I will reveal after The Trial tomorrow."

Aedan asked. "What plans? Why won't it matter to me?"

"After The Trial. Please trust me Aedan." Eldoran told his son.

Aedan sat back and accepted his father would not tell him anything until after The Trial. He considered bringing up the druid and challenging his father, but he didn't want to ruin the moment. He trusted his father. He let it go.

Eldoran turned to Kainan and continued. "And you must learn to love your people and lead them with purpose. You must learn to work with Aedan, and you must both complete The Trial together. This is essential to regain the faith of the people. There are murmurings amongst the populace they doubt your leadership, so you must make amends."

Kainan interrupted his father. "To hell with the people, father. We are their leaders. We should not have to pander to their whims. I will lead with strength and conviction, and I will not pretend to tolerate this fool and his insubordination, simply to appease gossipers in the streets."

"Son, please, I love you, and I need you to become who you need to be. I cannot allow this to continue. You must learn being a leader sometimes requires you stand behind and not in front." Eldoran's voice stiffened.

"Father, I believe in old age you are becoming weak and are too worried about things you never used to care about. Aedan has always been your favourite. Why don't you ask him to change? Why must I accept him?" said Kainan, raising his voice.

"Son, I asked him to follow your lead, but you must also show him respect." Eldoran tried to reason with Kainan.

"I will never respect him. He has shown me too much disrespect for me to ever see him as my equal. Besides, I am his leader. I am his superior," Kainan stated.

Eldoran replied. "Well, I have no choice but to warn you. If you are unable to grow and to learn the way a leader should."

Kainan snapped, "By grow and learn, you mean become more like Aedan?"

"Shut up, moron," barked back Eldoran. "You are smart enough to know exactly what I mean; you could not possibly be that stupid that you think it is all about Aedan? Enough is enough. I will delegate power to another noble family, and I will step down as leader. I have had it with this nonsense."

"You can't do that!" Kainan was enraged and stood over his father.

Aedan stood up at his father's defence, and Kainan shoved Aedan away. A fight was to ensue had not the most amazing thing happened.

Eldoran stated in a powerful and commanding voice, "Be gone, fool!"

Energy emanated from Eldoran's presence, which threw Kainan back, off his feet, against the door.

Kainan stood up in fear, unable to comprehend what just happened, and ran out the door.

Eldoran slumped in a heap and began to sob. "I have failed as a father."

Aedan was still in shock at what he witnessed. "Dad. What did you just do?"

Eldoran looked to Aedan. He saw fear in Aedan's face he had never seen before. "Don't be worried, my son. Forget what you just saw. It was nothing."

On hearing those words, Aedan could no longer remember why he was worried. He turned to his father and comforted him. "It's not you, dad. It's him. I don't know why, but he seems possessed by Akh. I try so hard too, but he just wants to hate."

"Just be quiet. It only makes it worse," Eldoran begged.

Aedan hugged his father. Together, slumped in the flickering, warm lights of the fire, their emotions ebbed and flowed in silence; until, much later, they each went to bed without saying a word.

Eldoran, propped up on his bed, gazed out his window at the moons Annah and Aura. He decided Sylvinar needed new leadership, and he would announce the transition of power after the festival. For now, though, he was worried about Kainan. If he quietened his mind, he was sure he could hear Kainan's suffering echoing in the cool, evening breeze. If only he knew how to help him. He wished Jasi was there to guide him.

Eldoran felt Jasi's hand on his shoulder. He looked over his shoulder, but no one was there.

The Trial

On the morning of The Trial, Aedan and Eldoran said few words to each other. Eldoran was worried sick because Kainan had not come home. Eldoran wished Aedan good luck in completing The Trial, but Eldoran was a man with half his heart missing, so he was unable to muster any excitement in his voice, "Good luck Aedan. May Nai bless you, guide you and give you strength."

They both dressed and ate in silence and left in silence. But the festival made no concessions. It was loud and gay.

Aedan stood in line with the other Sa'ami boys waiting to be issued with a beacon bracelet. The magical bracelet was a safety device given to all the boys descending into The Depths. If any of them were unable to complete The Trial or wished to quit, all they had to do was twist the top of the bracelet, which held a blue orb of pure manah, and they would teleport back to the amphitheatre.

In the centre of the Great Amphitheatre, the Maidens of the Festival danced to traditional Sa'ami music. The music was organic, earthy melodies, blown through large, hollowed-out tree trunks. Each trunk had multiple protruding branches, each sounding out different notes; creating complex chords that warbled with the musician's natural breath. A deep rhythm underscored the crunchy harmony sounded out on a mish-mash of percussive instruments, which galloped in time, increasing and decreasing in speed like an excited heartbeat.

The air smelled of roast vegetables, aromatic condiments, pungent spices, barbecued meats, flowers and morning mist. The odours saturated the city and flowed through the crowd into the Great Amphitheatre. Sa'ami wandered around munching on food, smoking pipes, and drinking tea from traditional little wooden cups with wooden straws. Vendors lined the pathway leading to the entrance, and it was nigh-on-impossible to resist eating or drinking something.

Aedan scoffed down a dip-and-fry tucker ball. He was poking his head up from the queue, trying to spot Ferni dancing amongst the other girls on the amphitheatre floor. But, instead, he spotted Kainan pushing his way towards the centre of the arena! An official confronted Kainan, who signalled for him to get in line to receive a beacon bracelet.

Kainan commanded the official, "Shove off, idiot. I am soon to be ruler, so don't bark orders at me, lest I have your head served on a platter."

The official stood aside and let Kainan walk past.

Aedan was issued a beacon bracelet and was granted access to the Great Amphitheatre floor. As he entered, his ears reverberated from the cheering all around him. The stadium was a tidal wave of people breaking over him. Such was the enormity of the amphitheatre; you felt dwarfed by its size when you walked in. On the opposite end from where he had entered, there was a sizeable vertical gate. The gate was the doorway to The Depths, which would change his life forever when he passed through it.

Aedan spotted Ferni, but she wasn't dancing. Instead, she fended Kainan, who was holding her by her wrists and trying to force himself upon her. Aedan bolted towards her, leapt through the air, and kicked Kainan in the chest. Kainan flew to the ground.

Aedan towered over Kainan and warned him, "This is something I will kill you for. Never lay a finger on her again."

Kainan forced out a laugh as he looked up at his brother. "You are pathetic that a girl can have such command over you. You are no leader." Kainan stood up, spat on the ground at Aedan's feet, and walked away.

"Are you all right? Did he hurt you?" Aedan asked Ferni.

Tears trickled down Ferni's cheeks. "It's ok. My wrists are a bit sore, but... Aedan, be careful. He said you don't have what it takes to make it back alive."

Up in the stands, Eldoran had seen everything transpire. He couldn't decide whether to go down or continue with the ceremony. He was so worried for Kainan yet, he, Eldoran, would not insult thousands of cycles of tradition over his son's stupidity, so he decided to push on with his duty as ruler.

Some Sa'ami approached Ferni to comfort her. Aedan put his arm around her and waved them away. A couple of the boys in the group, Fat Frango and Jonin, went off to confront Kainan.

Aedan whispered to Ferni. "Listen, he can't hurt you. My father will be handing power to another noble family after the festival. I suspect it will most likely be your family."

Ferni's eyes lit up, full of surprise. She wiped away her tears and looked at Aedan. "That means my father will be the ruler, and as his only offspring, I would be the heir!" She squealed with joy. "Don't you see what your father is doing? When I marry you, then you will be ruler with me!"

Aedan's eyes almost jumped out of his head from the realisation.

Ferni started dancing. She beckoned Aedan to join her. Aedan hesitated but joined her. As they danced, Aedan was startled by Kainan standing next to them. Aedan fronted Kainan, ready for a fight. Fat Frango and Jonin stood behind Kainan. Kainan glanced at Fat Frango and Jonin, who nodded towards Aedan. Kainan turned his gaze back to Aedan.

"I'm sorry, brother," Kainan offered sincerely. "I have been a bit crazy, and after yesterday's humiliation in the archery game, I lost my mind. I'm sorry, Ferni, I truly am. I've had too much pressure on me as a little boy to become a leader. I promise to never again come between you two. Will you accept my apology, brother?"

Aedan smiled ear to ear. "Of course I will!"

Aedan hugged Kainan in a tight embrace and mouthed, "Thank you," at Fat Frango and Jonin. Fat Frango and Jonin returned a smile to Aedan and then went back to their celebrations amongst the crowd.

Ferni was not sure she believed Kainan's apology. She thought someone couldn't have a change of heart like that. Doubt crossed her mind about Kainan's true intentions.

Eldoran was filled with joy to see both his boys hugging. Maybe what he said last night and whatever Fat Frango and Jonin had done had a positive effect on Kainan. Eldoran could now open The Trial on a high note. He took his stand and commenced his opening address. As he spoke, the music dwindled, the cheering subsided, and everyone's attention shifted onto him.

Eldoran boomed, "Today we lose many boys, who will return as men! Since we, the Sa'ami, first inhabited Sylvinar Forest, our boys have transitioned into manhood by descending into the dark abyss of The Depths where the great Traxys lumber. Each boy will need to find a Traxy and retrieve a scale from this colossal beast. The scale is a unique artefact that each Sa'ami will craft into their unique armour. I wish every Sa'ami boy the courage to be able to complete The Trial. The Trial is as much a test of knowledge as it is of brawn. Play to your strengths, focus on what you can do rather than what you can't, and you will find yourself back up here in four days with the rest of us. We thrive from our diversity as a society, and many Sa'ami are needed as teachers, scholars, traders, crafters, clergy, and entertainers. So, for those who relinquish in their attempt of The Trial, do not despair, for it is in Nai's design your destiny holds another calling. Today many young Sa'ami girls will become women. As Maidens of the Festival, they will be picked by those who complete The Trial. Should they return the grace in kind, they shall be united forever as husband and wife, wedded in the most highly-revered ceremony of unity."

The crowd erupted into applause. Sa'ami saw the union of man and woman for all eternity as the most sacred event in a lifetime.

Eldoran continued. "Shinar has begun. Nai is giving life. Our boys are becoming men. Our girls are becoming women. As proud Sa'ami of Sylvinar, let us never forget those who came before us and forever honour our people's free, independent spirit. Let The Trial of the Depths commence!" He concluded with such vigour and powerful expression it ignited an immense celebration from the crowd.

Down on the amphitheatre floor, officials were rallying the boys into a rough assembly facing The Depths' gates while ushering the maidens to the back of the arena. Ferni blew Aedan a kiss as he was shepherded away with Kainan. Kainan was all smiles with his arm around Aedan's waist.

Kainan laughed with joy. "Oh, brother, I can't believe we are finally going to complete The Trial. This is a moment I never want to forget. I have looked forward to it my entire life."

Aedan chimed in. "I agree, and I am so glad we are finally on good terms, and what timing! It couldn't be more perfect. Our father must surely be watching with pride as we attempt The Trial together. I am sure he will now retain power for you."

Kainan smiled at his brother's words because that was why he was doing it. He knew Eldoran would be watching, and he knew it would convince him they were both entering The Depths as a team.

"Ah yes, brother, everything is perfect," Kainan said with a countenance of deceit.

As the conglomerate of boys took shape before the gates, Eldoran gave his final blessing. "May Nai keep you and bless you. May she light your way and give you strength. May she be with you until the very end. We shall see you at the opening of Lum on the fifth day of Shinar. Open the gates!"

The gate tenders strained as they pulled on the massive ropes which drew open the enormous gates. The Sa'ami boys strode across the threshold towards their manhood. The sound of the crowd faded away, and the light from their beloved city dwindled far behind them. All they could hear was their stride and their breath. Their steps made a soft thudding sound. It was apparent the ground was becoming damper; its consistency was changing.

Aedan looked up at the canopy. It was becoming obfuscated with an ever-increasing number of vines and branches. It was also moving upwards, away from them. They were descending. The darkness was becoming thicker and more pervasive. The floor was becoming less dirty and more like bark. Aedan realised they were treading on an enormous branch of such girth and density it seemed to be the forest floor. Then it dawned on him: the forest he had known his entire life was the top of an enormous canopy, so thick, it was the ground upon which Sylvinar was built.

After an hour or so, the boys reached a place that split into multiple directions. About fifteen or twenty paths twisted and turned around each other and vanished into a labyrinth of immense branches and root systems. It was as if the boys were tiny ants in the soil beneath the forest floor. At this point, the boys all stopped and looked at one another for a moment. Then, they realised they could not continue as one; they would have to break up into smaller groups. It would continue to occur the deeper they went, dividing them all up.

Fat Frango already had enough of all this silly running around. He twisted his beacon bracelet. The manah was released. It consumed his entire body in a spectacle of magical glitter, and he was teleported, in a pod of bright light, all the way back to the amphitheatre, where he would treat himself to a nice meal and then go to bed. The rest of the Sa'ami boys continued ahead. They scattered down the branches like bread crumbs falling between fingers.

Aedan turned to Kainan and said, "Let's stick together."

Kainan was gone.

Aedan called out. "Brother? Where are you?"

Kainan did not reply.

Aedan thought it was a bit odd, but then again, he assumed Kainan wanted to prove he could complete The Trial independently. Many of the Sa'ami wanted to finish The Trial alone. Not only could they boast about it later, but it improved their chances of becoming great leaders in the Sa'ami army. Aedan thought nothing of it and took the opportunity to do the same: complete The Trial by himself.

Aedan knew what lay ahead in The Depths. He had studied all about The Depths in school. He decided he would move forward with a careful foot to avoid detection by the creatures which lurked below. Maybe he could make it down and back up without ever needing to draw his bow? Little did he know, the string on his bow had been frayed by Kainan, rendering the bow useless. Unaware of the sabotage, Aedan climbed down the branches, into the darkness, all on his own, to his impending doom.

A Druid's Concern

Grandor, a Beastmaster druid of Agwa'den, waded through the crystalline waters of the river Mhan. He fought against the raging current, bracing himself with his gnarly staff. The hem of his brown tunic was drenched and dragged along the surface of the water. It was a steaming hot day. The cool water of the river was a refreshing relief for Grandor. He had grown tired of his travels and knew he would have to settle down before nightfall, as he still had another quarter-day's journey before he reached the druidic grove. He hoped to convince the grandmaster druid, Magestrix, there was an evil rising on the country of Concordia which required immediate attention of the grove because the balance of nature was in dire peril.

His feet trod on the muddy riverbank. Gunk oozed between his filthy toes. It felt good. Then, he was knocked off his feet and fell onto his back. A savage timber wolf licked his face in festive delight. It was Tanke, his familiar and companion. Take was uniformly dark grey with a light grey underbelly and a white streak straight down his spine ending at the tip of his tail. Grandor wrestled him off and caressed the creature's mane.

"There, boy. You must have run at great speed to find a crossing and get here so quickly?" Gandor asked.

Tanke barked in affirmation.

"Looks like we'll make camp a little further up the shore, where the river bank rises onto that clearing," he explained to Tanke. "Let's go boy." Grandor led the way, with Tanke in tow. Tanke was always alert, minding his best friend's back.

This part of Sylvinar Forest was dazzling and beautiful. The closer one was to Agwa'den, the natural spring where the river Mhan erupted; the more life seemed to thrive. The immense volume of water was said to flow from Nai. The river carved a winding path through the forest and the mainland of Concordia until it flowed into the Great Ocean.

The waters flowing out of Agwa'den were rich in life-giving manah. The energy stimulated extraordinary growth in all living things near the grove. The trees were massive, covered in thick, luscious moss, draped in long locks of fibrous vine. The air was teeming with microscopic organisms swimming in the air, littering streams of light with speckled activity. Everything was moist, if not wet; small amphibians crawled, leapt and walked across almost every surface. The ecosystem was kinetic, lively, and harmoniously chaotic. The air was filled with a soothing cacophony; buzzing and humming to the melody of the forest.

Grandor settled down on the clearing and made a small fire to keep warm as the daylight ebbed away. He harvested wild berries, fruits, and greens for dinner. He brought to boil his herbal brew and gave thanks to Nai. As evening set, he had his fill and lay down to sleep. Tanke snuggled up next to him for warmth, and they both dozed off.

TWO DAYS HAD PASSED since the attack of Fort Bosk, and eight remained for the night of the ritual. Daylight broke. Lum was just above the horizon, reflecting the light of Usil onto the terrain, and Aura added her golden hue to the sky. The dew glistened in the morning light. Grandor opened his eyes. The fire had long been extinguished. Tanke's hind leg was on Grandor's face. Grandor moved it aside and stood up to stretch. He praised the morning light with an elongated pose reaching for the skies. Then he praised the ground, bending over and pushing against the earth with his hands. He lowered himself onto the floor and crossed his legs in one fluid movement, and began to meditate. Tanke woke up and, upon seeing Grandor meditating, decided to go for a morning prowl.

Grandor relaxed and focused his mind on everything around him. He absorbed the moment, forgot himself, and became aware of every sound in the forest. Even with the deafening sound of the flowing river reverberating around him, he was still able to discern the individual sound of a lady-beetle tumbling down a leaf. He could hear the pitter-patter of dew dripping onto the soil and the mating call of the local honey-frog. His mind absorbed everything. His mind processed everything. He lost himself. He was no longer an individual. He was one with nature.

The forest breeze kissed his skin. It transferred energy to him and charged his soul. He felt life flow through him, within him, out of him and, all around him. Now centred, he exhaled and opened his eyes.

Tanke was staring at him with a cocked head. *Are you ready yet?*

"Let's go, brother." Grandor smiled at Tanke and signalled for him to follow.

They walked through the ever more overgrown forest for a few hours. Thousands of creepy crawlies, amphibians and insects scurried all over the ground and fauna. Birds, small mammals and reptiles also darted around the place. Great forest creatures were hosts to hundreds of smaller lifeforms crawling over their bodies. The Panteras' spotted patterns were tiny newts feasting on mites. The symbiotic nature of life was omnipresent at the heart of Agwa'den.

Grandor looked up at the intense rainbow which glistened in the colossal jet of water that shot out of the cold geyser at the heart of the druidic grove. It was the heart of Concordia, where all water flowed into her veins, bringing life to the multitudinous creatures scattered across her terrain. The forest had been Grandor's home for a long time. He walked into the grove's antechamber where the druidic brotherhood mingled, sharing their experiences and reporting to their mentors.

Grandor was the head mentor for the few Beastmaster druids in the grove. Beastmasters were those druids who dedicated their lives to becoming friends with all living creatures. They learned to think like animals, communicate with animals, and form lifelong friendships with animals. Grandor knew every senior beast in Sylvinar Forest and Agwa'den. He had met many of their relatives and was aware of the politics between the numerous beast clans. His role as mentor was to guide the younger druids in their journey to become Beastmasters.

Grandor had gained favour with many of the animals across Concordia and other countries on Alteria over the cycles. He only needed to ask them for help, and they would run to his aide. As a Beastmaster druid, he had formed a special bond with one animal, Tanke, who was his familiar. A familiar was the animalistic embodiment of a druid. A familiar's life-force flowed from their druidic brother, and the druid's life-force flowed from their familiar—both separate entities and yet one and the same. Many of the other druids saw familiars as a weakness and, therefore, Beastmaster druids were not a popular life choice.

Ever since Magestrix had risen as grandmaster druid of the grove, and even before her rise, Shapeshifter druids had increased in unprecedented numbers. Shapeshifters dedicated their lives to manipulating their life force so they could alter their physical shape into another beast. Depending on the level of experience a druid possessed, they were able to turn into mighty beasts. When in beast form, though, a druid was unable to chant or invoke any magic.

Grandor believed this was the biggest weakness of all. Why turn into an animal when you could be friends with them all?

Grandor walked through the antechamber and noticed none of his pupils around. He thought they must be out bonding with animals. Many of the other druids in the antechamber averted their gaze, which he thought was quite odd. He knew the rivalry between Shapeshifters and Beastmasters was at times tense, but this was ridiculous.

He approached the grove's inner chamber and was greeted by crossed staves.

"Magestrix is not taking any visitors today," the tunic wearing guards stated with an angry tone.

Grandor looked at both guards in turn, "Are you two not the little boys from the outskirts of Mhan who were once caught nude, playing with themselves?"

The guards looked at each other.

Grandor continued. "Now look at both of you, how far you've come? Standing here. Telling a fellow brother to turn back. Quite a courageous task considering no one would dare challenge you out of respect. But what would happen if someone did challenge you. Say, myself, for example? Would you stand your ground and fight, or would you flee back to where you came from?"

The guards parted their staves and mumbled, "We don't want trouble, master."

Grandor let out a bellowing laugh. "You need to develop your sense of humour lest you be so easily fooled by an enemy." He slapped one of them on the shoulder and almost knocked them off balance. "Thank you, brother, for letting me through."

Grandor entered the inner chamber. It was much darker than usual. It seemed the daylight must've already dwindled from its apex, but he was sure Tanke and himself had made good time on their trek to the grove. He crossed the chamber and looked up through the open ceiling. The inner chamber was within a massive rock that had a colossal crevice parting the top. Light would shine through and cast dancing shadows as the foliage swayed in the canopy above. Animal sounds would reverberate throughout the chamber. But today, it was dead silent.

Magestrix sat atop her throne carved from an ancient Karkeha trunk.

She wore a black tunic draped in a cape made of large black, silver-tipped, Mountain Raven feathers. Green battle paint adorned her pale forehead, cheeks and lips. A headband made of twisted roots from the sacred Karkeha tree indicated her rank as Grandmaster. Her straight hair was pitch black and flowed down to her hips. She grimaced at Grandor's forced incursion.

"Grandmaster, how fare thee on this most beautiful day of Shinar?" Grandor asked with a formal bow.

"Fine," Magestrix snarked back. "Why do you insist on being insubordinate? Firar and Ernil are simply doing their jobs. You should have turned away and come back another time. I am busy."

"Apologies, grandmaster," Grandor continued as he stopped at the bottom of the stairs leading up to the throne, "I come before you with an urgent matter which requires the immediate attention of the grove."

"I will decide what requires immediate attention. Do not speak above your rank, druid," Magestrix corrected, pointing at Grandor.

"Apologies. If I may continue?" Grandor bowed again.

"If you must," Magestrix gesticulated for Grandor to speak his mind.

"I have witnessed an attack on Fort Bosk." Grandor paused to let Magestrix respond.

"So? Why is this our problem? Forts are there for battle," Magestrix quipped.

"The attack was by animals from the forest of Sylvinar. More troubling is many of the creatures in the ranks of this 'army' were beasts from beyond The Depths, which I have not seen since the Great Manah Wars." Grandor was about to continue when Magestrix cut him off.

"You think I would not be aware if animals had risen from The Depths?" she chastised Grandor.

Grandor spoke with command. "I do not think anything of the sort, grandmaster. I am simply reporting on what I believe I have witnessed. What I also believe is these beasts are undead. Reanimated with magical force to serve a greater evil. Thus, I believe, not only is the ruling power of Concordia at risk of being usurped, but the balance of nature is about to be completely soiled and polluted."

"Even if any of this were true druid, which I am pretty sure is simply your deluded perceptions, what would you have me do? Dispatch the entire grove on a quest to fight this army? To shed the blood of fellow druids on an irrelevant battle?" Magestrix cackled.

"I merely ask if you would sanction an official mission for me to attend to Castle Mhan on behalf of the grove or other such druid you see fit to warn the queen and offer our assistance," Grandor replied.

"I will do no such thing. You have interrupted my mediations so I could listen to your imagined concerns, and now you ask I provide you with the official druidic seal so you may recount your deluded tales to the queen as an official druidic matter?" Magestrix snickered to herself as she belittled Grandor.

Grandor became defiant. "Grandmaster, I find it disturbing you distrust a fellow druid, namely myself. Someone who is potentially your equal and does not have a history of imagined concerns or delusions as you so eloquently described. I have lived through many cycles of conflict. Enough to know when I see a festering evil rising up against this land. Do you not sense it in your meditations?"

"Find it how you will. I am your leader, and you will do as I command. I sense nothing except your silver tongue. I am not Firar or Ernil to easily manipulate your words so that you may have your way. Begone from here. Go to Castle Mhan if you wish. The further away you are from the grove, the better. But your so-called 'mission' will not be sanctioned," Magestrix slammed her fist.

"If I must," Grandor concluded and exited the inner chamber. He rushed through the antechamber and met up with Tanke outside. "We must go on our own, Tanke. It seems Magestrix is too preoccupied with exerting her authority than listening to reason."

Grandor broke into a jog. He gained speed on his feet. He hummed and chanted to the winds, and feeling in tune with the flow of the air was light on his feet. The residual manah in his body from his morning meditation, and the forest around him, gave him haste. He sprinted over the ground. He flowed through the forest. He was one with the wind.

The Descent

Aedan descended into The Depths. It was pitch black.

Aedan was the only Sa'ami with red eyes that provided him with excellent night vision. Aedan could sneak in pitch darkness at speed and still take stock of his surroundings with little effort. But, as the darkness of The Depths set in around him, even he began to struggle to see the environment. He relied on his ears and nose, much more than usual, to discern what was coming up ahead.

Aedan stopped in his tracks as he took a few sniffs of the moist air. He was convinced he could smell a dead animal. He worried scavengers might be in the area, or even worse, an egg-laden Sukted victim. When Sukted eggs matured, they burst, launching hundreds of baby Sukteds, the size of tiny coins, in every direction. Any living creature in the vicinity would get all of their blood drained by the ravaging larvae in a matter of seconds.

Aedan became tense when he realised the smell of decay was getting stronger and stronger. He held his breath out of fear. Whatever it was might hear him inhale. A Kun's unmistakable silhouette lumbered into his view on the branch below. He was sure it was the source of the rotten odour. The smell rose from the branches beneath, which obscured his sight, but he was confident he could hear many more Kuns walking past. Aedan did not move a muscle and relaxed himself to hold his breath longer and avoid gasping in panic. The first Kun stopped and looked up at him. Aedan reached for his bow. His hand hovered over the bow, ready to react.

Instead, the Kun lowered its head and continued along with the rest of the pack.

Aedan's chest burned from a lack of oxygen, but he waited until they had long left before taking a breath. He was glad he had practised holding his breath from a young age. Aedan used to wonder when the things Eldoran forced him to learn would be of any use in real life; well, he wasn't wondering anymore.

Aedan heard a branch crack. It sounded like a footstep. He spun around and studied the dark but couldn't see anyone approaching. Kainan was training his bow on Aedan and was deciding if he could make the shot. His hand twitched. All he had to do was let go of the arrow.

AEDAN SNUCK DOWNWARDS. He was startled by the sounds in the dark. He wasn't sure what the sounds were, but he attributed them to Monos. Monos, he learned in class, were tiny hominids with a furry, white coat. Their eyes were the size of a racquetball, which allowed them to see in The Depths with great clarity. They possessed lightning-fast reflexes bordering on precognitive ability, which, when coupled with their incredible speed and agility, made them nigh-on-impossible to catch. They only ate Sukteds, which reminded Aedan, the sounds he could hear might be Sukteds. He stopped dead in his tracks.

There was a deep, panting sound. Aedan could hear it coming from up ahead. He studied his surroundings for an alternative route. To either side of his branch, there was only darkness. He reached out with a long stick but was unable to feel anything. His only option was to continue along the branch he was on and hope for the best. But there was no doubt there was something up ahead, and it didn't sound friendly.

According to his studies, at this level in The Depths, the most dangerous creatures were Hunting Horrors, Yeshi Salamanders, and Kuns. He could not smell the stench of a Kun, and, he was sure, Yeshi Salamanders did not pant. Thus, he concluded he was approaching the nest of a Hunting Horror. After all, it was the start of Shinar, the beginning of new life; so, it would not be surprising to find a Hunting Horror nursing her young. Nothing is more dangerous than a mother defending her children.

Aedan decided he would sneak past the creature rather than try to kill it. He did not want to interfere with the cycle of life. Eldoran had taught him that avoiding a fight is better than winning because when you fight, even when you win, you have lost. You have just lost the least.

Aedan walked to the edge of the branch he was on and laid on his belly. The branch was covered with an intricate system of thick, vein-like ridges. It provided a grip for Aedan to position himself on the underside of the branch. One of his feet would push against a ridge while he shuffled along with his hands. It was a slow process. It took half an hour to traverse the branch. He could hear the panting above. Finally, his curiosity piqued, he convinced himself to take a peek. He pulled himself towards the edge of the branch, where he caught a glimpse of the Hunting Horror.

The beast was much taller and broader than a Sa'ami, Human, or even a Ras'i. She had a thick, canvas-like membrane stretched between her fore and hind limbs, with giant paws and razor-sharp claws. Her face was flat, dominated by a large wet snout and mono-like eyes. Hunting Horrors were large, stupid animals that were relatively easy to kill. But Aedan was saddened to think they had been hunted to near extinction by the Gnoss.

Aedan looked in awe at the beast. She was not paying attention to anything except her brood. Aedan took a gamble, knowing if she grabbed hold of him, he would be torn limb from limb and climbed up a protruding trunk just beyond where he was perched. As he climbed past the Hunting Horror, he spotted her young. From beneath her furry underside, a petite babe popped its head out, screeching for attention with a tiny, delicate voice, at a frequency almost imperceptible to Aedan's ears. The mother leaned down, regurgitated food into her baby's mouth, and then covered the infant with her fatty skin. Aedan thought back to all the drawings he had seen of this beast in his school books and how fearsome it looked. Yet, here, he saw a vulnerable and fragile mother tending to her family. After a while of admiring the scene, Aedan thanked Nai for the opportunity and climbed down. He reached the bottom and crept away.

Crack! He stepped on a dry twig. The mother shot up on her hind legs and let out a deafening scream. It reverberated throughout the entire nothingness. The multilayered vocals of varying frequencies penetrated Aedan's soul, freezing him in his tracks. He looked up. He saw the beast leap off her perch and dive-bomb towards him. He drew his bow and an arrow.

Twang! The bow's string snapped.

Aedan's life was about to end. He leapt back into the abyss. The creature's underbelly was the last thing he saw as he fell into the darkness.

AEDAN WAS FALLING.

He grasped at the darkness. He was unable to see or feel anything. He closed his eyes and concentrated. He remembered scaling a trunk, so there had to be something just beyond his grasp. He tossed his grapple into the blackness.

Nothing.

His heart was pounding at the thought of his body splattering on the ground.

He threw his grapple again. His hands burned against the rope as it unravelled. He had hooked onto something. He clenched his fists. The rope pulled on his arms with so much force he thought they would be ripped from their sockets. Then, his fall changed direction. He swung downwards towards whatever he had hooked on to. He braced his legs to absorb the impact, which shattered him, and he blacked out.

THE NUMBNESS OF HIS lips was the first thing Aedan felt as he regained consciousness. Every muscle was sore, bruised and battered. His right eye was half closed from the swelling. Blood trickled down his face. He moved his right hand, struggling against the pain, and touched his mouth. A sharp pain shot across his face. His lips were split and smashed.

Aedan lay there for a long while, staring into the darkness above, feeling the pain all over his body. How far had he fallen? He tried to survey his surroundings. He had landed on a branch near a trunk. He could smell the rotten odour rising from The Depths' primordial ocean of gunk. He figured he was close to the bottom of The Depths. At this level, danger was everywhere, and this close to the bottom, Yeshi Salamanders ruled the roost. Aedan panicked. He knew he had to keep moving lest he falls prey to their lust for meat.

He checked his body for broken limbs. His arms were sore, but he could move them. Likewise, his neck, torso, and legs seemed to be fine; bar the excruciating pain from the numerous bruises, cuts and grazes. His left foot responded well; but, the pain from his right foot paralysed his entire body. His right foot, he deduced, must have been fractured.

Aedan clenched his teeth and rolled over onto his left side. He propped up his body with his right arm. Everything hurt. He looked around. His rope and grappling hook were nearby. *Thank Nai, it did not fall on my head*, he thought to himself. He took a deep breath and pushed himself up onto his knees.

"Aaaaaannnnnngggggghhhhh!" Aedan let out a scream. The pain felt like a battering ram was wailing against his right ankle. His yell echoed throughout the darkness. He knew every creature, beast, and animal would have pricked its ears in his direction. His only option was to get away as soon as possible. He made haste, got up, and let out a moan of pain. He grabbed his rope and hopped over to a nearby branch. He used his axe to lop it off. Then, using a section of rope, he bound the branch to his leg, making a rudimentary splint.

With each movement, he yelped. Creatures from the dark responded with cackling and yapping. The Depths had come to life. Aedan was unarmed except for his small axe and hunting knife. He lopped off another branch, about his height in length, and sharpened the end of it with his knife into a makeshift spear. Aedan hated spears. He did not like that once it was released, you were left without a weapon in hand. Well, at least he could use it as a crutch while he walked.

Maybe creatures will confuse me for a mage and flee at the sight of me? He wished.

Aedan limped away from the scene of his blood-splattered landing; wincing, and clenching his teeth to avoid moaning from the pain. He was sweating. He thought it was weird how lots of sweat always accompanied great pain.

He could see much better than in the upper levels of The Depths. It was not bright by any means, it was still dark, but he could discern shapes, shadows, and details he could not see before. There were speckled orbs of light floating in the nothingness, like dust floating past a bright window on a hot day of Kalor, except these particles glinted in the darkness. They were tiny but provided just enough light to see the environment. Aedan was sure the creatures of The Depths would be able to see as if it were day.

He felt a presence behind him. The branch he was on vibrated. There was the slithering, soft hissing, and unmistakable acrid smell of a Yeshi Salamander. He turned and saw what, until this moment, he had only ever seen in his study parchments, never in real life.

The Yeshi Salamander was a reptilian beast of human stature with a masculine upper body fused between a snake's head and tail. He knew salamanders were fast and agile, able to close great distances in the blink of an eye. The human torso and arms allowed it to wield weapons. Salamanders were the creation of evil sorcerers from the middle-ages of the Great Manah Wars. Since then, Salamanders devolved from intelligent spell-casters into savage beasts. To make matters worse, they spat and bled acid, making them very difficult to kill without being killed.

It leapt at Aedan! It spread its mighty arms to tackle him. Aedan jumped aside, avoiding the impact, but fell over. He dragged himself towards the edge of the branch, ready to drop down in a vain attempt to save himself, but he knew another fall would render him unable to move and would be his demise. He knew this encounter would be over in a moment.

"Arrrghhhh-tooooooth!" The Salamander spun around and hocked a massive spitball of acid at Aedan. Aedan rolled out of the way. The branch, where the spit hit, seared as the acid dissolved it. Aedan felt a burning sensation on his right arm; there was a spot of the creature's deadly saliva singing his flesh.

The beast darted towards him! Aedan heard its deep throaty gargle as it prepared to hock another ball of acid. Without thinking, Aedan aimed and threw his sorry excuse for a spear at the salamander. It was a fantastic shot. It travelled straight, strong, fast and true on target. It would have skewered the salamander had the creature not dodged it with such agility to render Aedan's attempt futile. Instead, the spear impaled itself on the trunk behind the beast. The shot did disrupt the creature's attack. Aedan saw an opportunity to run for his life; and, maybe slide down the tree trunk; and, maybe he could hide, and maybe he could lose it?

Aedan got up and hopped as fast as he could towards the trunk. For a moment, he felt he had a chance. He peered back at the salamander and saw it standing there, looking at him, and he saw it had a smile on its face. It was savouring the moment, watching its prey attempting to escape with futility. Aedan's helplessness and vulnerability pleased the beast. It decided to end the confrontation, slithering towards Aedan with conviction and purpose, salivating and hissing in torment.

Aedan hopped faster, but there was no way he could outrun the salamander. He reached the trunk just as the salamander growled an unholy growl and pounced on him. The beast pinned Aedan underneath its bulk. The beast looked at him and smiled.

"Look before you leap," Aedan advised.

The spear stuck in the trunk was skewered through the salamander's chest, straight through its heart. Blinded by lust, Aeden had led it to its doom. It shuddered and went limp.

Aedan struggled with all his might to shift the massive bulk. Acidic blood was dripping onto Aedan's chest from the creature's wound. It burned. He cleared his mind and focused his thoughts for a moment. He grabbed the spear and pushed it as hard as he could. Using the weapon as a fulcrum, he was able to shift the beast for a brief moment so he could escape. He rolled away from underneath the animal. He clutched his chest and burned his hand as well.

Aedan lay there, clenching his teeth, holding his breath, waiting for the pain to fade away. He looked at his hand and chest. He knew it would get infected in a day or so. He had endured enough. He did not want to go on. His right foot was shattered. His chest and hand were burned. What would he do if he confronted a Traxy?

As he lay there, defeated, with his eyes closed, he had a vision of Ferni. She approached him, wearing her pretty, frilly dress. She leaned over him. He could feel her breath. He could see the detail in her eyes. Her hair dangled onto his face, and it smelt like flowers. She kissed him.

Aedan's eyes snapped open. He remembered why he was there: to complete The Trial; to marry Ferni; to become a man.

He forced himself up. He cut cloth off his tunic with his hunting knife and bandaged his hand and chest. It hurt like Akh, but with each shot of pain, he found strength, for it proved he was becoming a man and was no longer a boy.

He continued climbing downwards, hopping from branch to branch, scrunching his face in agony with each movement, with each impact, with each stride. The pain became his ally, his companion and his friend. He no longer hated it. He embraced it.

He could see the bottom. He was sure.

He hooked his rope around the nearest branch and descended.

The Depths

Aedan gazed at the massive ocean before him of bubbling sludge composed of decaying animals and plant life which The Depths had digested. The rancid odour was an assault on Aedan's senses. Rising out of the ocean, at great distances from one another, were cyclopean trees. The trees fanned out above, connecting to form the lower canopy from where he climbed down. Down here, it was dead silent. He could hear his breath as loud as if a hornet had dug itself into his ear. Aware of his vulnerability, he decided not to waste time and get moving.

Aedan left his rope dangling where it was. He gathered some bark, wood, and leaves and made a heap. He planned to lure a Traxy out with fire. He recalled from his studies Traxys were drawn to warmth. He also needed a place to hide. He camouflaged himself with twine, bark, and fronds. He lit the heap, starting a fire, then rowed, on a large branch, towards a tree in the distance. He couldn't look at the fire; his eyes had become acclimatised to the dark. The light from the fire was brighter than anything he had ever seen. With the light to his back, he was able to see far ahead. Eyes were glinting in the darkness, staring back at him. They darted away on Aedan's approach. He heard scampering all around him.

After a while, he reached the base of the tree. He glanced in the direction of the fire. It was a mere speck of red and yellow flickering in the distance. Aedan climbed the trunk. His splinted leg dangled. He relied on his arms to pull him up. He secured himself to the tree with twine so he could sleep without fear of falling, then pulled out rations from his leather pouch. He ate some berries, bread, cheese and drank cold tea from his flask. Then, with his mind focused on his breathing and his belly satisfied, he lost himself in his thoughts and fell into a deep sleep.

Aedan awoke to a rumbling sound. He felt well-rested and refreshed. He panicked, thinking he'd overslept and missed the Traxy, but, as he peered into the dark, he saw it. It was a mountain, moving at a snail's pace. Aedan had read in books that Traxys were colossal, but he never imagined that seeing one would be so unfathomable. The ocean surface did not break but, such was the animal's momentum, ripples as tall as a person radiated from its bulk.

It had a head like a turtle but with fat, bony spikes jutting from its crown. A large horn stuck out from its nose. The Traxy was close, oblivious to Aedan's presence. Its eyes were focused on the fire, which had been extinguished for quite some time, but its embers still burned with enough heat to attract the dinosaur. The Traxy's mountainous back, covered in its coveted iridescent scales, passed Aedan. All Aedan had to do was jump down onto the creature's back and hope he had enough strength to overcome whatever happened next.

AEDAN JUMPED DOWN.

The drop was not too far but, far enough, his right leg gave way. He fell and tumbled across the beast's bouncy back. Aedan stood up and could feel the flesh squish beneath the scales. He looked around. He wondered if he was dreaming. He wondered how it was possible. He wondered what would come next. His life had led to this very moment, and he was here. Everything he had been through seemed trivial now that his eye was on the prize. Of course, he still had to make it back up to Sylvinar, but even that seemed straightforward compared to what he had already endured.

Aedan surveyed the back of the beast, looking for a suitable scale to craft his armour. He limped from one scale to the next. Each one was too small for him. They suited a normal Sa'ami, but his lanky body would require a longer scale. His eyes transfixed on one jutting out from beneath the rest. It was abnormally long. He knew this was meant to be. He approached the scale and, using his hunting knife, severed it from the feather-like tubing which connected it to the under-skin.

Something scampered past behind Aedan. He turned around and saw nothing. He strapped the scale onto his back. The scampering sound surrounded him! There were a few bugs, the size of his foot, with long, sharp stingers curved over their backs. More bugs crawled out from underneath the scales of the Traxy. They were symbiotes protecting their home.

Let me guess; these guys are poisonous, he thought.

The killer insects closed in on Aedan. Aedan saw the camp fire site was close. The bugs tried to sting his legs. He limped, hopped and jumped his way towards the beast's head. If he were lucky, for once, on these most wretched of days, the Traxy would be close enough to the campfire site that he would be able to swim the distance to shore. But the swarm of bugs, all hellbent on ending his life, were closing in on him; and, all he could do was hop and hope.

What a predicament to be in! If only Ferni could see me now, he thought. But, alas, she would hear the retelling and doubt the accuracy of his story. "You have such a wild imagination," she would say.

The bugs closed in with each hop he took. He could feel the stingers nipping at his heels. He looked over his shoulder and saw a sea of beady, yellow eyes chasing after him. He turned back and saw the campfire site within reach. It was now or never. He threw himself off the side of the beast just as a bug stuck his right boot with its stinger. Aedan fell, and tumbled, and rolled, and bumped, and bounced all the way down the left side of the beast. The Traxy stopped at the destination, oblivious to what had transpired on its back. It leaned down, ate the embers, relishing in the warmth they provided.

Splush! Aedan splashed into the primordial ooze. The stench almost crippled him. He poked his head out of the gunk and doggy-paddled towards the clearing. He had landed not too far from shore and was there within moments. He watched the Traxy hulk away. Aedan screamed with joy. He'd made it. And, all he lost in the process was one of his boots. He took off his other boot and threw it in the sludge. He saw his rope was still dangling where he left it. He got up and limped, barefoot, towards it.

AEDAN COLLAPSED FROM a sudden, sharp pain in his abdomen. He looked at his gut. There was an arrow protruding from the side. He was confused. Who would be hunting at these depths? A Gnossian? A Gautarian? Maybe a Ras'i far from home?

"You're such an idiot, brother," chuckled Kainan.

Aedan's was shocked to hear his brother's voice but also glad: *What great fortune Kainan would turn up to help him in his darkest hour.*

"Be careful. There is a hunter nearby. I've been hit with an arrow," Aedan warned his brother.

Kainan laughed. "Like I said. An idiot."

"I don't understand. What are you saying?" Aedan held onto his disbelief.

"I'm the hunter, you ridiculous excuse for a Sa'ami. I shot you. I will take your scale and leave you here to die. Is that clear enough for you?" Kainan yelled, spittle ejecting from his mouth as he knelt next to Aedan. "Then I will tell Ferni how I tried to save your life when you tripped over a rock, but you fell to your death like the clumsy idiot that you are. Don't worry. I'll make sure she forgets your name once we are married, and she bears my children."

Aedan threw a punch at Kainan, but he was too weak; Kainan caught Aedan's hand and used it to roll him over. Kainan removed the Traxy scale off Aedan's back, severed the beacon-bracelet off Aedan's wrist, and threw it into the ocean. He stepped on Aedan's back and climbed up the rope with the Traxy scale slung over his shoulder.

"See you later, brother. Good luck finishing The Trial," Kainan cackled.

Aedan rolled over and watched as his brother vanished into the darkness above. A few moments later, the rope fell into a heap next to him.

AEDAN WAS NOT SAD. He was not upset. He was not even worried. He was angry. He was furious. He was fired up. He had not endured everything to give up now. He knew he could get back home if he did not give up.

Aedan pulled himself up against the tree trunk. He grabbed the arrowhead and pulled the arrow through his body. It hurt like hell, but he was used to pain. He threw the arrow to a side and applied pressure to the wound. He dressed the wound as best he could with pieces of his clothing. One more injury to add to the list. He'd have to lose his head to stop now.

"Kainan must be possessed or under some spell," Aedan thought to himself.

Aedan found a branch big enough for him to stand on. He cut it in half, so he had two. Then craft them into flat wedges. Next, he chopped the tree trunk making a deep incision at shoulder height. He stuck one of the wedges in, climbed onto it, then cut another incision, stuck the other wedge in and climbed that. Then, he removed the wedge below and repeated the process. It was slow and painful, but he was climbing. Aedan would never quit now. Not even death could stop him.

A Formal Request

Maya crouched deep, flexing her left leg, ready to leap. She spread out her right leg sideways, stabilising her lithe frame. Shun, her Drayph monk guardian, threw three crispy apples in the air. The round fruits flew in confusing trajectories across the royal chamber. Maya fanned out three feather-darts in her right palm. She leapt up, twisting and twirling her body through the air. Her garment's tassels and frills swirled around her in perfect symmetry. Her long ponytail added to the mesmerising corkscrew effect. She blew the darts from her hand as she spun like a tornado over Shun's head, splitting each fruit straight down the middle. The test was over in a few seconds. Maya landed semi-prone, with her hands braced on the floor and her legs posed, ready to launch into a sprint as if to run from some unseen attack. With a cheeky grin on her face, she looked up at Shun.

"Pretty good. Wouldn't you agree?" Maya spoke with the voice of an eager child.

Shun spoke with a measured, stoic voice gesticulating with her right index finger as she adjusted the white rope belt around her orange silk gown with her left hand. "Good, it may be. But do not be satisfied. Satisfaction leads to procrastination."

Maya nodded. "You are right. I could have been faster, and I did hesitate for a small moment."

"We will work on your form. It is through the familiarity of form that you will achieve speed in execution," Shun lectured. "We are done for the morning. You should now seek nutrition to replenish your stores. I will meet you in the breakfast garden." Shun bowed with her right hand across her chest, holding her blond, braided ponytail and exited the royal chamber.

Maya entered her ornate bedroom. It was themed in white with the red and blue colours of Mhan accentuating details and gold trimmings and tassels on the edges. The four-post bed was made of a single carved piece of white marble draped with curtains and a fine mosquito net. Dotted along the white marble wall was her white wood armoire and dressing table with effigies of her family carved into the edges and handles all pressed with gold and dashed with accents of lapis lazuli and red onyx. Two tall windows opened onto a grand balcony with a pillared balustrade overrun with creepers covered in sweet-smelling flora. Adjoining the main room was a lavish boudoir as well, leading into her private bathing chamber.

Maya wore titanium bracers and anklets and Symbian boots with knee-high, diamond-weave stockings capable of deflecting blades. Maya preferred to leave her upper legs bare for freedom of movement. She also wore a high-cut, single piece bodysuit in Nai blue embellished with white frills and trimmings. Maya donned a short front and rear train made of the same magically reinforced, flowing silk as her tight one-piece. Her hair was braided into a long ponytail down to her waist, held together by multiple ribbons, and at the end, she weighed it down with a tail-blade; a weapon wielded by Drayph monks. Maya removed everything until she was naked.

She submerged herself into her free-standing bathtub of such girth she could stretch out. The water was steaming hot and sprinkled with beautiful smelling musk petals. She closed her eyes and relaxed. She relaxed as much as she could, but she was unhappy. She was a young girl who should have been enjoying the life of a princess under the tutelage of her queen and king, but instead, she felt overwhelmed to be without parents and be responsible for an entire country. Her mother had taught her well, but some days she could not be bothered dealing with the politics of keeping the royal court and nobles in check. It sometimes felt like members of the court were trying to manipulate her. For the good of their own people, which she understood but, at times, it was avarice which drove their hearts.

Oh, how she would have loved to be a village girl for once. To sit idle under a tree all day and watch her flock. To dress however she liked, no matter how skimpy it may be. To be able to kiss a boy and talk about it with her friends. But, alas, she was doomed to sit in Castle Mhan and carry the burden of an entire nation until her dying days. She thought of stepping down, but the power vacuum it would create was a terrible thought. It would, without a doubt, lead to civil war. And, what if her mother or father returned?

She must've lain in her bath for quite some time. Her skin had pruned. She decided she couldn't stay in there all day and had to confront the irritations of her station. She pat dried her body and then draped on each layer of her undergarments and clothes. Even during the warmer months, she was expected to wear her complete, royal attire.

Why can't I just wear a lovely frilly dress? She pined.

Exhausted, she sat down half-dressed and stared out the window at the clear blue sky. She watched the swallows sweep across the sky in coordinated unison. How she longed to fly away from her problems and travel to a distant land where she was unknown and could disappear into anonymity.

"Your majesty. Everyone is waiting for you in the royal court. I suggest you dress, have breakfast, and tend to your daily duties promptly." Shun encouraged Maya from the doorway.

Maya looked up at Shun with tears welling in her eyes. "Not today. Please, not today. Can I just sleep today and have a rest?"

Shun walked over to Maya and stood her up. She continued to dress her. "Life is there to be lived. Not to be avoided. We must do what we must because there are those who depend on us."

Maya just stood there as Shun finished dressing her.

"But who can I depend on?" asked Maya.

"You can depend on me, my lady," Shun said with the deepest sincerity.

They both exited the room side-by-side with their heads held high.

MAYA GRACED INTO THE royal court. No matter how she felt, she always walked with regal confidence. While her stature was small, her presence in the room was all-encompassing. The royal court bowed before her as she glided past each member. She took her place on the throne.

Rheal, the stout court scribe in a red suit with white stockings, approached her, twirling his pencil moustache and mumbled, "Good morning, your majesty. We have President Gonzel of Antillia here today who wishes to establish a trade route for...."

Maya could not remember what was discussed or what was said in detail. However, she could recall not being well-liked for her decisions. Many nobles wanted her to grant tax-free trade routes to specific nations, others wanted criminal laws relaxed, and some wanted more resources for their fief.

Maya ruled with logic. Tax-free trade would deplete the nation's coffers, benefiting the noble who wished to line their pockets. Relaxing criminal laws would encourage wrongdoers to do more wrong. More resources would be nice, but, in all honesty, if a fief was unable to sustain itself, it should relocate or join the capital. Maya declined all requests with royal politeness.

Back in her bedroom, she removed her royal attire with the assistance of Shun. Her morning tasks completed, she would have lunch before doing her rounds across the castle and other establishments in the capital. Her evening would entail another round of political requests and negotiations before she could have her dinner and retire for the evening.

She switched into a relaxed, flowing dress but of extreme elegance fit for a queen. She combed her long hair over her shoulders and applied some afternoon shades of Tinian powder onto her eyes and lips. She was a stunning creature of such beauty that with a simple glance of her eyes, she could distract even the most resolute man.

"You have a guest for dinner tonight," Shun advised her.

"Who!?" Maya spurted out. Guests were far and few, so this was some excitement in her dreary life.

"An old friend," Shun responded.

Maya jumped up, dropping her hairbrush as she ran out of the room towards the dining hall. Her feet skipped across marble pavement. She burst through the hallway entry and saw her father's oldest and dearest friend, Lord Venon of Thule. She had grown up calling him uncle as a young girl, back when he visited more often. Lord Venon and Maya's father, King Kanon, had been on campaigns together during the Great Manah Wars. It was through their alliance order was established, and Concordia inaugurated. The nobles voted King Kanon of Mhan to rule Concordia, but Lord Venon had always had the most significant influence in the royal court as the most respected lord.

Venon's height and slender build radiated authority. He wore the dark purple colours of Thule. He looked like he was in his late thirties, lest he betrays his true age by saying it. His eyes were a deep brown, almost black, matching his short tussled hair adorned with a jewelled band. He had a haughty countenance that melted away with a warm smile when he saw Maya.

Maya darted towards him. "Oh, Venon! How glad I am to see you!" She leapt on him and hugged him the way a young girl hugged her father after not seeing him for a long time."

Venon chuckled and grabbed hold of her by her shoulders. "Let me look at you," he said as he gazed all over her body and then into her eyes. "You grow more beautiful every day. Just like your mother."

Maya blushed. "Oh, you! I can't believe you are here. What brings you to my home?"

"Am I not welcome?" he quipped with a tilt of his head as Maya laughed. "I have come to see how things are. It has been almost a year since I last came, and it was on official business. It seems unless there is business, we do not make an effort anymore."

"You are always welcome here. I sometimes wish I did not have to rule so I could visit you more," Maya pined.

"You do not sound content," Venon enquired.

Maya gave a half-hearted smile in sheepish acknowledgement. "Is it that obvious?"

"Let us talk with some food in our bellies and drink to our lips," Venon suggested with a beaming smile and uplifting tone.

They sat opposite each other on a quaint little table perched on one of the many royal balconies overhanging the castle's royal gardens. It was a beautiful afternoon with local birds chirping amongst the trees and flowers. Lum radiated a loving warmth, and the air was breezy enough to ward off the encroaching heat. The main course was fresh fish from the great ocean with a crisp garden salad. The fish was a large Crimson Royal. It was the size of a small child with flaky, delicate flesh. Its flavour was accentuated with the local zesty lemons and aromatic herbs. The royal cooks had prepared a selection of the most exotic fruits, coupled with coarse spices, seeds, and nuts for dessert.

Venon sipped tea from the tiny, decorative teacup. His eyes engaged Maya over the rim of his cup. Maya felt embarrassed and looked down at her cup. She had always thought Venon to be quite handsome for an older man. Maya was at a point in her adolescence where she was very conscientious of her looks. She tried her best to look disaffected, cool and pretty because she felt she had to.

Venon sensed the opportunity to speak his mind. "Maya, my dear. I must admit with quite a bit of shame that I have actually come here on what is not purely a visit for the sake of a visit. I do have an ulterior motive."

Maya felt somewhat confused by Venon's statement. Though she appreciated the candour, all of a sudden, she felt manipulated. "Really? So this visit is all show? And here I thought it was purely out of friendship. To see an old friend and say hello."

"Well, it is quite more than that. This visit is out of courtship," Venon leaned towards Maya, expecting a response.

Courtship? Maya was stunned. She was nineteen years old and Venon, if she was not mistaken, was at least seventy-five, if not eighty years old. "I must admit I am shocked you would think courtship appropriate. My father. Your age. I assume you must have an excellent reason or a sense of humour?"

"I do have a sense of humour, but I am not joking about this. My age is irrelevant if you feel I am strong. My age would play to your advantage. You would acquire more land and wealth for your kingdom in our union. You know me and trust me. I am good friends with your father, and you can safely assume he would approve of our union," Venon replied.

"They are valid points, my dear old friend," Maya paused and took her time thinking of how to say what she needed to say but said it the only way it could be said. "But I do not love you."

"You do not? Yet you call me dear friend? As your dear friend, do you not love me?" Venon asked, furrowing his brow.

Maya was becoming uncomfortable with his questioning. "Venon, please. Of course, I 'love' you as a friend, but not romantically, and I do not see marriage as an option between us."

"Romance, passion, love are but fleeting emotions. You need someone who will be there for you when things are difficult. I am reliable, honest, trustworthy, sincere, gentle and strong. I am a man who knows what it is like to be young and alone. We share much in common. At least do me the honour to grant me a few more opportunities to court you and convince you we should marry?" Venon pleaded with the most gentle and loving intonation.

Maya snapped back. "No Venon. There will be no courting. I intend to marry someone I love. I intend to marry for the right reasons. I intend to wait until my father returns so he may give me away to the man I love. Everything will be right with the world when I marry. I must also marry someone I feel drawn to physically so I may bear their children. As far as needing someone to be there for me, I have Shun. My father was wise to bring her into my life. If you do not mind, I must excuse myself. I have much to attend. My aides will provide you with anything you need so you may commence your trip back to Thule."

"I do mind," Venon replied with a slight irritation in his voice. "How can you be so rude to me, your majesty? We have grown up together. Your father is like my brother. You can not rule this kingdom without a king. Surely you must feel the discomfort in the royal court. Surely you've heard the murmurings. Your father's return is unlikely. After five years, many suspect he is with Nai now. You must marry. You need a king to help you rule these lands before you have an uprising. Don't be a foolish child. Listen to me."

"Shut your mouth. I am your queen, and you will not speak to me like that!" Maya burst out. "How dare you come here on the presumption of friendship to convince me I need a king, a man, to rule. You speak of my father as if he means nothing to you. If he were like your brother, why have you never bothered to search for him? Why did you not go into the Underworld and return with him? Your actions betray your words 'dear friend'. Lest you offend me anymore, I would suggest you say nothing further and head back home. I will dispatch an emissary so you may pay your taxes, and I will see you in the court for any formal matters."

Maya stood up and was about to leave.

Venon grabbed her by the wrist. "Maya! Stop!"

Before he could say another word, Maya twisted his arm around. He dropped onto one knee. "How do you choose to die, cretin?" Maya yelled. Shun leapt up from the balcony below and placed a dagger to Venon's neck.

Venon pleaded. "I am so sorry, your majesty. I do not know what came over me." Tears began streaming down his face. "I am such an old fool. I have fallen in love with you and thought I could court you. Please forgive me. I will pay any penalty."

Maya released him. "I should have you beheaded for trying to manhandle me. Venon, you are truly an idiot. Our friendship is no more. That is your penalty. Out of my sight forever. I never want to see you again. All communications are to be through proxy. Now, be gone."

Maya stormed off the balcony. Shun placed her dagger back in its sheathe.

Venon shambled through the hallways, back to his royal carriage in the forecourt, and commenced the long ride back to his kingdom of Thule.

Battle at Fort Watch

South of Mhan, on the border of Thule, Fort Watch was under attack in the cloak of the night by an undead army of beasts and men. Unlike Fort Bosk, this fort was well garrisoned, with a full complement of soldiers, cavalry, spearmen and archers, but the enemy outnumbered them a hundred to one. The army flooded the front gates and surrounded the fort like a sea of death.

Commander Shep, an Exquisite Swordweaver of the Mhan Royal Army, lead the defence with outright confidence. Like all Swordweavers, he wore tight leather armour buckled up the front. His arms were bare, and the leather was in thin segments held together with titanium links for freedom of movement. The armour ended in a short front and rear train. His leather boots were knee-high and edged with gold like his armour to indicate his rank of Exquisite.

His soldiers had been training for years. They had tried, many times, to convince their commander to take it easy, but he would make them practice every day. Thousands upon thousands of drills forged the cohesive battalion he commanded on that night. The soldiers took their stations without hesitation, without fear and without thought; ready for combat, ready to die.

The enemies' mindless bludgeoning of the front gate belted it in an inch at a time. The garrison within the fort braced the gate with steel struts. The foreyard was filled with spearmen and cavalry, ready to absorb the inevitable wave of enemies.

"This is nothing, my brothers and sisters. We have prepared for this. This will be the day you become heroes of Mhan!" Commander Shep boomed. The intonation of his voice penetrated their souls, filling them with courage; so, their chests grew in size and their hearts in resolve.

"Hurrah!" they cheered.

The enemy was relentless. It clawed, banged and bashed every inch of the fort perimeter; if there were a weakness, they would find it. As a result, the fort looked like a dead insect surrounded by hungry ants feasting on its corpse.

"Sir. What is that?" asked Regaz, a young female archer. She pointed to a black cloud approaching the fort.

Shep squinted, trying to see what it was. *Maybe it is some kind of magical conjuration?* he thought and wondered how a host of this size, with mages in its ranks, could get this deep inside Mhan undetected. However, he did not wonder for too long and immediately took action.

"Prep your boom-arrows!" Shep ordered.

The archers pulled out the special arrows from their quivers. Boom-arrows had fat heads filled with silver powder known as dragon's meal.

"Aim at that black mass in the sky. Fire on my command." Shep took station next to the line of archers. He stared at the black cloud, squinting his eyes. It was a swarm of Ranhi: flesh-eating bats indigenous to the caves of Ras'Fahem. If they breached the fort perimeter, every soldier would be eaten alive in a matter of minutes.

Shep signalled the archers. "Fire!"

Woosh! Ka-boom! The arrows created a massive explosion on impact, blasting the bats into oblivion. The swarm swirled like a tornado made of fire as it rolled and tumbled down to the ground near the fort's front gates, setting alight everything around it.

The battlefield in front of the gate was lit up as if it were day. The Harbingers stood out from amongst the other beasts. They were giants with deformed heads and mutated bodies. Some had three legs and others two heads; sometimes, it was hard to tell where their bodies started and ended. They were the bastardised result of Gnossian experiments in creature manipulation. Noble giants turned into mindless, deformed beasts who craved pain. These monsters were those same giants raised from the dead to crave pain once again.

Scattered between the Harbingers were the Batyles. They were no larger than a Kun, resembling tiny Traxys with the addition of a long tail with spiked bones on the end. They were also capable of extending their necks and snapping their crocodile-like snouts. However, their turtle-like appearance and lumbering gait was deceiving as they could dash short distances with blinding speed.

The enemies burned, but the flames did not deter them. They continued to barrage the gate. Their burning bodies gave off a dark, intense smoke, which obscured them. If it continued, they would burn through the gate. That was something Shep had not considered when he ordered the explosive arrows to be fired upon the enemy. No one in recent times had been trained for battle against an undead army; lest of all, confront one.

Shep studied the smoke covered front line of enemies. He ran around the top of the fort to get a better view of something he noticed at the enemy's rear: a dark figure on horseback. It looked like a human but twice as large. It would gesture, and the front line would respond in unison, controlled by magic.

"Concentrate all fire on that target!" Shep screamed his order with an emphatic signal of his hand.

The archery contingent opened fire on the figure. A volley of arrows rained down on the target, but it had vanished. Shep lost sight of the enemy. It was too dark and too distant. He knew whatever it was; it was the head of the army.

The horde at the gate was clambering over themselves. The bodies piled up and started to form a smouldering mound. One beast piled on top of the other, and the mound grew in size in only a matter of moments. Then, the shadowy figure on horseback galloped out from the dark towards the gate.

"Keep firing! Do not stop until I tell you to!" Shep pointed at the rider.

With each stride, the undead stead was struck with a volley of arrows, but it had no effect on the creature's forward momentum. The person astride deflected every projectile fired at them with deft sword work.

As the figure galloped towards the gate, Shep took a long, hard look at his enemy. Then, knowing he was gazed upon, the rider looked up at Shep. The vampire bared his fangs, then leapt off his ride in a powerful forward summersault, flew through the air, landed near the pile of undead, and started running up the mound. The vampire climbed the mass, like a flight of stairs, and was atop before anyone could even train an arrow on him. He leapt the last few metres over the battlements and, in what seemed to the casual observer like a whirlwind of incomprehensible sword moves, slew all the archers nearby. Shep, with a contingent of enraged comrades, led the charge towards the vampire.

In a single stride that defied logic, the vampire darted to the gate's draw ropes and sliced them with a single sweep of his sword. The gate rose as the counterweights came crashing down. The burning mound toppled over, and the sea of enflamed enemies flowed into the foreyard. The cavalry charged into the horde of doom. They slew as many creatures as they could but would watch them rise back up off the ground unharmed. The beasts swarmed the horsemen, pulled them off their rides, and disembowelled them on the floor.

Shep stood face to face with a Ras'i vampire. Like all Ras'i, it towered over humans and had a broad, muscular body. His yellowy-green, lizard-like eyes glinted in the moonlight, and his matte red, rock-like skin was covered in sharp, bony protrusions on his knuckles, brow, shoulders and knees.

The vampire swung his sword at Shep. Shep blocked the blade inches from his neck. The vampire cocked his head in confusion; Shep was not cannon fodder to be disposed of without effort. Two of Shep's soldiers flanked the vampire but were decapitated by a swift, spin attack. Shep took the opportunity to thrust his blade into the enemy but almost lost his balance when it was parried away effortlessly. Such was the vampire's skill; even a Swordweaver of Shep's calibre was unable to trouble him. The vampire attacked Shep with multiple strikes in quick succession. Shep worked very hard to fend off the fast swordsmanship. The vampire was efficient and precise with his sword work. Shep was tiring in his effort to keep up, and the vampire could smell the blood pumping through the exhausted commander's veins.

The men slain by the vampire rose from the ground. Vampires could amass massive armies of undead because each enemy they slew became a servant. On this night, Shep was witnessing this vile magic rise up against him and his country.

The vampire closed in on Shep. Shep knew he needed a better position, more support, and some luck to even hope of defeating this thing. Shep jumped off the concourse to the portcullis below and slid down the Mhan royal banner into the foreyard. Amongst the horde of his army, the vampire lost sight of the commander.

Shep hacked and slashed his way through the flailing, rotten limbs that tried to tear him apart from every angle. He almost killed a soldier of Mhan by mistake. The soldier tried to bite him. Shep pushed him back and realised he was wearing a shredded outfit from Fort Bosk, but he was undead. He was a beast, like all the other creatures in this army. Shep hesitated for a moment before slicing him in half. He evaluated the battlefield and saw many soldiers from various forts and smaller establishments in its ranks.

"Some look like our comrades but have been turned to darkness. Show no mercy!" Shep yelled.

He wondered how to turn the tables in this unwinnable situation. He knew two knights of the Order of Caval were due for a training drill the next day. Maybe they had sensed danger, with their clairvoyant powers, days ago and were rushing to the fort to provide aid. Perhaps they made good time and would arrive any moment. Shep's wonderment turned to faith. He knew they would be here soon. He knew Nai was on their side. He knew this was not to be their defeat.

"The Order of Caval will join us soon! Fortify towards the rear of the foreyard. Let's hold them off until our friends arrive!" Shep's commands reverberated throughout the entire fort. All the soldiers retreated and formed a sizeable defensive unit at the back of the foreyard. Their shields, swords, spears, lances and arrowheads formed an interwoven barricade, impenetrable to the enemy. The undead soldiers, Kuns, Harbingers, and Batyles, swarmed the men, but every enemy was met with a blade.

Shep coordinated the movements and defences. "Watch them move. Leftward. Heave!"

The men flocked one way then another, deflecting, slicing, and pushing back with determination. The men's teeth clenched, brows furrowed, and sweat poured over their sinewy muscles as they worked for their very survival. But, as each moment passed, their energy drained; they became less responsive and more sluggish.

The vampire ran over the top of his horde like a sheep dog and straddled a Harbinger. He studied the formation of the soldiers.

He knew if Shep fell, the rest would falter. He knew they had no means of defeating an undead army. It was only a matter of time before the soldiers gave way to exhaustion. The vampire sat atop the Harbinger, waiting for an error in the defensive line to penetrate and drive his blade into Shep's chest. *What a slave Shep will make!* Savouring the thought, he grinned and clenched the hilt of his sword in anticipation.

Shep noticed his soldiers' formation breaking up in parts. "For Nai's sake, keep focused! The knights are but upon us. Hold your ground. Our salvation is almost here."

But his words could not undo what the tired muscles of his soldiers felt. Their limbs burned and throbbed. Each push and impact wearied them. The gap in their formation increased in size. The vampire perched himself on top of the Harbinger's shoulders like a feline about to pounce; his blade pointed back and skywards, ready to slice through the heart of the defence.

A bright ray of light cut through the horde.

Undead dropped to the ground clutching their eyes. The angelic radiance of the beam carved a straight path. The source was Relianstar, a Champion Cavalier of the Knights of Mahn in shining silver armour upon a white steed riding to the soldiers' aid, followed by Browbearer, a more miniature Champion Cavalier decked out in Gnossian battle gear, riding a brown and white horse. The mere sight of these two heroes reinvigorated the soldiers.

Relianstar chanted, "By the blessing of our Lady, rise up and slay her enemies!"

The soldiers felt refreshed. Their blades glowed with magical energy. They could fight back! They smote the undead, gaining strength with each one they fell.

Relianstar leapt off the white steed, which galloped away into the dark, and joined the battle. She lifted her face guard. Relianstar was a veteran woman with cool blue eyes and warm, tanned skin. She wielded a sharpened lance and sliced through hordes of the enemy with each swing.

Browbearer's battle-axe was molten hot, powered by a red manah capsule embedded in the hilt. Browbearer wielded his weapon with gusto. It was a tornado of death and destruction.

Crack! Crunch! Smash! The axe came to a sudden, jarring stop on impact with a Kun's skull. Browbearer dislodged it with his plated boot and continued to mow through the undead army.

"You must escape. Take what rides you have and make haste to Castle Mhan. Stay here at your peril," Relianstar commanded the melange of fighters.

"And abandon the fort?" Shep retorted.

"It is the only way." Relianstar had but just finished her sentence when she was struck hard on her side by the vampire's blade. The impact dented her armour and sent her flying across a pack of Kuns.

The vampire darted towards her fallen body to kill her.

Blut! Blut! Blut! Blut! Blut! Browbearer unloaded an entire clip of bolts from his mechanised cross-bow. The vampire's rugged body was hammered. He dropped to the floor in a daze.

"Run!" Browbearer's deep voice boomed out of his sound grille. Like all Gnoss, his armour was a self-contained biome, made of a flexible material covered in various polygonal plates of titanium, which enabled him to survive above ground, away from his natural environment beneath the surface of Alteria.

Shep led his men through the path the knights had carved. Browbearer pulled Relianstar up. Her magic armour popped back to perfection.

"M'lady," Browbearer growled.

Relianstar charged the vampire with Browbearer by her side. The vampire shook off his daze, pounced up, and scaled the fort's inner wall like a lizard. He was afraid of these two knights. He was not prepared for this type of enemy. With a gesture of his hand, he commanded his minions to swarm the knights at the expense of allowing Shep and the fort's soldiers to escape.

"You go. I'll deal with these beasts," Browbearer snorted.

Relianstar nodded in affirmation. Browbearer boosted her up the wall towards the vampire. She thrust her lance skywards. A bright aura emanated from her weapon, cutting through the dark, threatening the vampire's very existence. The vampire jumped back out of the way and mumbled arcane words. He was forced to channel his dark magic in defence, acknowledging this knight as a true combatant. A dark forcefield surrounded the vampire's body that absorbed Relianstar's holy magic. This duel would, therefore, be settled with their blades.

Shep and his men mounted their steeds, three to each horse, and headed northwards, at speed, into the night.

Browbearer was outnumbered. The undead swarmed him. He aimed his crossbow up at the concourse and fired a bolt with a steel line attached. The bolt lodged itself onto the fort wall, and the manah powered mechanism on his right bracer winched him upwards. He dropped a small ball onto the floor as he flew away.

Ka-boom! The ball, a Gnossian grenade, exploded in a massive fireball of intense heat. The undead creatures caught alight and burned to a cinder.

Browbearer landed on the concourse. Relianstar was locked in a heated duel with the vampire. She thrust and swooped her lance and, with a twirl, leapt into an overhead attack. The vampire dodged her attacks with clever footwork and countered with a combination of thrusts and strikes of his own. Relianstar had to backpedal while blocking with her lance. The vampire was leading her to the edge of the wall.

Browbearer loaded a lightning bolt into his crossbow. The Gnoss designed these bolts to paralyse and kill powerful vampires, but the shot had to land on the heart. Browbearer pressed a jewel on his crossbow, and a crosshair sight popped up. He aimed. The vampire stopped for a moment. Browbearer took the shot. The bolt was on target, but the vampire leaned back and watched the bolt fly inches past his chest. He knew he was lucky not to have been killed, so he took the opportunity to leap over the fort wall and escape into the darkness.

"You missed," Relianstar glared through her faceguard at Browbearer. "You can not miss."

Browbearer jumped up onto the fort wall and searched the darkness, switching through the various viewing lenses on his multi-vision goggles. But the vampire was nowhere to be seen. Then, Browbearer heard a thunderous stampede, so he turned to look at the source of the racket. A second wave of undead flowed into the foreyard and filled it like water fills a lake.

"I'm sorry m'lady. We better make haste our escape." Browbearer spoke with a down-beaten voice.

Relianstar observed the foreyard. Her steely mask glistened in the moonlight. "Very well."

She jumped up onto the wall next to Browbearer. Browbearer fired dual grapples from a gas-powered, double-barrel shotgun. The grapples unravelled two steel ropes from reels attached to his left thigh guard. The steel ropes wrapped around a pillar on the wall, twenty metres away. Browbearer handed one of the ropes to Relianstar and dropped off the ledge. Relianstar followed him. Each of them let out a sharp, long whistle, which crescendoed into an arpeggio. Browbearer's arpeggio was legato and drone-like, whereas Relianstar's arpeggio was staccato and uplifting.

They ran on the surface of the wall, along the pendulum trajectory inscribed by the length of the ropes. As they swung toward the bottom of the arc, their steeds galloped into view, having responded to the whistled calls of their masters. Relianstar and Browbearer pushed off the wall, still holding onto their ropes; they glided directly above their respective horse's back and let go. They landed on their mounts, took hold of the harnesses and turned away from the fort at speed, heading northwards, back to Castle Mhan.

The Ras'i vampire seethed beneath the canopy of an old weathered tree whose leaves had just started to bloom but withered and fell to the ground in the presence of his blight. He held a fort soldier, who was clinging to life, by the hair. The vampire thrust his black longsword into the man's back. A few moments later, the soldier's eyes flickered dead open, and he stood up ready to serve his new master.

The vampire spat his words. "It is only a matter of time, and you will all bow before me."

The End of the Trial

Kainan puffed on his pipe and drank wine from a flask while he gobbled down some roast quail. He admired the massive Traxy scale. *The lanky idiot had to pick the biggest one*, Kainan thought to himself. It was such a pain to carry on his back. He had to lean forward so it wouldn't drag on the ground. He loathed his brother. He knew he shouldn't but, it wasn't fair. Nai had blessed Aedan with everything he wanted. When he thought about it, he hated Nai as well. Everyone worshipped her, but she was not a fair god when you thought about it. *I probably would have done the same thing to Nai. After all, no one is going to give you anything in this world. You have to take it for yourself. Might is right.*

Kainan had marked the trees with his blade when he descended so that he could find his way back up. He killed anything he came across just to be sure, like the stupid Hunting Horror on the upper canopy; he riddled her with arrows and burned her nest. Those babies would, one day, kill someone. He couldn't help but laugh to himself. Now with Aedan out of the picture, he didn't have to worry about Eldoran playing favourites. His father would have no choice but to honour his right as tribal leader, and Ferni wouldn't want to marry anyone else. Kainan hated his father for being such an idiot. *What moron doesn't choose their first son to lead the tribe?*

Kainan was tired. He sat down and checked his backpack. He didn't have any food or wine left. He boiled up some water and made himself some tea. He took his time. There was no point in rushing.

He drank his fill and smoked a session on his pipe before continuing his ascent.

He heard a loud noise as if something dropped from above onto the branch he was traversing. He looked around and saw nothing, but he was sure something had jumped down. He pulled his bow out and aimed at the void. He couldn't see very well in the darkness, but it wasn't too bad; he was close to the surface, and some light was leaking in through the canopy. He scanned the shadows with his arrow, waiting for something to jump out.

Silence.

Kainan relaxed and continued walking. He reached a drop and realised he had made a wrong turn somewhere. He would have to backtrack, but there was a rustling noise behind him. He drew his short sword, stolen from his father, and walked towards the noise. His hand was shaking, soaked in sweat; the blade was slipping from his grip. He was terrified. He didn't want to get hurt. He didn't want to feel pain.

Then he saw three of *them* walking towards him. They looked like soldiers from Mhan. Outpost soldiers, maybe from Fort Bosk? But they walked with an unnatural gait. It was jarring. They walked with a sudden flinch at a time. They walked as if driven by something else. He could smell the rank of their flesh. He could tell they were dead, and they wanted him dead too.

"Hey there," Kainan struggled to pronounce the words.

They broke into a jog towards him. They let out a gargled squelch from their rotten lungs. It was disgusting and disturbing.

Kainan froze. He didn't know what to do. Within moments the three undead minions were upon him. They raised their weapons and were about to smash him to death. But then, a blur swung down from a branch above and knocked them down.

It was Aedan. Bloodied, bruised, broken, but unstoppable.

"Get up. We need to run," Aedan commanded Kainan.

Kainan stared at Aedan in shock.

The minions were rising.

"Now!" Yelled Aedan.

Kainan jumped up.

"Run after me." Aedan led the way.

Kainan followed Aedan, who strode ahead aided by a makeshift crutch. The minions got up in a rage and gave chase. Kainan's legs were shaking and almost gave way under him.

"Try and keep up!" Aedan demanded.

Spurred by Aedan's courage, Kainan stopped and shot a few arrows at the undead. The arrows impaled themselves into the enemies but had no effect.

Aedan yanked Kainan. "They're undead! You can't kill them with arrows or swords," Aedan explained as he dragged Kainan along. Kainan kept tripping as the Traxy scale clipped his heels.

"This way." Aedan led Kainan up a very steep branch.

The undead minions closed in on them at an alarming pace.

"You idiot," yelled Kainan, "they're going to catch us and kill us!"

"Shut up, brother. I'm here to save your life," Aedan said.

Aedan and Kainan reached the top of the branch. The minions were a few metres behind. Kainan collapsed from exhaustion.

Aedan faced the oncoming enemies. As their heads came into view from below, Aedan pulled back some shrubs. There lay the dead salamander he'd slain the day before. With a slash from his hunting knife, he disembowelled the beast. Its acidic blood sprayed all over the undead soldiers. They melted, they slumped, they contorted, they pooled, and turned into a gooey heap.

Kainan stared at his brother in disbelief. He watched as the last remains of the undead evaporated in smoke and seeped through the melting trunk. He looked back at Aedan and noticed the crutch, braced foot, beaten face, burned chest, and, of course, the bloodied arrow wound. At that moment, Kainan realised his brother was incorruptible.

"Why did you help me?" Kainan asked in genuine confusion.

Aedan looked at him square in the eyes and said, "For you will always be my brother."

Kainan stood up, removed the Traxy scale off his back, and placed it on the ground, "I believe this is yours."

"We can share it," Aedan responded.

Kainan looked at Aedan dumbfounded.

"What's wrong?" Aedan asked.

"What's wrong?" Kainan retorted. "I'll tell you what's wrong." His rage festered. "Nai has gifted you with everything I could ever want. You have been blessed with looks, with skill, with luck, and with strength. Not to mention, you also have the love of the girl I want and the favour of our father. But, for all the generosity Nai has bestowed upon you, this is not enough to quench your desire. You also wish to take my birthright: To rule all of Sylvinar. You have so much, and yet you want more. I, on the other hand, have nought but the ridicule of the town and now your pity. Of all things, there is nothing more repugnant than to be pitied by you," Kainan stole a breath, "And you ask me what is wrong?"

Aedan was disarmed by the revelation. It had never occurred to him that Kainan felt like nothing. He did not know what to say and offered the first words that came out of his mouth. "I am sorry Kainan. I am sorry, my brother. What would you like me to do?"

"Whatever in Akh's sake you wish to do. But I will never be your brother." With his last word, Kainan turned, jumped off the branch, and vanished into the lower canopy.

THE REST OF THE ASCENT was uneventful. It took a half-day more after he last saw Kainan. So close to the end, he felt exhausted.

Like he could not go on anymore. He broke through the upper canopy of The Depths and was almost blinded by the brightness. He waited until his eyes adjusted and continued his stride to the end.

Aedan loved the sensation of the warm sunlight on his skin as he walked the final stretch of The Trial, Traxy scale on his back, towards the Great Amphitheatre. He would soon arrive, to the cheers and adulation of his fellow tribespeople. He would hold Ferni in his arms and share stories from the last three days of his life. What a wonderful feeling it would be. He could not believe this was happening. He had dreamed of this moment his entire life. He felt the love of Nai, Ferni and his father in his heart. Aedan was on top of the world.

He hoped to convince Eldoran to make Kainan tribal leader. He was sure Kainan would rise to the challenge and become a better person. After all, Aedan would rather cuddle Ferni all day than being tied down with the responsibility of ruling Sylvinar.

He was surprised he couldn't hear anything as he approached the amphitheatre gates. Maybe he was a day late, and everyone had already celebrated and left? Maybe Ferni had already picked a husband? Perhaps it was Kainan? Aedan panicked; so, he ran into the amphitheatre ignoring the pain in his foot.

He passed through the entrance. The arena was empty. All he could hear were his footsteps. Sylvinar was dead quiet. Not even the milling sounds of the populace, which he expected to hear crackling through the air, could be heard. It was as if everyone had shut their mouths and stopped moving at the same time.

The sunlight cut through the dusty air. The wind rustled through the city. Off in the distance, wind chimes percussed. Aedan walked out of the arena, a little disorientated; the whole situation was disconcerting. The streets were empty. The balconies were empty. Never had the city been so dead.

Maybe father has responded to the threats by the hooded man? But surely he would not have evacuated the city without me? He thought.

Yet, it seemed like the entire city was empty.

He knocked on a door and waited. No one answered. He pushed the door open and looked inside the home. It was empty. He knocked on another door. No one answered. He looked inside. Empty. He banged on another, pushed in, looked; empty.

Everything and everywhere was empty.

He ran from door to door, hollering. "Hello? Is anyone here at all? What is going on?" It made him agitated, so he begged out loud. "For Nai's sake, what is going on? Please, Nai, help me!"

He ran as fast as his legs would carry him to his home. He smashed through the door and found Eldoran standing there; or rather, it looked like his father except made of stone. The doppelganger was posed with his right hand up as if telling someone to stop, and with his left hand, he was shielding someone behind him: it was Ferni. She was also petrified. Her eyes were wide open in fear. She was clutching onto Eldoran's tunic in despair. What cruel joke was this? All of Sylvinar had vanished, and the two most important people in his world were statues.

Grrrrawl! There was a loud snarl. Aedan spun around. His senses kicked back into gear at the sight of five ferocious, undead Kuns. He darted through the door and bolted up the stairwell as fast as he could. He ran for his life around the home tree but was unsure where he would run to and what he would do. He was alone. He did not have a plan. His pain was unbearable, and he was sure he was injuring his leg further by putting so much strain on it. The Kuns burst out the door and chased him.

Aedan felt all the energy drain out of his legs, and his thighs and calves burned from exhaustion. He was about to collapse at any moment. He began to stumble as he crossed the rope bridge from his home tree. The Kuns shoved one another out of the way as they pushed towards Aedan. Aedan dropped to his knees a metre before reaching the other side. He looked up at Kainan, who was standing there, right in front of him.

"Brother?" Aedan asked in genuine confusion and reached out to his brother, with his left arm, for help.

Kainan raised his sword, high above his head. He shifted his focus from Aedan to the Kuns, then back to Aedan. "I'm sorry," he said. He took hold of Aedan's left arm and yanked him clear of the bridge while striking the bridge's support ropes. The bridge collapsed, swung downwards, and the Kuns fell. They bounced and banged along the side of the tree, smashing platforms and barricades, as they tumbled to the bottom, landing with a solid thud on the ground below.

Aedan looked with eyes wide open at Kainan. "Brother?"

"Yes, Aedan," he grunted and let go of Aedan's arm. He stood up and sheathed his sword. He surveyed the surrounding area looking for any other possible threats.

"You saved me?" Aedan asked, confused.

"I do not like you, brother. But, Sylvinar is my home, and you are a Sa'ami. So I must protect you." Kainan's face was full of hatred towards Aedan, yet there seemed to be an air of responsibility surrounding him.

Aedan asked, "Have you seen Ferni and–"

Before he could finish, Kainan responded. "Yes, I have. And I do not wish to think about it."

"What are we going to do?" Aedan asked.

"We will board ourselves up at home until you are healed. Then you will go to Castle Mhan to seek assistance while I remain here to watch over the city," Kainan commanded.

"But what can you do if an army comes? What if you get turned to stone too?" Aedan asked his brother, worried for his safety.

"My fate will be no different to theirs. You run and seek help. That is what you are good at. I will stay here. I am tribal leader now until father is restored, so you will do as I say. If not, it is insubordination, and I will punish you with death. Right here. Right now." Kainan glared at his brother.

Aedan knew this was the closest they would ever be. "Ok brother. I will follow your lead," he responded.

Kainan looked down at where the Kuns had landed. They were no longer there. "We better move."

Kainan lifted Aedan off the ground and threw his left arm over his shoulder for support. There was no way to cross back to their home tree from where they were. They had no other choice but to go down.

"We must go down, but the Kuns will be waiting for us. Are you able to stand on your own?" Kainan asked Aedan.

"Yes, I can stand. Walk a little. But, beyond that, I am useless," Aedan sulked.

"Ok, follow me. We must be stealthy. Here take this." Kainan gave Aedan a short sword and a bow.

Kainan led the way. They crouched with their backs against the tree and snuck their way down the spiralling staircase. Their hands clenched around their swords' hilts. They approached the final flight of stairs. On the ground below, they saw the pack of Kuns milling near the entrance to their home, snapping at each other in frustration.

Kainan signalled Aedan to shoot an arrow at a line of pots above an archway about sixty metres away. Aedan nodded in agreement to the plan. The jars would crash to the ground, distract the Kuns, and they would sneak past.

Aedan placed his sword down, then drew his bow and an arrow. He lined up his shot and pulled the string back, flush against his right cheek. He let out his breath to steady his aim and was about to release the arrow when one of the Kuns spotted them. It growled to alert its companions. They bolted towards Kainan and Aedan.

Kainan grabbed a rope supporting the staircase, severed it, and yelled at Aedan, "Hold onto me!"

Aedan did not hesitate. He grabbed on for his life. Kainan kicked off the platform, and they swung over the Kuns, who nipped at them as they flew past overhead.

Twang! The rope snapped, and they both fell. Aedan and Kainan had almost made it, but now one of them would die.

"You can make it. So save yourself," Aedan told his brother.

"There's no point if I survive alone. I need you," Kainan corrected Aedan and took a swipe at one of the Kuns with his sword. "Come on, you piece of Akh-trash!" he yelled.

Aedan shot an arrow at another, landing the shot on its forehead. The undead beasts snarled back in defiance. The Sa'ami's weapons did not affect them, so the Kuns circled them and prepared to close in for the kill. Their beady, dead eyes flickered as they licked their rotten lips in anticipation.

A flutter of beating wings in the sky drew the attention of the Kuns for a moment and that of Kainan and Aedan too. A flock of ravens swooped down on them. Grandor and Tanke walked out from amongst the bushes. The ravens mobbed the Kuns like a flock of flies. They tore the flesh off the beasts. Tanke jumped on one of the Kuns and ripped it apart, limb from limb, with his powerful jaws. Grandor darted towards the other Kun, like a rush of water, and struck it with his staff; with such might, the Kun shattered against the tree, splattering like rotten fruit. The last Kun flailed about, running into the bushes, trying to shake off the flock of ravens. Tanke chased after it. Sounds of crunching and smashing were followed by a dead silence. Only the flapping wings of the ravens could be heard. The birds perched themselves around the place: on tables, chairs, railings, and branches. Tanke strode out from the bushes with a confident swagger. He sat down and licked a small wound on his right hind leg.

"Thank you, my friends." Grandor signalled to the ravens. "You two need to come with me now," he instructed Aedan and Kainan, who had not moved a muscle since Grandor and his entourage had appeared. They both stared at the druid in complete shock.

Aedan blurted out, "It's you!"

Grandor looked at him and smiled. "Yes. I remember you hiding inside the tent. It is not polite to eavesdrop on a private conversation."

Aedan approached the druid, and Kainan followed suit.

Kainan asked, "What do you know of what has happened here?"

"An undead army has risen from beyond The Depths. It has swept across Concordia conquering smaller establishments, forts and villages, building up its host from those it has slain. It eventually became a considerable enough force it attacked Sylvinar," Grandor explained with a straight face.

"What of our people? Have they been turned to undead?" Aedan cried out in panic.

"I do not know," Grandor replied.

"Why is our father and Ferni made of stone?" Kainan asked.

"Why their fate is different to everyone else who has met this horde perplexes me too. A possibility is an enemy wishes to use them as a ransom for some, yet, unknown reason."

"Who leads this army and why?" Aedan asked.

"Undead armies are usually led by an elder vampire of immense power. Sometimes sorcerers or mages have been known to lead undead forces, but none of this size. In ancient times it was the Revenants who lead those from the dead side," Grandor explained, "but we must not waste time discussing these matters here. Instead, we must head to Castle Mhan immediately and advise the queen of what has transpired here. I believe there is a great evil rising and, if we do not act quickly, the entire world will be covered in darkness."

"I am not going anywhere. I am staying here," rebutted Kainan.

"Remaining here is pointless. Come to Castle Mhan with me," Grandor reasoned with Kainan.

"I will not leave our father or Ferni. I will protect them. A Kun might shatter them, and then there will be no hope of restoring them. Aedan, you go with...." Kainan stalled, realising he had no idea who this druid was. "What is your name, druid?"

"I am Grandor. Beastmaster of the Druidic Circle in Agwa'den. I serve the balance of nature," Grandor stated.

"Very well, Grandor," Kainan replied with superiority. "Aedan, go with Grandor to Castle Mhan and see what reinforcements you can bring back. Find out who this enemy is and where they hide. Then, we will crush them for what they've done here."

Aedan leaned into his brother. "Should we be trusting this druid? I overheard him threatening our father to evacuate the city. So far, the undead have mostly been Kuns. He's a Beastmaster, after all. Maybe this is all a ruse?"

"If I wished you dead, I would have killed you by now. If I wished to kidnap you, I would have thrown you into a knapsack filled with Dormir leaves, and you would be fast asleep by now. What ruse could I possibly be attempting here, young Sa'ami?" Grandor grew impatient. "We must leave now. Stay here if you wish, Kainan, but board yourself up well and do not engage the enemy at any costs."

"How do you know my name?" Kainan snapped back.

"You are the heir to Sylvinar, are you not? Your father spoke highly of you. Enough discussion. We must leave now." Grandor walked away. "Tanke, let's go. Come Aedan. We have a long walk ahead of us."

Tanke got up and trotted behind Grandor. Aedan stared at his brother, unsure what to do.

Aedan thought out loud. "But I should get some things? Or maybe I should...."

"Go! That's an order and take your Traxy scale. Make yourself some useful armour," Kainan demanded.

Aedan touched the Traxy scale on his back, almost having forgotten it was there. For a moment, he remembered The Trial. It all seemed like a distant memory now. There was to be no celebration. There was to be no happiness. He looked at the druid who was gaining distance. The druid seemed to be his only way forward. His only way to try and make things right, but he felt so powerless. He felt so useless. Aedan was struck with immense sadness.

"I will miss you, brother," Aedan leaned in to hug Kainan.

Kainan shoved Aedan off. "Do not touch me. Go on your mission and be gone." Kainan turned and ascended the stairwell back to their home tree. Tears welled in Kainan's eyes. He had never felt so much pain as he did right now. He would cry for days on end."

Aedan stumbled after Grandor with a sick feeling in his stomach. He was not sure what would happen next. He felt torn, leaving behind Ferni, his father, his brother and his home. Yet, he had no choice but to push ahead towards an unknown destiny, towards an unknown future.

He caught up to Grandor and walked beside him. He looked up at the druid's hooded face. Grandor seemed stern yet soft. Grandor looked at Aedan with a firm gaze, which comforted Aedan.

"Once we have gained enough distance from this place, there is something of great importance I must tell you. Something which weighed on your father's mind. It is something which will change everything you have come to know," said Grandor.

"What?" Aedan pleaded.

"I will tell you soon enough," said Grandor.

They both crossed the threshold of the shattered Sylvanarian gates into the wild, tangled forest beyond. Their shapes were consumed by the mist and shadows of the woods. They melted away into the distance.

A Country at War

Vera sat cross-legged on a baroque cushion on the floor in the middle of the throne room before Maya and her ever-present bodyguard and aide. Maya watched Vera like a fox studying its prey. Vera turned her head as if she could see something to her right through the white silk blindfold she had worn since birth. Her long grey locks swayed before her pale face, obscuring her countenance. She was blind to that before her, but her clairvoyance covered great distances and spans of time. She connected her mind to Relianstar and was living through her experience.

"There is darkness," Vera stated with a slight tremor in her voice. She could feel evil penetrating her mind like tendrils of ominous vapour consuming her sanity.

"What darkness?" Maya asked as she leaned forward on her throne. She felt the hairs prick up on the back of her neck. She was agitated at the imagination of what Vera might say next.

"It comes from below. There is a vampire. An army of undead. An unholy army which is rising out of the ground." Vera's voice quavered. She felt her composure slipping from her. She felt herself falling into an abyss.

"What is this army's intention?" Maya asked, her eyes widening, her fear escalating. During her short rule, she only had to deal with politics, never war.

"It is not clear, but I sense it intends to consume... to consume all living things." Vera turned her head to the left and looked up and down as if someone was standing right next to her.

"What is it?" Maya cried out, almost jumping out of her throne.

"There is something I can not see, but I know it is there. There are so many unknowns." Vera paused and then *looked* at Maya. "Your majesty, this is a battle we can not win."

Maya did not know what to say. She was stunned by the seer's revelation. "What do you mean we can not win?" She asked with her heart full of worry and confusion. Then, she turned to Shun, "Shun, what does she mean?"

Shun did not reply. She nodded towards Vera. Maya turned to face Vera once more.

Vera maintained her invisible gaze on the queen. She did not flinch; only her lips moved. "We will not win the war. All will be lost. Everything we know, and everything we take for granted, will be wiped off the face of Alteria." A single tear rolled down her cheek from beneath her blindfold, and then her body toppled over.

"Shun!" The queen uttered, turning to her aide.

Shun had already darted over and caught Vera before her head hit the floor.

Maya knelt next to Vera and helped lift her off the ground, "Are you ok?"

Vera extended her legs and stood on her own, nudging Shun and Maya away from her, so they let go. She collected her pillow, bowed before the queen and glided out of the royal chamber. Her long silver hair camouflaged against her white silk gown trailing along the ground.

Maya turned to Rheal, "Bring me the general at once."

"Of course, your majesty," acquiesced Rheal, bowing and exiting the chamber.

Maya leaned over to Shun and whispered, "So there will be bloodshed, it seems. I'm not sure, but I believe preparing for battle is essential. What do you think?"

"We must first know our enemy, and we must know ourselves," Shun replied as she turned her eyes from where Vera had exited the room back to her queen.

"Ah, of course. We will take stock of all our resources and send out spies to report back on the host as it advances," Maya pontificated, walking back to her throne.

NAUGHT BUT A QUARTER-hour had passed when General Uriah charged into the throne room. The general was a blue coloured Ras'i who joined the Mhan Royal Army to mend the bonds between his people in Ras'Fahem and Concordia. Ras'i were feared and loathed across all of Alteria. Their size, strength, demonic appearance and natural magical powers were not the reason. But, their tribal lifestyle and isolationist civilisation on Ras'Fahem was seen as greedy because they blocked access to the Crater of Akh, where the largest reserves of manah were left untapped. His people saw his actions as traitorous, and he was banished, never to return to Ras'Fahem. He remained in the Mhan Royal Army, enduring discrimination and hatred from the people of Concordia. In the face of all this oppression, he rose through the ranks of the Mhan Royal Army through his dedication, commitment and saving every soldier's life at some point or another. He was revered for his unmatched combat ability, strategic vision and unwavering obedience to the queen.

He dropped on one knee before the queen. "Queen. What will you have me do?"

"Rise, general. I need you to prepare us for war," Maya replied.

The general stood to attention. His size dwarfed the queen. "War? When? Who?"

"The Seer has spoken of an undead army led by a vampire rising out of the ground. It could be today on our ground. I need our defences ready. I need my army ready now," Maya ordered, pointing her right index finger at the ground.

The general looked down at the queen; old memories long repressed in his mind were bubbling to the surface. "A vampire leading an undead army? This is bad. This is very bad. Are you sure the Seer is not mistaken? For even I wish this not to be true."

Maya nodded. She could feel panic welling inside her but kept her composure.

Uriah spoke with ire, "I have not fought undead in a long time. But I do not forget how tough they are to kill. We need manah. Lots of manah. We need the gryphons. All of them. All our steel needs to be blessed with manah or kimikels. I need immediate access to all of these resources without restriction if we hope even to stand a chance against an undead army."

"You will have whatever it is you need, general. Rheal will immediately issue you with a royal order on your way out. Now stop wasting time and get moving," Maya commanded.

General Uriah bowed. "As you have me do, my majesty." He turned on his heel and marched out of the royal chamber.

GENERAL URIAH STOMPED through the castle foreyard flocked by his lieutenants. He had been born in war, raised in war, educated in war, and fought in wars so many times it was routine for him to give orders in preparation. He did not doubt himself. He did not doubt what he knew. He was confident of his strategy and knew the outcome of any scenario if his information was complete. He had never lost a single battle except against an undead army many years ago in Ras'Fahem when he led his tribe against the pestilence of an evil sorcerer who led a charge to steal the manah from beneath their village. Women and children perished that day. The pain in his heart had never left, and every waking moment of every day, it bled in agony because of his failure. Now he felt the pressure of that failure again. He did not know how they would win, knowing what he knew about their defences and capabilities. All he could do was issue orders based on sound strategy, respond to new intelligence, and hope something would turn the tide before the hour was upon them.

"Marko, prep the mechanised defences with dragon's meal. Cycle units on watch twice as often at all stations. Nothing must get through. Understood?" Growled Uriah as he turned to glare at Marko, Chief of Mechanised Munitions, the commander of the mechanised munitions division of the Mhan Royal Army.

"Yes. Right away. We will be ready by nightfall," Marko snapped back.

"Nightfall will be too late. Before then!" Uriah collared the lieutenant. "There are women and children who rely on us. Think of them and push yourself to the limit. I want it all done before I complete my rounds of the castle." Uriah shoved Marko off.

"It will be done." Marko ran off yelling orders.

The urgency electrified the air. It was contagious. Mhan City came alive. Its citizens ran around gathering their families. The soldiers ushered those they could towards safe refuge in the production halls behind Castle Mhan, deep in the cave system under Mount Firtina.

Uriah continued his march towards the city gates. With each of his powerful strides, his feet pounded the ground with purposeful punishment. The civilians in Mhan City who lived in the enormous forequarter of the castle's fief watched in awe as the Ras'i dished out orders to his lieutenants with such ferocity it instilled a definite sense of confidence in everyone: Uriah was the greatest general who ever lived.

"Sena, all the clerics must immediately begin imbuing our weapons with manah. The queen has provided unlimited access to the royal stores. We are fighting the undead, so place half your clerics on the battlefield to heal and buff our soldiers and the other half to meditate and chant from the upper halls. We need blessings of faith and light if our soldiers are to stand a chance." Uriah looked at Sena, Grand Cleric of the Mhan Royal Army, with a piercing gaze. His eyes were fireballs of passion awaiting a reply.

"It will be done before you complete your rounds." With those words, Sena turned and ran to the Temple of Nai near the castle's western wall. She lifted her red and blue gown's hem off the ground so she could run faster while holding her silver tiara with her spare hand.

"Gallastrian, Relianstar and Browbearer will lead the charge. Attack in a flat formation, split, let the enemy flow between and annihilate them as they try to regroup. Most undead are stupid; we use this to our advantage. Do you understand?" Uriah smashed his right fist into his left palm, emphasising his question.

"Yes. But I recommend Suverchant and Bastrolar to lead the charge. They are young and able." Gallastrian, Champion Cavalier of the Knights of Mhan, blurted out his suggestion. He wanted to give his favourite knights an opportunity to prove themselves on the battlefield.

Uriah stopped and, with his right arm, collared and lifted Gallastrian, who was wearing full plate armour, off the ground and faced him, "Do not waste time questioning me. Otherwise, you will find me as your enemy. I give orders, and you take them. Suverchant and Bastrolar are inexperienced and will soil themselves when they witness an undead army for the first time in their lives. Relianstar and Browbearer eat undead for breakfast." Uriah threw Gallastrian onto the floor. "Do as I command so that we may prevail. Each delay you create with your idiotic questions leads the enemy one step closer to victory."

Gallastrian stood up and bowed his head trembling. "I'm sorry, general. I will get on the preparations right away." He marched off, ready to prepare the cavalry.

"Felgar, your archers must use boom, flame and acid arrows. Set long-range bows across the top of the perimeter wall and each archer to ensure they have adjusted their bows to perfection. We will be falling back here." Uriah pointed at the inner walls. "And over there is where we will eventually fall right back to the castle towers."

"You think the enemy will breach our walls?" Felgar, Exquisite Sniper, Chief of Ranged Combat, asked.

"Yes. They will overwhelm us, and we will not win. We will survive. Your job is to make sure only soldiers die. Not civilians. We are warriors born to die so others may live. Repeat that a thousand times before I return and ensure all our units are ready to hail destruction on our enemy." Uriah shoved Felgar away. Uriah stopped before the main gate. He turned to face Felgar, who was still reeling from the shove.

Felgar stood to attention and replied with a passionate exclamation, "Yes, immediately," as she ran off to prepare her contingents.

Rygar, Juggernaut Berserk Reaver, Commander of the Frontline Fighters, remained in tow. "What about your footmen? What will you have us do?"

"Bring the footmen here to me. I will address them personally," Uriah stated.

"Yes, my general." Rygar ran off to rally the footmen out of the barracks nearby. Within minutes all one thousand were assembled in front of the gates in ten rows of a hundred fighters each. Uriah walked up and down the assembly blasting his speech like the colossal inspiration that he was.

"You are to support the cavalry's formation. Protect the knights from the ground. Do not break away. Do not attempt isolated combat. Stick to the plan. You will need all the buffs and blessings to survive long enough because you will all die. Each and every one of you. But survive long enough, you must. Why? Because I am here to remind you, you are here to die courageously in battle, so the enemy does not ravish your women, your children, your babies. Bards and maidens will sing of your glorious deaths until the end of time. Future generations will name their children after you and give thanks in prayer before they have a peaceful meal. We are here today because our forefathers died for us. Each breath we take is a gift. Each day we live is a gift. Each feeling, each sensation, is a gift that is taken with death. Death can come for us at any time, at any moment. But today, we get to choose how we die. Today, I, your general, will be right here by your side when the enemy breaches the gate. Today, I will be right here when the enemy floods in. Today, I will charge the enemy with you. Today, I will be right by your side until your last moment in this life, and I will see you in the next. Because today I choose to die gloriously with you so our women and children can live on and sing about us. You are my brothers. My sisters. My blood bound brethren. And I am here to ward off the darkness and cowardice with honour and bravery!" Uriah spoke with so much passion that everyone felt moved in the deepest part of their soul.

Uriah stood atop the main gate with his right foot perched against the wall. His yellow eyes twitched in every direction as he studied the terrain. He was visualising the battle, thinking through every possible outcome. He looked back at the foreyard. It was teeming with activity. His lieutenants were assembling all units ready for war at any moment. Uriah looked up to his right at Mount Firtina. A web of electrical veins crackling with thunder and lightning capped the peak. He knew without the Gryphon Riders to aid them; they would all be turned to undead.

This thought haunted him. His sleep was soaked in nightmares.

Revelations

Night had fallen. The campfire burned. Aedan stared into the flames. He did not move, except to steal a glance at Grandor, who was mixing some herbs in a small mortar and pestle. Aedan could feel his stomach-churning. He wanted to throw up. He wanted to cry. But he held it all in. Ferni used to tell him it was ok to cry, but it was always so embarrassing. It made him feel like a child.

"Show me your wounds." Grandor's voice snapped Aedan back to reality.

"I'm fine," Aedan replied.

"Show me your wounds, child. I am not here to judge you. I am here to heal you," Grandor retorted.

Aedan lifted his tunic. The arrow wound was filled with white pus and was turning purple.

"This will hurt. Clench your teeth on this," said Grandor as he shoved a stick in Aedan's mouth. He wiped away the infection with the herbal concoction he had prepared.

Aedan bit hard on the stick. His face turned white, and sweat poured over his brow. He clenched his fists and fought hard not to contort his body. The pain was intense. He had forgotten the pain he experienced in The Depths. This was a reminder.

Grandor finished cleaning up the wound and covered it with some Albacca leaves. He secured the dressing with some Chato vines wrapped around Aedan's abdomen. Aedan slumped. He had passed out. The combination of exhaustion and pain took its toll.

Grandor continued to clean up all the injuries Aedan had all over his body and dressed them. He also treated the fractured foot and splinted it. Finally, he lay Aedan next to the fire and wrapped him up in a thick blanket of leaves and bark so he would keep warm.

A few hours passed, and Aedan roused from his sleep. He was hungry. His eyes fluttered open, and he looked around. Grandor sat opposite the fire, eating food.

"Hungry?" Grandor asked, offering up a morsel.

Aedan nodded.

"Well, come over here and have some food with me," said Grandor.

Aedan pulled off the covers and shuffled over to Grandor. Grandor handed him a bowl of beans, nuts, berries, fruits and sweet roots. Aedan studied the food. He was expecting chicken, fish or even rabbit.

"Something wrong?" Grandor asked.

Aedan shook his head and dug into the food. The food was flavoured with aromatic spices and condiments. It tasted fantastic. He shovelled it into his mouth and chewed like a starved lion.

"Here, have some water." Grandor passed a water gourd to Aedan.

Aedan drank from the gourd with desperation. Grandor put more food into Aedan's plate. Aedan continued to eat. His emotions were driving his hunger, and his hunger was driving his emotions. Everything was building up. The more he ate, the more he could feel his heart sinking until he started crying. He sobbed.

Grandor put his arm around him. "I know it does not seem like it now. But everything will be ok."

"But everyone is gone." Aedan wailed. "There is nothing left. I just want to go home. I don't want to go to the castle. I don't want to see the queen. I just want to hug my father. I just want things to go back to the way they were." Aedan's crying subsided after he blurted out his last words.

"I understand," said Grandor. "But what has happened has happened. There is no other way. Except to believe you will find a way to make things right. Do you understand?"

Aedan shook his head.

"When you fire an arrow, do you ever doubt yourself?" Grandor asked.

"Doubt myself?" Aedan asked back.

"Do you ever think you will miss?" Grandor replied.

"Of course not. I don't think I will miss, but sometimes I do. Not often. But sometimes I do." Aedan recounted.

"This journey you are on right now is no different than firing an arrow. You should not think you will miss. Let your actions drive your purpose. Believe they will succeed, and you will find yourself back home before you know it," explained Grandor.

Aedan thought about what the druid said. It made sense to him. "Like an arrow, I should focus on my target? And keep moving forward?"

"That's right," Grandor confirmed.

"But what is my target? I still don't understand what is going on. You said there was something important you had to tell me?" Aedan had forgotten his tears and was alert, full of questions.

"Your target is to establish contact with the queen. I am certain they would be preparing for battle by now. I have seen the undead army destroy Fort Bosk and can only assume many other forts across the land have also been attacked. The Royal Seer would have sensed it by now, and General Uriah would be preparing the castle defences. When we arrive, we will see what use we serve and how we can help in the coming battle, for there must be a battle. The undead army will not surrender. They must be destroyed. How does that sound to you, young Aedan?" Grandor asked.

"I'm not sure. I think I saw the undead down in The Depths. Three skeletons covered in rotting flesh. I used the acid of a Yeshi Salamander's gut to stop them." Aedan replied.

Grandor laughed out loud. "That is excellent, child. If only the rest of the residents of Concordia are as resourceful as you, we will win this war in no time."

"But what of this important news you must tell me? I think father hinted at it just before The Trial." Aedan pushed for answers.

Grandor looked at Aedan square in the eyes. "You are not a Sa'ami."

Aedan stared back at Grandor without blinking for a while before replying. "What do you mean I am not a Sa'ami?"

"Eighteen years ago, your mother Jasi was walking through the forest on the outskirts of Sylvinar with your father, Eldoran. Your mother was pregnant with your brother and due any day. As they strolled back towards the city gates, they heard a baby cry. The sound came from the Mhan riverbank. They walked over and found a straw basket. Inside the basket, they found a small baby. This baby was you," Grandor said.

"They found me?" Aedan asked.

Grandor continued. "In the basket, they found a note, which said: 'Please give this child a life as I am unable to care for him.' Your mother's nurturing instincts meant she was immediately compelled to keep you and care for you. Your parents took you back to Sylvinar and decided to keep you a secret until your brother was born, at which point they revealed you as his younger fraternal twin. They did this to avoid scandal in the city and to protect you. They both suspected you had been abandoned due to some malevolent or nefarious reason and thought you were the child of a Sa'ami, maybe from Antillia. To this, they confided in me and asked me to examine you. This is where I noticed you were actually a common human, like myself. Do you understand what I have told you?"

Aedan laughed. "You tried to scare my dad in the tent, and now you are trying to manipulate me." He stood up. "I think I will return to Sylvinar and stand by my brother's side than listen to your lies anymore." Aedan gathered his belongings.

"Haven't you always wondered why you are the tallest Sa'ami in all of Sylvinar? Haven't you always wondered why you have red eyes? Haven't you always wondered why you are so different to your brother?" Grandor asked.

Aedan ignored the druid and continued to pack.

"It is nightfall. The enemy will be about. I have a perimeter of animals keeping watch for us tonight. You are safe here. I will take you back tomorrow if that is what you wish to do. But, before you make your decision, read this letter from your father. He wrote it to me shortly after your brother's birth." Grandor held out a letter.

Aedan turned around and stared at the parchment in the druid's hand. Then, he reached out and took the letter. He unfolded it, sat down and began to read it in the flickering firelight. It was his father's writing. It read:

> *Grandor, you big lug. I am writing to you because ever since finding this boy and taking him in, things have become... concerning. You know I think you are a fear-mongering moron, who always has to make things sound much worse than they are, but what you said and what has been happening can not be a coincidence. My powers have become much more acute. I can now focus my magic so much easier. I can manipulate reality and confuse and dumbfound everyone I see with a few simple words or a glance. I am confident this flow of manah originates from the boy. The more I love him, the stronger I feel. But, it is not all fun and games. It seems to be having the opposite effect on Jasi. She has been feeling down and low on energy recently. She*

spends entire afternoons staring out the window, depressed. Some days she will be delighted, but mostly sad. Maybe you are right. But what am I to do? He is only a baby. If we hand him over to the capital, they will place him in an orphanage, and many evildoers will want him for his manah. I think we have no choice but to keep him until he is old enough to know the truth, and then he can make up his own damn mind. I just hope we can teach him to use his powers for good. Whatever they may be.

With tears streaming down his face, Aedan looked up at Grandor. "Did my mother die because of me?"

"No. Your mother passed back to Nai because her time had come," Grandor replied.

"Is my father a mage?" Aedan asked.

"Yes, he is indeed. He is a great illusionist. But he is not bound to the capital via phylactery and, as such, an outlaw should his secret ever get out," Grandor replied.

"What am I? What is my father talking about? What do you think about me?" Aedan asked as he wiped his tears away with the back of his hand.

"It is such a long story, and you need rest. We shall talk about it tomorrow," Grandor stated.

"No. You will tell me now, druid. Or I will fight you to the death." Aedan stood up and trained an arrow on Grandor.

"Don't be such a stupid child. Sit down. I will tell you," Grandor barked back.

Aedan sat down, brooding in contempt.

"Have you heard of the legend of the three?" Grandor asked.

Aedan shook his head.

"Do you know how the Great Manah Wars were brought to their dramatic and conclusive end?" Grandor asked.

"Yes. The armies of Uro marched onto the western front of Shefar, the Guatarian homeland. At the same time, the Gnossian Battleborn rose from their city in the Underworld and marched on the eastern front. The Gautarians were pushed to near extinction as they refused to surrender. The Drayphs of Uro eventually negotiated a withdrawal on both fronts, and the conquest of the Gautarians was brought to a stop. In a final display of military might, the kingdom of Mhan dropped a Gnossian devastator from a dirigible on the kingdom Eerak, which is now the wasteland between Concordia and Shefar. Shortly after, treaties were negotiated with the Ras'i, and other paynims hid amongst the archipelago of the Great Ocean. Small skirmishes continued for many years after, but the massive casualties of war had ended, and there was no manah left to fight over as most of it had been claimed by the newly formed country of Concordia," Aedan recounted his textbook teachings.

"So it would seem. That is what is written. Yet, there is the untold story. Do you believe in Nai and in Akh?" Grandor asked Aedan.

"I guess so," Aedan replied.

"All the manah which was harvested, mined, consumed and ravaged from our beloved Alteria has left Nai very weak. Akh is all-powerful. Akh rose from his resting place in the volcanic land beyond the mountain ridge of Ras'Fahem. His slumber was disturbed by the imbalance in nature. Akh gave the Gautarians a blessing of immense power on the condition they destroy all who oppose him and join him as his army. This is why the Gautarians rose so prominently to power. But Nai had designed in her infinite wisdom a fate which would ensure Akh did not rise ever again. This is the legend of the three, simply referred to as The Champions of Nai. The three champions are the warrior, the mage and the rogue. The warrior is the force of passion, the mage is the force of wisdom, and the rogue is the force of intelligence. These three faced Akh in the final days of the Great Manah Wars, and they sealed him back into his tomb. Otherwise, he would feast on all living things on Alteria and make it a living hell. After he was sealed back away, the Champions returned to their normal lives. The mage was a sorcerer of immense power called Yama. I had the pleasure of meeting him when he sought refuge in Eerak just before the kingdom was wiped off the face of Alteria by the devastator. Yama had red eyes, just like yourself. I believe you are imbued with manah energy like the great sorcerer Yama. Roj'ah manah energy, to be precise. The most destructive type. It is the same energy that flows from Akh. Ah'zul, which is the creative energy, is the polar opposite. Since Yama, I have never met anyone else with red eyes, and as you can tell from your father's letter, you gave him strength in his magical ways. This is a testament to the manah which flows through you. I believe your existence in Concordia has become known to a great evil force that wishes to harvest the manah from your body. It is a valuable resource, and manah from a living soul is exponentially more powerful than any manah stone found in nature. The manah in your body would be equivalent to an entire mountain. So you see, young Aedan; you are an orphan, raised by your Sa'ami family until the time your secret could not be kept a secret any longer because your father's biggest fear was the kingdom of Mhan would bind you via phylactery to serve their purpose. This is a worry, but we have no choice as you will draw the attention of the undead wherever you go." Grandor finished talking and sat in silence.

Aedan stared at the fire. His mind was trying to make sense of everything he heard. Then the first question popped into his mind. "Then who is my real father and mother? Yama is my father?"

"Impossible. He was destroyed while he was in Eerak when the devastator was dropped almost twenty-five years before you were found in Sylvinar by your parents," Grandor replied.

"Then who are my parents?" Aedan asked.

"I do not know. It will be tough to find out unless they are to step forward and claim you as their own," Grandor explained.

"That is what I want to know. I don't care what the queen wants. I want to find out who my parents are. I want to find out why they abandoned me. I want to know why I have red eyes. I want to know who I really am," Aedan stated.

"What about Sylvinar? Do you not care for your parents anymore?" Grandor queried.

Aedan stalled. "Yes, I love Eldoran. I love Jasi. I love Ferni. I tolerate, Kainan. Maybe not so much anymore as he is not really my brother. But I still want to spend the end of my days in Ferni's arms. That will never change, but I want to know the truth. I cannot believe my entire life is a stupid lie. I cannot believe everything I have held dearly is not what was meant for me."

"Then what shall we do?" Grandor led Aedan's thoughts.

"We shall go to the castle. We shall do what we must to bring an end to all this conflict. We shall free my family in Sylvinar. Then, I shall marry Ferni, then I will seek out my real parents in Concordia, and I will get my answers," Aedan concluded and stood up.

"Very well. For now, let's remove these bandages." Grandor removed the bandages from Aedan's wounds. They were completely healed, including his fracture. Aedan's body was as good as new.

"How is that possible?" Aedan asked.

"A druid's strength is found in the natural manah found in all living things. Nature provides us with everything we need. Here take this and study it." Grandor gave Aedan a pouch full of herbs, seeds, and roots, plus a little set of parchments full of notes and diagrams.

"What are these?" Aedan asked.

"These are recipes and the ingredients to treat many ailments. Learn them well. You may find yourself in danger and need to treat your wounds one day." Grandor smiled. "We should sleep now. It is not long before daylight. Lumbra is already revealing Lum's light."

Aedan stayed up a bit. He flicked through the notes and diagrams in the parchment. He pulled out some of the herbs and roots and compared them to the drawings. He tasted them and tried to memorise as much as he could. He did it because he could not sleep. After everything he had learned, he was not going to sleep anytime soon. He kept thinking of Ferni's petrified face and how terrified she looked. Whatever had done this to her was because of him. He brought this upon everyone. He felt great sadness well up in his heart. He knew he had to make things right. The brightness which was his life had dwindled away. He no longer could sleep in and rely on his father to slap him awake. He would no longer have fights with Kainan. How happy Kainan would be to find out they were not brothers. How happy Kainan would be to find out Aedan was not a real Sa'ami. Aedan nodded off to sleep. His sleep was full of visions of his fellow Sa'ami dying. Aedan would try to save them, but he would always get there too late, and their eyes would close. Then moments later, they would snap open, black as death. They would bare fangs and try to bite his neck. A tall Ras'i figure kept walking towards him. Aedan would run, but he would always be in the same spot. The figure raised its black sword high in the air and struck Aedan in the back. Aedan died in his dream, and the last thing he saw was Kainan kissing Ferni and laughing at Aedan as he was buried alive.

Return of the Knights

The watchmen above the gates of Castle Mhan signalled the bell and hollered, "There be soldiers on the approach!"

Relianstar and Browbearer led the entourage of horses weighed down with the soldiers from Fort Watch. They galloped at full speed towards the gate. One of the guards lowered the colossal drawbridge across the moat and raised the portcullis. The horses' hooves thundered across the bridge. They traversed through the encampments in the front quarter of the city. Finally, they made their way to the barracks on the western wall, where general Uriah was inspecting the soldiers' preparations.

Uriah turned around to the oncoming party. The horses slowed down to a halt. Relianstar and Browbearer dismounted and made their way to the general.

Relianstar spoke over her left shoulder to the Fort Watch soldiers still on horseback. "Take your horses to the stables, eat, and have a rest. Return to the barracks by nightfall." She then addressed Uriah. "How fare thee general?"

Uriah spat on the ground. "Who cares. Report?"

Relianstar spoke fast. She was good friends with Uriah and had known him for many years. So she was very familiar with his personality and curt manner, a cultural trait of the no-nonsense Ras'i tradition. "Fort Watch was attacked by an undead army led by a vampire. The army had Kuns, Harbingers, Batyles and many sentients races converted to serve. I counted four of our fort banners amongst the chaos. I am certain I saw civilians amongst the ranks.

Some seemed to have been reanimated from graves. This army may have amassed corpses from all graves across the land. It is hard to estimate the numbers as it was very dark, and we discerned approximately 10,000 strong, but my educated guess is an army of 30,000 units or more."

Uriah barked back, "Who was the vampire?"

"It was a Ras'i master swordsman. I am certain it was Maleh of Iz'amu. Who raised Maleh from the dead and turned him into a vampire? I did not find out. So whether he is unbound or a puppet to a master is uncertain," Relianstar explained.

"Maleh? He will seek to destroy all of Concordia if he has risen as a vampire. How he crossed from Ras'Fahem into Concordia without detection is my first concern. I suspect treason. Whoever is controlling him would need to be very powerful and have a strong understanding of the history of the Iz'amu's animosity towards Mhan. I can not imagine a Ras'i turning one of their own into a vampire, as it is a spiteful form. It would have to be an outsider." Uriah walked off back to the castle. "We will report to the queen."

Relianstar and Browbearer followed the general towards the castle.

URIAH FINISHED RECOUNTING the knight's report to Maya as she sat on her balcony overlooking the city. She was observing the battle preparations taking shape while she ate lunch.

"Is there anything else?" Uriah asked the two knights.

"That is all," Relianstar replied.

Maya pondered before speaking. "If I recall correctly, from my father's tales, Maleh was found washed ashore twenty years after the end of the Great Manah War, on the beach of Vida just east of this very castle. I was a child when he told me these stories, and I do not recall anything else. So it is highly likely Maleh's body has been in

Concordia all this time. Maybe even in our mausoleum within the catacombs." Maya turned to her scribe, Reahl, a short older man in a white gown with a flowing beard and thick moustache, with thick spectacles and a white fez. "Reahl organise an immediate and urgent investigation in our catacombs. We are looking for any desecrated tombs. We need to know if anyone who was buried there may have been turned into a vampire."

"Your majesty. Keeping a Ras'i body from being buried amongst its people is a sacrilege. Maleh was a great warlord of the Iz'amu who singlehandedly repelled the Gautarians out of Ras'Fahem," Uriah explained.

Maya looked at the general with annoyance at his political comment. "You are speaking beyond your station general, but I will answer your hidden question. Maybe he was tossed in the ocean by his people? The Ras'i are fickle in their cultural interpretation and easily turn on their own. Are you not an exile simply for asking to negotiate rather than fight? Do not question the integrity of my father ever again, or I shall have you beheaded. Do you understand?"

"My apologies, your majesty. You are right as always." Uriah bowed out of respect. "What shall you have me do now?"

"Continue preparations for war. Report to me at nightfall on the status of our preparations," Maya ordered.

Uriah turned and walked out of the balcony.

"You two," Maya referred to Relianstar and Browbearer, "I need you two to head to Agwa'den with the moonstone and have Magestrix recharge it to full power."

Uriah stopped before exiting the balcony and hollered back at the queen. "Your majesty, we need the knights here for battle. Send Suverchant and Bastrolar in their stead."

"You were dismissed. Why do I still hear your voice?" Maya quipped.

Uriah took a deep breath and left.

Maya continued talking to the knights. "While you are there, request the druidic grove's assistance in this upcoming battle. If they excuse themselves by quoting some allegiance to the balance of nature, threaten them with destruction. I can not have freeloaders in our kingdom who do not contribute to its defence."

"As you wish," Relianstar responded.

"Reahl will issue you with plenty of manah so you may hasten your trip. Do not take more than a day there and back. Now go." Maya waved them away.

"We have already left," Relianstar said as she turned heel and left with Browbearer.

Shadowy Savannah

Six days had passed since the attack on Fort Bosk and only four days remained until The Ritual. Lum's light dwindled in the sky as Lumbra eclipsed it. The stars twinkled into existence as the darkness of night crept over the land. Grandor and Aedan walked side by side, followed by Tanke across the long-grassed savannah. The bright green weeds swayed to and fro in the gentle evening breeze. It was tranquil. They had all been walking since first light from the edge of Sylvinar Forest. Grandor had led them around Fort Bosk to avoid any possible confrontation with undead stragglers from the attack days ago. The detour added considerable time to their journey, but he felt it best to be safe than risk being outnumbered by the enemy and killed.

Aedan was stern, for once in his life. He was no longer the same person. He didn't believe he was a human. *Grandor probably isn't intentionally lying. He is just confused*, Aedan thought to himself.

He would look at Grandor from time to time to study his true intentions. But, as always, the druid would look back with a stoic and comforting gaze, putting Aedan at ease.

Aedan spotted civilisation up ahead. It looked like a few homes bunched together like a colony of mushrooms atop a hill.

"Do you see that?" Aedan asked no one.

"That is Hilltop Hamlet. We will be staying there the night," Grandor replied.

"Will we be staying at an inn?" Aedan asked with genuine interest. He had never stayed anywhere outside of Sylvinar Forest.

He was interested in what might happen. They were going to interact with people. What bizarre strangers would he come across?

"No. I have friends there. We will stay with them. I hope," said Grandor.

"You hope?" replied Aedan.

"Yes. From here, it looks like the hamlet is abandoned. Let's slow down our pace while I have a friend scout up ahead."

Grandor stopped walking and whistled to the sky. It was a series of short shrieks which echoed across the savannah.

"What are you doing?" Aedan asked.

"Calling a friend who frequents these parts," Grandor said with a smile.

A few moments later, there was a reply—a series of short shrieks from the south. In the sky, a bird flew towards them. It was a giant crowned eagle. Grandor shrieked back in acknowledgement. The bird descended at speed. Grandor raised his left arm. The bird swooped down and perched onto the druid's forearm.

"How are you, my friend?" Grandor stroked the giant bird's neck.

The eagle cocked his head, and with his right eye, he studied Aedan.

"This is Aedan of Sylvinar. Aedan, this is Y'a'rer'ghek. A proud father of five?" Grandor looked at Y'a'rer'ghek for confirmation, who let out a shriek in affirmation. "And the master of the skies in these parts."

Aedan looked at Grandor, then back at the eagle. "Um. Nice to meet you," Aedan struggled to pronounce the name, which required the syllable to be strained through the throat like a bird's call, "Yahhhh-rarrrr-ghaak."

Y'a'rer'ghek shook his head, stretched his neck out and spread his wings while squawking.

Grandor laughed. "He welcomes you into his home but asks you to learn to pronounce his name properly."

"Oh, I'm sorry. I didn't mean to offend him," Aedan said.

"It's ok. He's used to it. I will teach you how to say his name later," Grandor then spoke to Y'a'rer'ghek. "My friend, can you take a look up ahead? I fear monsters may have taken the homes of my friends."

Y'a'rer'ghek leapt off the druid's arm and started to climb skywards towards the hamlet.

"Let's continue. He will signal me if it is safe or if the place is overrun." Grandor signalled with his hand for Aedan and Tanke to follow as he walked off.

In the distance, Y'a'rer'ghek circled the hamlet. Then, he swooped and dive-bombed around to get a good look near the ground.

After a while, he headed southwards and let out a few short shrieks. Grandor waved and shrieked back.

"He says the place looks empty. No sign of monster tracks. Only human footprints heading northwest towards Castle Mhan a day or so ago. We shall make ourselves at home then, but I doubt my friends would have fled to the castle," Grandor said.

"Why do you think that?" Aedan asked.

"You will see," Grandor replied.

Night had fallen as they neared the hamlet. Tanke stopped dead in his tracks and snarled.

"What is it boy?" Grandor asked his companion.

Tanke kept very still. His eyes locked on the horizon behind them. He sniffed the air and continued to growl.

Grandor could not see anything except darkness. "What about you Aedan? What do you see?"

"The grass is moving. Looks like something. Maybe a pack of animals? I'm not sure. Could just be the wind," Aedan thought out loud.

Tanke barked a few times.

"He is not sure either as we are not downwind, so he can't smell anything. Let's not waste time here. We are but a few footsteps from shelter." Grandor led the way towards one of the smaller homes in the hamlet.

Tanke kept turning around to have a look back at the horizon.

Grandor knocked on the door. They waited for a long while.

"Knock again?" Aedan asked.

Grandor shook his head. "They heard the first one."

Tanke leapt up off the ground, where he had laid down to rest for a moment, and charged into the grass. Grandor drew his staff from behind his back and stood on guard, ready to fight. Aedan drew an arrow and aimed his bow. They could hear Tanke chomping on something. A few moments later, he strode out from the long grass with a willowshent: a medium-sized, crimson coloured rodent.

"Always thinking with your stomach," Grandor quipped.

"And so am I!" a voice bellowed behind them.

Aedan spun around. He was pointing his arrow at a very tall human with a gut the size of five watermelons. There stood a sweaty, fat man with mangy blond hair and a mutton chop. He was in long johns held up by leather suspenders. His shirt was stained brown and soiled with sweaty residue.

"You need a bath," Grandor replied.

"Good to see you too!" The man shoved Aedan's arrow out of his face and proceeded to hug Grandor.

Grandor turned his head away. "Your stench will keep any enemy at bay." Grandor introduced Aedan. "This is Aedan of Sylvinar. This is Gnaw of Hilltop Hamlet."

"Pleased to meet you." Aedan offered his hand.

Gnaw grabbed Aedan's left hand and, in one move, pulled him, spun him around and grabbed him in a reverse headlock. Aedan was unable to move. Gnaw proceeded to rub young Aedan's head with his right hand's knuckles. "Nice to meet you. Hahahaha."

Aedan was left with a sore head and tousled hair. He wasn't very impressed.

Gnaw laughed a bellyful laugh. "Gotta love kids."

"I'm not a kid. I would have your head in a moment's notice!" Aedan snapped back.

"Woah! He's also got bite. Freida's gonna love this kid," said Gnaw with excitement.

"Who's Freida?" Asked Aedan.

A fat woman with enormous breasts in a low-cut gown pushed past Gnaw. "Oh, what a cutie!" She squealed and proceeded to bury Aedan's face between her bosom.

Aedan turned his head to the side so he could breathe.

"Nice to see you again, Freida," Grandor said with courtesy.

"Oh, shut up. We haven't seen you in over a season. What's been keeping you?" Freida asked as Aedan managed to push himself away from her tits.

"Druidic matters," Grandor replied.

"Druidic matters? It sounds like a support group for disenchanted tree huggers!" Gnaw spat back in amusement. "Well, don't just stand there talking like you have a stick up your backside. Come inside. Let's have some food and some ale."

Aedan, Grandor and Tanke were ushered into the couple's warm and smelly home.

Gnaw hit Grandor on the back as he closed the door and bellowed, "Oh, that's right, you only eat vegetables and sh–"

The door slammed behind them.

The long grass moved against the wind.

GNAW BIT INTO A LARGE, roasted leg of lamb. The greasy meat left a glistening coat on his facial hair. Freida downed a pint of ale in two gulps. She burped and slammed down her brass cup. They both devoured the food in such a disgusting manner. It made Aedan a little sick. He tried to eat the food on the table, but he couldn't help think of all the saliva on the two hosts' hands which touched everything in sight.

"Eat up, boy! You need some meat on them bones of yours!" Freida ordered. She threw some meat on Aedan's plate. "Now, dig in!" She yelled as her inebriation took control.

Aedan strained a smile back and decided best to talk about something so he could avoid eating the slosh in front of him. "So, how do you two know Grandor?" Aedan asked.

Gnaw slammed his fist down. "Hasn't this good for nothing Beastmaster told you anything?"

Grandor smiled.

"What good are you, aye? Who the hell is this kid anyway? Are you evacuating to Mhan like everyone else?" Gnaw asked.

"It seems so," Grandor replied. "What can you tell me about this evacuation?"

"Undead, they say. A few fighters from the castle came through and told everyone to evacuate back to the capital. I know Fort Bosk was overrun, and the residents in the northern port town of Mara were destroyed or turned as they say," Gnaw babbled as he stuffed food in his mouth.

"Why are you here?" asked Aedan.

Gnaw stopped eating and stared at Aedan square in the eyes. "During the Great Manah Wars, we used to eat undead for breakfast. Ask your druid friend there. I saved his hide a few times. My missus is the only one I'm scared of!" He let out a bellowing laugh.

Freida smacked Gnaw in the back of the head so hard, Gnaw's face hit the table top. "Show some respect, you fat-arse bully," Freida snapped.

Gnaw lifted his head off the table, shook off his concussion and grunted. "She calls me the bully. She'll drive away your undead army with her fists alone." He turned around and winked at his love.

Freida smiled, "You always had a way with words."

Aedan could not help but stare at the weapons hung on the wall in the dining room. First, there was a massive ice axe. Ice coalesced around the blade from the surrounding air and dripped onto the floor. There was also a short sword with a burning blade of fire. Finally, completing the collection, hung a cat o' nine tails rippling and crackling with electrical veins.

"I see your eye is caught on those three there. The axe is Chomp, and the sword is Bite. The whip is Crack. That's Freida's," Gnaw explained.

"Are they magic?" Aedan asked.

"You're a bright kid. You one of them Gnossian scientists or something?" Gnaw winked at Grandor as he made fun of Aedan.

"Leave the poor boy alone. He hasn't even had a chance to touch his food. Go ahead and eat my son," Freida coaxed Aedan.

Aedan took a tiny bite out of the ribs. It was so squishy and oily. He did not want to eat anymore.

Grandor nodded at Tanke, who jumped up and snatched the food off Aedan.

Freida took a swing at Tanke. "Why, you little...!"

"Let him be," Grandor spoke.

Freida stopped. "Only your mutt can get away with that under my roof. What will Fabian eat now?"

"My name's Aedan!" Aedan retorted.

"Sorry, Damian," Freida replied.

Aedan rolled his eyes and gave up on trying to correct her.

"I've come here to ask you to join the war," Grandor stated.

Gnaw, and Freida stopped eating.

"You know we don't take sides anymore," said Gnaw. "We just want to stay here. We are happy here."

"The enemy will come. Their numbers are great. You cannot defeat them on your own," Grandor reasoned with them.

"Maybe not, but to be honest, I think the enemy has already gone past. They think this place is abandoned. We like to keep it that way. Sorry my dear friend. All we can offer you is food and a bed. Beyond that, we must say no," Gnaw added with a polite tone.

"You two could be the deciding factor in the battle. All of Concordia. All of Alteria is in danger. You two could save an immeasurable number of lives." Grandor pleaded.

"They sold us the same stories when we were growing up. Remember Freids?" Gnaw sought affirmation from his woman.

Freida nodded. "I've heard it all before. End of the world nonsense. It ain't gonna happen. Someone's always gonna fill the void that's left. The smart ones stay away and keep living their lives. Let the idiots battle it out over shiny gold and imaginary power."

Grandor did not want to argue and decided to stop reasoning with them. The night drew out, and they told Aedan stories of their time growing up in the orphanage at Thule, how they met as young children and fought side by side in some of the greatest battles in Concordia's history. Aedan was blown away to learn these two slobs were responsible for some of the most famous skirmishes he had read about in school. He was in the presence of those who he had admired and wondered how they had done the things talked about in story books. Finally, Gnaw and Freida drifted off to sleep in their chairs. Their snoring resembled thunder.

Aedan, Grandor and Tanke shared a bare room. As they lay down, ready to sleep, Aedan wanted to ask Grandor something.

"Grandor, how did you call the eagle today?" Aedan asked.

"He is my friend. I have known him for many cycles. I knew his father and mother. He listens to me," Grandor explained.

"But how did you learn to speak eagle? He obviously couldn't teach you," Aedan queried.

"Why not? How does anyone learn a new language? You learn through empathy and care. You pay attention to facial expressions, look for repetition, sense emotions," said Grandor.

"Can you teach me eagle?" Aedan asked.

"It would take a very long time. But I can teach you something else. Animals understand us. We just don't understand them. They know exactly what we say, but we think they say nothing to us. Next time, pay attention to any animal, and you will see in their eyes, in their movements, and tone of their voice a message. You will realise they are trying to communicate with you. Reply in your own tongue and see if they reply to you in their tongue. You will be surprised." Grandor smiled as he explained.

"Can you also teach me magic? I saw what you did in Sylvinar. The way you moved. That was magic," Aedan pressured the druid.

"Magic is not taught. It is merely revealed. Magic means different things to different people. How is it you shoot an arrow with such skill, with little effort, where others struggle? That is your magic," Grandor stated.

"What do you mean? How is that magic?" Aedan asked.

"We are tired and need rest. We shall continue this conversation at a more opportune time. Now go to sleep. At Lum's first light, we will commence the final leg of our journey and arrive at Castle Mhan before night." Grandor lay down to sleep. Then he rolled over and handed a bowl of fruit, nuts and vegetables to Aedan. "Eat this if you are hungry." He rolled over again and went to sleep.

Aedan scoffed down the food and also went to sleep.

AEDAN WOKE UP TO THE sound of Tanke growling. Grandor was already awake, peering out the window.

"What is it?" Aedan asked.

"You stay here with Tanke. No matter what you hear, do not leave this room. Do not look out the window. The enemy must not know you are here." Grandor leaned into Aedan to emphasise his last question. "Do you understand?"

Aedan nodded.

Grandor then spoke to Tanke. "You heard what I said, boy. Take care of him."

Tanke growled in a hushed tone in affirmation.

Grandor exited the room. He walked into the dining room.

Gnaw and Freida were putting on their battle armour. The large pauldrons and chest plates fell into place, held together by chainmail reinforced studded leather. Gnaw tightened the side straps on Freida's armour, and she returned the favour.

"You sensed it too?" Grandor asked.

"Aye. There's a pack of wild animals outside. They don't sound friendly. We'll be cornered in this small house. Where's the boy?" Gnaw replied as he pulled Chomp and Bite off the wall. Freida grabbed Crack.

"He is in the room. Tanke is guarding him. He is safe as long as the enemy doesn't spot him. But, if they do, they will descend in full force upon this place in an instant," Grandor warned.

"Don't keep secrets from me, druid. What about the boy?" asked Gnaw.

"He is an infused. The first I've seen since the war," Grandor replied.

"An infused? They're trouble if you ask me. Whatever druid. I just want to survive this." Gnaw snorted.

"Like old times," Freida remarked as she and her husband took point at the front door.

Grandor took his place behind Freida.

"You protect me," said Grandor.

Gnaw and Freida nodded in affirmation. Gnaw held up his open right palm and counted down from five, one finger at a time. On the last count, he kicked the door open, and they ran outside.

A Kun leapt from the right at Gnaw. Gnaw swung Chomp outwards and cleaved into the Kun. The beast was snap-frozen by Chomp's magical force. The Kun smashed against the wall and shattered into a million pieces.

Out of the tall grass, thirty Kuns flowed out and swarmed the party.

Grandor knelt onto the ground and held his staff upright in front of him. He looked to the heavens and started chanting. Clouds swirled and moved above him.

Freida cracked her whip with superior efficiency. She was fast at cracking left, then right, then back. Crack! Crack! Crack! Each beast was met with a surge of electrical energy, which sent them reeling back. Their rotten flesh was singeing. She was radiating lightning in every direction.

Gnaw cleaved and shattered Kuns with Chomp and fended off the smaller ones with Bite. He swung and froze and smashed and crashed and burned and kicked and headbutted. But, amongst the violence, he managed to spit some words. "Hurry up druid. We don't have all night."

Aedan could hear the battle outside. He wanted to look out the window. He went to get up, but Tanke stood over him and snarled.

"Whoa! I'm on your side," Aedan reasoned with Tanke.

Aedan tried to get up again, but Tanke snapped at him. Aedan pulled back and sat on the floor again. Tanke sat opposite him and stared at him. Aedan stared back.

"Fine. I'll sit here then," said Aedan.

Grandor's eyes rolled back and turned white as he closed them tight. The swirling clouds above him had grown in size and were rippling with electricity.

A Kun darted past Gnaw. It ran straight for Grandor. It opened its drooling jaws and went to close them around the druid's comparatively tiny head. Crack! The Kun was ensnared by Freida's whip and electrocuted to a cinder.

Another Kun grabbed Freida by one of her legs and started to shake her. Gnaw leapt on top of the animal and drove Bite straight through the animal's skull while striking at another Kun with Chomp.

"Must we die first before you are of any use?" Gnaw yelled at Grandor.

Aedan could hear the battle and Gnaw's words. He looked at Tanke.

Aedan was sure he could see distress in the animal's eyes. Maybe Tanke was just as scared as he was something would happen to their friends.

"We need to help them, Tanke," Aedan said to the timber wolf.

Tanke cocked his head and looked to the window.

"What if Grandor dies?" Aedan reasoned.

Tanke whimpered.

"I'm good with my bow and arrow. I went to the bottom of The Depths and back. I rode a Traxy and survived an attack by a Hunting Horror and a Yeshi Salamander. I slew three Skeletals. Don't tell me I can't fight. I can fight. Will you fight with me?" Aedan stared Tanke down.

Freida sat against a wooden pillar, cracking her whip as best she could. Her left leg was bleeding out. Gnaw was striking at a Kun, which had grabbed him by the arm. He fell to the ground as another Kun pounced on top of him. Another Kun grabbed Freida by her left arm and pulled her towards the bushes. She wrapped her whip around the pillar and held on as the Kun pulled on her other arm.

"It's now or never, you stupid druid!" Gnaw yelled.

The sky was covered in electrical activity. The clouds swirled around a vortex. Grandor thrust his staff skywards. Lightning shot up from his staff into the clouds. Then a moment later, lightning rained down on the Kuns. A bolt of lightning struck each one. Streams of electricity rained down. The energy. The spectacle. The night looked like day—Flash! Flash! Flash! Flash! Flash!

The air was filled with the smoke and smell of burning fur and flesh. The Kuns lay limp as the final surges of lightning struck them. A few more flashes and the clouds dissipated. The enemies were vanquished.

Gnaw darted over to Freida and pulled her upright. "Aye?" he asked.

"'t is but a scratch." Freida quipped. Her left leg had a massive open wound which was bleeding. Her right arm was riddled with bite wounds.

"Help her, you idiot!" Gnaw yelled at Grandor.

Grandor drew a bottle of ointment from his pouch and poured it over her wounds. He immediately wrapped the wounds with nettle-weaved bandages. "They will heal in a few hours."

"The pain is already relieved. Thank you," said Freida.

"You took your time," Gnaw complained.

"I'm sorry. It was a clear night. Summoning the storm took longer than usual." Grandor explained. "Let's gather our belong–"

Before he could finish talking, a Kun pounced on him and pinned him on the ground. A fresh wave of the relentless beasts poured out from the long grass. Freida got up on her legs and cracked the beast off Grandor. Gnaw smashed the scouts leading the packs.

Grandor pointed his staff at the long grass and begged it for aid.

The grass came alive and tangled the beasts which were running through it. The Kuns struggled to break free.

"That will only hold them for a little while," said Grandor. "Let's retreat and hold the fort."

"They will overrun us inside," Gnaw argued.

"We have no hope out here," Grandor reasoned.

Gnaw was unhappy with the suggestion but had to concede it was their only tactical option left. "Very well."

Gnaw pulled Freida back towards the home. Grandor walked ahead to open the door, but a pack of Kuns had flanked them. They blocked the entry. The Kuns in the grass had shredded their way through.

Grandor, Gnaw and Freida stood in an outward-facing circle as the Kuns closed in.

Thwat! Thwat! Thwat! Thwat! A volley of arrows hit the rear bunch of Kuns. Aedan stood at the doorway, firing off his arrows in succession. Tanke bolted past him and led the charge into the Kuns.

The undead beasts turned on Aedan and charged at him. Their beastly senses overwhelmed.

Aedan led them away to the end of the long veranda. He climbed onto the roof and kept firing arrows at them to taunt them, for he knew he could not hurt them with his weapon.

"I told you not to come out!" Grandor yelled as he crushed one of the Kuns with his staff.

"I'm helping," Aedan yelled back just as he noticed something rising out of the ground beyond the horizon. "What is that?" he pointed.

Grandor looked at the army rising out of the ground. "That is why you should not have come out. They know you are here."

"Haven't seen Harbingers in a long, long time." Gnaw whistled the words in surprise as he slashed through another Kun. "No point boarding up now," he said with a smile.

"We stand and fight until our death then." Freida blurted as she electrocuted another undead beast.

Aedan stared at the approaching army. He was stunned with fear. He managed to mumble, "What do we do now?"

Grandor did not have a reply. He knew they could not outrun the army without horses. He knew there was no escape. But there was one very slim hope. He yelled, "Aedan!"

Aedan turned to Grandor and made eye contact.

"If you believe you can defeat this army. Then you will." Grandor told him.

"But I don't," Aedan replied, confused and looked at the approaching army again.

"Just trust me and believe you can. You have no other hope. You have been in this situation before. Haven't you? Remember what you told me about The Depths?" Grandor kept a Kun at bay with his staff as he reasoned with Aedan.

Aedan looked at the army. He looked at the Kuns on the ground snarling up at him. He remembered how he overcame The Depths. He remembered how it felt to rise up against all odds. He figured if he could kill the Kuns just below, they could make a retreat somewhere and from there create a bottleneck. Maybe destroy the entire army? Was he dreaming? Of course, but so was he when he was left for dead in the depths. He had twenty-three arrows left. There were about twenty Kuns below. He looked up at Nai and asked her for help. No, he *believed* she would help. He drew his first arrow, which started to glow with magical energy. He fired it. The Kun was struck in the forehead and convulsed on the floor in anguish before laying still. *It worked! How did it work? Who cares! It works!* Aedan fired off his remaining arrows in quick succession, and the Kuns fell dead.

"Excellent. Come down. We must go. There is an outcrop of rocks up ahead. We might be able to hide there," Grandor yelled with glee.

Gnaw and Freida laughed. Freida yelled out, "You're my kind of boy!"

Aedan leapt down and joined his friends. Tanke, covered in ghoulish stains, leapt on Aedan in festive delight. Aedan caressed Tanke's mane, "We did it. We helped them."

"Was this your idea Tanke?" Grandor said with annoyance.

Tanke barked and whined a little.

"We were fine. You need to do as you're told," said Grandor as he looked over towards the army. "We have about a five-minute head start. Let's go."

Grandor ran ahead, and everyone followed, but Gnaw was smashed in the head by a Batyles powerful tail-club. The armoured creature lumbered out from the grass with his fellow pack.

Gnaw was out cold. Freida ran over to protect his body. "You two keep going. This is our end," she yelped with tears in her angry eyes.

"Not tonight!" Browbearer boomed as he galloped to a grinding halt next to her. He fired a cone-shaped object out of his gas-powered shotgun. It exploded on impact with the ground amongst the Batyles and shattered them into pieces.

Relianstar pulled up next to Browbearer and spoke to Grandor. "Take this manah and moonstone. We need the stone back before the enemy sets upon the castle."

Grandor pocketed the items and nodded in affirmation. "Protect the boy. He is what the enemy seeks. He is an infused."

Relianstar looked at Aedan. The first thing she noticed was his red eyes. They made her unsteady. Not since the time of Yama had she seen red eyes. She was compelled to strike the boy down as a precaution to avoid further conflict, but her oath to Nai prevented her from doing such things.

"Very well," she grabbed Aedan and pulled him onto her steed.

"What's happening?" Aedan asked.

"Go with them to the castle. I must attend to Agwa'den. I will be back before you know it." With those words, Grandor ran southwards. He snapped a small amount of manah dust between his finger and thumb, and he darted away at a blinding pace with Tanke by his side.

Freida pulled Gnaw and herself onto Browbearer's horse.

"You two really need to lose weight," Browbearer grunted in disgust.

The army was but moments away. They turned towards the castle and galloped away. Browbearer and Relianstar sprinkled some manah on their rides and whispered in their ears. The horses' legs became a blur as they cheated time and space.

Maleh, amongst his horde, watched as they galloped away. He could have caught them, but on his own, he would not stand a chance against them. At least he knew where the fabled boy was. So, it was true. There was an infused in Concordia. Maleh thought his master not so ignorant now. But, what he wanted to do, was strike his master down and take the boy for himself. Alas, the phylactery his master possessed stole him of his free will.

The City of Mhan

Castle Mhan thrust out of the earth with regal authority. It had many spires, landing platforms and balconies as if many castles had been fused to form this cyclopean conglomerate of steel and stone dressed with flowing banners. The royal chamber was at the highest point above the court and the city. The city's perimeter wall was a colossal barrier made of gargantuan stone blocks surrounded by an artificial offshoot from the River Mhan as a moat. Crenelations, machicolations and loopholes provided excellent defensive options from within the city walls.

As Aedan approached the city on the back of Relianstar's stead, he noticed mounds rising out of the ground. Thin barrels arranged in cylindrical fashion pointed outwards and were trained on the horses as they galloped by. He was able to catch a glimpse of a soldier within the mounds through the loophole.

"What are those?" asked Aedan, interested. This was all new to him. *What could those mounds be?*

"They are defensive pillboxes," Relianstar replied through her mask, without glancing back.

"What's a pillbox?" Aedan pushed for more knowledge. He had not learned about them in school.

"They are what you see. Men inside wield automatic crossbows, which can fire a shot every second. Gnossian technology Concordia acquired during the Great Manah Wars. Any enemy who invades the castle must first get past these defences." Relianstar pointed out the mounds all over the ground.

"There must be nearly a hundred of them!" Aedan cried out in surprise. Then a shadow blotted out the sky. He looked up and saw the city walls dwarfing the sky. Yet, they were still a few minutes away on horseback.

The drawbridge started to drop. It squeaked and creaked as it was lowered over the river moat. The reinforced steel gates were opened outwards by long steel chains, with links the size of giants. Within the gates stood a Ras'i. It was General Uriah.

Gnaw, who was well awake and annoying Browbearer the whole trip, hollered across to Aedan. "Aye! This place will poison your mind if you're not careful."

"Shut up, don't scare the child," Freida snapped back.

Browbearer wanted to kick them both in the moat just to watch them flail about in the water. Listening to them bicker the whole way was getting on his nerves.

Relianstar and Browbearer pulled to a halt just inside the gates. They both dismounted. Gnaw and Freida rolled off their ride, but Aedan stayed astride his. He was too busy taking in the sight of the city before him.

Sworders, archers, spearmen, cavalry, armoured warriors, clerics, and what he was sure were paladins like Relianstar were moving around to various parts of the city perimeter. All along the long wall, there was activity. Soldiers were talking, practising drills, tending to their weapons and exercising with iron weights and bars. At some distance to the left from the entrance, there was a large square building with enormous barracks. Off to the right, there was a similar but taller building with an effigy of Nai at its pinnacle.

Towards the castle, there was a city. Stone and Tudor buildings littered the colossal area navigated by cobblestone roads linked to a principal, polished stone road, wide as ten horses, leading up to the main castle complex jutting out of the mountain behind it. The precipice rockface enveloped the castle's semicircle footprint.

Within this semicircle, seven prominent spires shot out of the castle's main body. The tallest spire was in the middle, surrounded haphazardly by six other spires of varying height. Smaller spires popped out from different parts of the castle. There were enormous platforms built out of each of the central spires linked with winding pathways and stairways.

"I know these two." Uriah signalled at Gnaw and Freida. "Always good to have more help. But who is this vagabond?" He asked with a wave of his hand at Aedan.

"This is Aedan of..." Relianstar looked at Aedan so he would finish the sentence.

Aedan sensed he was being watched and looked at Relianstar. He then looked around and saw the general. *A Ras'i! What is a Ras'i doing here?* He thought.

Relianstar sensed his thoughts and replied, "He is the General of the Mhan Royal Army, and his name is Uriah of Mhan. But you should address him 'general.'"

Aedan looked at Relianstar in shock. *How does she know what I'm thinking?*

"I am a Paladin of the Light, and I am clairvoyant in some way. Now can you tell us where you are from?" Relianstar asked as she raised her face guard to make eye contact with Aedan.

Aedan replied, "Of Sylvinar," with a proud intonation while keeping a cautious eye on Uriah.

"Sylvinar? But you're too big to be a Sa'ami," Uriah barked back with a slight annoyance in his voice.

Aedan did not reply and looked away from Uriah's unsettling gaze. He thought to himself how he would kick the stupid Ras'i in the face when he got the chance.

Relianstar chuckled. "You better watch out, general. It looks like he wants to teach you a lesson."

"Hm. As you were saying...." Uriah prompted Relianstar to finish her report.

"We sensed them at Hilltop Hamlet on our way to Agwa'den. The undead besieged them. I blessed them from a distance and embued Aedan's arrows with my magic." Relianstar pointed at Aedan.

"That was you?" Aedan asked, for up until this point, he thought *he* had used magic.

"Yes, it was me," Relianstar replied, then continued to report to the general. "We saved them from a small contingent of Batyles and made contact. Grandor set off with a ration of manah we gave him to Agwa'den to recharge the moonstone. He advised this young boy is infused and requires immediate protection. He believes this army may have something to do with this boy. Then we returned here with what you see."

Uriah walked up to Aedan and studied him. "He has red eyes, but that does not mean he is infused. I do not feel any manah when I am near him. You?"

"Neither do I. Which is a relief," Relianstar replied.

"Hm. Take him to the queen. Let her decide what to do with him. I am sure Vera will be able to tell if he is infused or not. Browbearer, Gnaw and Freida, we have some battle preparations we need to go over." With that, Uriah dismissed Relianstar.

She leapt onto her ride and galloped down the broad road towards the castle, through the city of Mhan. "You get to meet the queen, little boy. Try not to be rude," Relianstar warned.

Aedan thought of what he knew of the queen. He recalled the things Eldoran said about her and her politics. Aedan did not like the idea of a queen. He did not like the idea of authority. He just wanted to go back home to the way things were. At that moment, he thought of Ferni and his father and how much he missed them.

Relianstar looked at him with a warm gaze. "Your family needs you to be strong, little boy. Find the strength within you. Ask Nai for guidance."

So, Aedan did, and he felt better.

THE HALLWAY LEADING to the tower of the royal court was as wide as the River Mhan itself. It was made of polished marble, which looked like flowing water. The pattern within the stone wibble-wobbled from the light refracting through the multiple layers of varying density. Aedan looked up at the convex ceiling made from translucent crystals of iridescent colours interlocked together depicting the history of Mhan. From the rise of creation, when Akh and Nai descended from the heavens to fertilise Alteria, to the end of the Great Manah Wars when King Kanon, Yama and the Unknown confronted Akh, the lord of destruction. Or so the legend went, which many people doubted even occurred.

Light from the sky shone through crystals designed to animate the illustrations. Either side of the hallway was host to arched panes portraying the heroes of the Great Manah Wars. Aedan noticed a depiction of Relianstar astride her stallion, leading a charge into a horde of Gautarians. She seemed to leap out of the window as if the flat image had forward volume. Her likeness towered over the barbaric Gautarian hordes beneath her.

"Is that you?" Aedan asked with a pointed finger.

"Indeed it is. That is the battle for Antillia. With the aid of the great Daryph commandos of Myrah, Mhan led a counterattack against the barbaric hordes of Shefar, who had all but conquered the eastern front towards the end of the Great Manah Wars. If they had succeeded in enslaving Antillia, with her beautiful resources and abundant lands, they surely would have multiplied in numbers and continued conquering the rest of the world." Relianstar clenched her right fist in anger at the memories which came flooding back to her.

As they walked further along the hallway and approached the royal court, Relianstar pointed out a few more images. "There is my knight mate, Browbearer. The only Gnossian Battlemade left above ground as a diplomatic symbol of unity between the Gnoss and Mhan. Near the entry is General Uriah. King Kanon is on the other side of the hallway, and Queen Ain is opposite him. We now enter the royal chamber of their one and only offspring and current ruler of all of Concordia, her royal highness, her majesty, Queen Maya. Bow before her when you enter. Only speak when spoken to. Follow my lead."

The two royal aides by the door, draped in blue and red satin in honour of the two opposing forces of manah, pulled the tall doors open while bowing at Aedan and Relianstar. Relianstar returned the gesture by touching the three middle fingers of her right hand to her forehead. Aedan tried to copy her and placed his hand on his head.

This is so stupid, he thought to himself. He wasn't fond of having to bow or show unnecessary respect. He just wanted to wave or shake hands with people. That was *real* respect and demonstrated true homage to your fellow people.

Reahl announced to the Queen, with Shun by her side, "We have Relianstar entering your chamber. She is here to present before you an issue which requires your decision." He proceeded to scribe what he said and what was happening.

"Your majesty. I come to you on the gravest of circumstances. I am sure the general has already painted a bleak picture, but I come bearing news from Sylvinar Forest." Relianstar knelt before the Queen with her head down.

Aedan stood there. He made eye contact with Maya and smiled.

Maya was not sure what to make of it. She was too busy looking at Aedan. His red eyes captivated her. He seemed to be so raw as to not even belong in her presence. He was pretty dirty, and his dark, earthen skin was alluring. He looked like a ruffian whom she would never associate with, but something interested her. She felt compelled to smile back but held her composure. "Do you not recognise me as your queen?" Maya asked in her most stern voice.

Reahl was motioning his head in Relianstar's direction, trying to give Aedan a clue. *Copy her.*

Relianstar spoke beneath her breath, "Kneel Aedan and lower your head."

Aedan looked at Relianstar and, realising he had missed her cue, knelt while smiling at Maya.

Reahl nodded downwards, indicating he must also lower his head.

Aedan lowered his head. He snuck a glance up at Maya then kept his gaze down.

Maya wanted to smile and tell him it was ok, but as his queen, she could not. "Rise. Tell me, Relianstar, what is your news? And who is this boy next to you?"

Relianstar stood up, so Aedan followed suit and dusted off his clothes. Dirt fell all over the spotless ground.

Relianstar motioned towards Aedan, "This is Aedan of Sylvinar."

"Sylvinar? But they are Sa'ami. He looks human to me, except for the red eyes," Maya said in confusion.

"Indeed, he is from Sylvinar. He was raised as one of their own. But he is a human orphan–" Relianstar was interrupted.

"That's what everyone keeps saying. But I haven't seen any proof yet." Aedan retorted with a cheeky tone.

"Quiet! Only speak when spoken to," Maya snapped.

"Why?" Aedan asked.

"It is disrespectful to interrupt someone," Maya replied.

"What if I forget what I was going to say? My father always taught me to speak up for myself..." then imitating Eldoran's voice, "... lest it slips from your tiny little brain."

"Well, I am not your father. I ask you to remember what you need to say and say it when it is your turn to speak," Maya added in a calm but definite voice.

"Yes, your majesty," Aedan said with a curtsey.

Maya was annoyed but let it go. "Please continue, Relianstar."

Relianstar added, "Grandor saved him and Kainan from a pack of wild Kuns. Eldoran and the missing girl, Ferni, were petrified. Kainan refused to leave but ordered Aedan to go with Grandor. Grandor was bringing Aedan before you because he believes he is an infused, and the undead army seeks this boy for its own purposes."

Aedan looked at Relianstar, wondering. *The missing girl? What is she talking about?*

"You look puzzled Aedan. Is this all news to you?" Maya said with a gentle breath.

Aedan looked at Maya gauging if her question was genuine, "Why is she referring to Ferni as the missing girl?"

"You have not been told? The Sa'ami evacuated the city on royal order back here to Mhan," Maya explained.

Aedan's heart raced, "Why didn't anyone tell me?"

"You didn't ask or think it, so I assumed it was not worrying you, or you knew," Relianstar stated.

"Where are they now?" Aedan asked with an excited warble in his voice.

"They are safe in the industrial caverns behind the castle," Maya explained with a casual gesture to the rear of the castle.

Aedan ran to the balcony off the royal court and looked at the precarious drop from the spire he was on. He could see walkways leading to the rear of the castle. They were large and melded the castle into the mountain behind it. The castle had no aft windows, and the precise masonry transitioned into rough stone melding into the mountain. With his gaze, Aedan traced a path down the spire to the base and saw a hallway through a window that seemed to connect to the part of the castle that led into the industrial caverns. He leapt off the balcony and grabbed hold of the royal banner, which dangled to the bottom. He descended to the base of the spire, landing on the lower platform and leapt into the window he had spotted from above.

Relianstar arrived a fraction of a second too late to stop him. She peered down and watched him vanish into the window below. Maya joined Relianstar on the balcony and also looked down.

"I will fetch him immediately." Relianstar turned heel and headed outwards.

"Don't be silly," Maya retorted. "We are about to head into war. You have more important preparations with the general. I will have an aide fetch him. He is obviously distressed about what is happening. I will talk with him once he has had a moment with his friends."

Relianstar was surprised at the queen's forgiving nature towards Aedan and worried she had forgotten the real problem, "Your majesty, if he is infused, we need to know now so the general can consider the impact on our battle plans."

Maya did not like being spoken to like she did not know what was going on. Besides, she felt empathy for Aedan, and she also thought he was, well, handsome. "Relianstar, do not tell me what is important, for I already know. I do not rule this country through guessing and gambling. I rule through well-thought-out and calculated efficiency. If I put too much pressure on this boy right now, he can easily escape, as you have seen. Vera will assess him in an hour or so after he has calmed down and is open to it. Sooner is pointless. His mind will be blocked. Don't you agree?"

"As always, you are right, your majesty. Your logic is impeccable." Relianstar bowed and headed out the chamber.

Maya kept staring out the window, wondering what Nai's plan was for this boy and if she was part of it. Finally, she ushered Shun, "Escort me down to the caverns. I want to make sure he is alright."

AEDAN RAN DOWN THE dank stone hallway. There was meagre candlelight illuminating the way. He bolted past filthy labourers carrying garbage in wheelbarrows and a couple of scruffy guards armed with short swords and torches.

"Halt there!" hollered Baraf, a black-bearded, greasy guard in a studded leather chest plate and dirty, grey pants with strapped cloth boots.

"Stop running!" yelled Lari, a blond-headed guard with long, sticky locks in the same attire as Baraf.

They both chased Aedan down the hallway.

Aedan ignored them and continued his run at top speed. His heart was racing. He was excited to see some familiar faces soon. *The Sa'ami were safe!* He wished there was some way he could tell Kainan. Then he remembered poor Kainan, who stayed back. He would have ordered the whole city to return to defend Eldoran and Ferni. He would have whoever was in charge condemned for abandoning Sylvinar. Then Aedan wondered, *who is in charge?*

The men were gaining on Aedan.

"I said stop!" Baraf yelled out as he threw his torch at Aedan.

Aedan turned a corner, and the torch shattered on the wall. Hot splinters and embers scattered in the air. Baraf and Lari were both enveloped in the hot dust. They slowed down to rub ash out of their eyes and to brush off ash on their clothes.

Lari grumbled as he caught sight of Aedan up ahead, "Why, you little twerp!" He grabbed Baraf and dragged him down a hallway to the left, "Let's go this way."

Aedan looked behind. He had lost them. He spotted a cleaner with a mop and bucket trying to clean up a spill of black fluid on the ground.

Aedan stopped to ask the cleaner a question, "Which way to the caverns?"

The rotund, balding man looked up at Aedan, "Who are you, son? What are you doing here?"

"I'm a Sa'ami. My people evacuated Sylvinar city here to the caverns in this castle. But I do not know where to go. Can you please help me?" Aedan asked with his hand on the man's shoulder.

The man looked at Aedan's hand because no one ever touched him. He was a filthy cleaner, after all. He looked back at Aedan and pointed down the hallway, "Head down that way, turn left and then the third hallway on the right leads to the antechamber where you'll find the cavern's entrance."

Aedan gave the man his rations pouch, "Here, take this. Thank you."

Aedan ran off at speed. The man peeked inside the pouch, pulled out one of the orange roots, and took a bite. He grimaced at the taste and spat it out.

Aedan turned left in the next hallway and pushed as hard as he could. He could not wait to hug his fellows.

Lari and Baraf popped out from a hallway and grabbed Aedan by the arms.

Lari spoke in Aedan's face, "We got you now."

Aedan kicked Lari between the legs, smack bang, right in the gonads. Lari groaned and let go of Aedan.

"You'll pay for that," Baraf barked as he wrapped his right arm around Aedan's neck.

Aedan manoeuvred his head so he could bite Lari's forearm. Lari resisted the pain by clenching his teeth and tightening his grip on Aedan. Aedan bit harder. Lari bit his lower lip as his face turned red. Finally, he erupted in a yelp and let Aedan go. Aedan turned around, kicked him between the legs and ran off.

Lari and Baraf were both left clutching their crotches, rolling around on the floor, moaning in pain.

Aedan turned at the third hallway and entered the antechamber. It was an enormous chamber about a quarter the size of the Great Amphitheatre but made of stone with flickering torches all around the edges. It was dark, but he could see the piles of rubbish being shovelled by workers into carriages that were heading into dedicated tunnels off to the sides. The floor was barren dirt, and far across on the other side, there was a sizeable opening. It was the entry into the caverns. Beyond the entrance, there were lights and activity. There were immense, block-like structures with many levels surrounded by soft amber lighting. Aedan could smell coal and snoot in the air and feel the smog crawling over him.

He jogged the final distance across the chamber past the piles of rubbish. Workers looked up at him but took little notice. Aedan nodded at some of them, but no one returned the acknowledgement. Aedan felt sad for the workers. It was such a beautiful world outside, and here they were, stuck in a dark, barren hole, shovelling garbage.

Then he heard the sound of murmuring voices. The murmuring sounded very familiar. It sounded like a late afternoon stroll through the markets in Sylvinar. It was the Sa'ami. He could see them all assembled in a giant morass near the middle of the cavern. They were huddled together around sack tents and campfires. Some were cooking soup in large cauldrons; others were sharing bread and water.

Aedan looked around at the large stone buildings pumping smoke and hot air into the cavern. He would catch a glimpse into one of the buildings and spotted obese men and women hammering away in time against molten hot steel blades or armour. Sweat poured off their bodies and pooled on the floor. The heat in the rooms distorted their silhouettes. Another building had a pile of trees next to it as high as the cavern ceiling itself. Workers strained on large chains, controlling a soot-covered pulley as they hauled a tree into an opening in the side of the building. The grinding and screeching sound of steel against wood reverberated as sawdust shot out the side in a rooster tail arc, landing in a pile surrounded by a scaffold made of log. Workers on either side shovelled the sawdust into bags and loaded it onto carriages. On the other side of the building, planks of wood, spear shafts, arrow shafts, crossbow bolts, shield frames, and other contrivances of war were being lowered onto carriages heading to the same tunnels on the side of the rear cavern. The whole chamber was a mechanised war machine churning out the utilities required to fight the onslaught about to hit the castle.

Jonin looked up and spotted Aedan. It took him a while to register what he was seeing.

Jonin stood up and walked towards Aedan, "Aedan, is that you?"

Aedan stopped looking around and turned to Jonin. He smiled at the sight of his friend.

"It is you!" Jonin yelled. He let out a celebratory laugh and ran towards Aedan.

Aedan ran towards Jonin.

A few of the Sa'ami looked at what was happening. They murmured amongst themselves. They began to realise it was Aedan. They stood up one by one and started flocking towards him.

Jonin and Aedan leapt onto one another and hugged in a tight embrace, laughing and crying with joy.

"We thought you were dead! But, by Nai, how good it is to see you," Jonin proclaimed.

Aedan laughed, "And I, you."

They broke their embrace and looked at each other square in the face, hands on each other's shoulders.

Jonin looked around, expecting to find someone, "What about Kainan? Where is he? Did you find Ferni? Is Eldoran ok?"

Aedan shook his head, "They are both turned to stone. Kainan stayed to protect them."

A sea of Sa'ami surrounded Aedan. They were all trying to touch him, congratulate him, welcome him. Every Sa'ami in Sylvinar within this cavern wanted to see the second son of Eldoran.

A group of six Campesino warriors in Traxy armour cut through the crowd, parting them with their spears. Aedan looked at the group and in the middle was Ferni's father, Santo. Santo reminded Aedan of a happy Eldoran. He was short and old and dressed in formal attire but was always smiling and calm. Aedan looked at Jonin for a clue.

Jonin hinted at Santo with his head, "Your father left him in charge to lead the city to Mhan."

Santo walked out from amongst the Campesinos. He looked very distressed and knelt before Aedan and spoke with well-enunciated words. "My leader."

All the Sa'ami followed Santo's lead and knelt before Aedan as well.

"Kainan is alive and protecting Eldoran and Ferni. Do not kneel before me." Aedan waved with his hand for everyone to stand up.

Santo leapt up with hope in his eyes and begged, "Ferni is alive?"

"She is turned to stone. The same fate has befallen my father." Aedan comforted Santo with a hand on his shoulder.

Santo turned around to think. He turned back to Aedan and asked, "So what are we to do now? What were Kainan's orders?"

"He wished me to bring back an army from Mhan to hunt down whoever turned Eldoran and Ferni to stone. We believed, at the time, all of you had been murdered or turned to undead." Aedan could feel everyone hanging on his word, their gazes staring into his soul, begging for leadership, "But he would not wish anyone to risk their life on a gamble crossing the savannah. The general here is preparing for battle against the undead. Campesinos, we must aid the royal army in battle. I will confer with the queen and find out how to break this curse that has befallen our loved ones. Do not worry. I will rescue them."

Jonin pointed at the Traxy scale on Aedan's back, "You completed the trial!"

Aedan turned his head to look at his forgotten scale, "Yes, I did." He removed it off his back and handed it to Jonin, "Here, take it. I don't want to see it ever again."

"No." Santo stepped forward and grabbed it, "You are the only Sa'ami we know of to have completed the trial this Shinar. All the others were recalled by their beacon bracelets when we commenced the evacuation. But you and your brother did not return. What happened?"

"We lost them completing The Trial together," Aedan said with a straight face.

Santo studied Aedan's face. He could sense there was something not right, "We will take this scale and forge your Campesino armour with it. You have become a man Aedan. You are no longer a boy."

Aedan nodded in thanks but felt empty. He thought of Ferni. He thought of her beautiful eyes, her lovely smell and her enchanting smile. A tear was about to roll out of his eyes, so he turned heel and walked away, "I will confer with the queen. Campesinos prepare for battle. Women and children will need to head deeper into the cavern and set up comfortable refuge. Should this castle fall, your presence must remain unknown to the enemy." At that moment, Aedan felt he needed company and someone to relay messages to his fellow people. "Jonin, you come with me."

Jonin ran to Aedan, “Yes, I will follow you anywhere.” He slapped Aedan on the back.

Aedan looked at Jonin and managed a smile.

Jonin smiled back, “I was scared. But with you here, I am not.”

Aedan's Path

Aedan walked back through the hallways with purpose. His head held high, with Jonin walking tall beside him. Aedan asked guards for directions, and they did not question his authority. As they headed out the last dank hallway from the castle's rear and approached the servant quarters, they came across Baraf and Lari guarding the exit.

Baraf pointed at Aedan, "I knew you'd come back this way."

Lari punched his right fist into his left palm, "I'm going to teach you a lesson."

Aedan kept walking towards them. He whispered something to Jonin.

Jonin nodded.

Aedan pointed at the guards, "Step aside. I am the leader of the Sa'ami here in Mhan on my way to counsel with the queen."

Baraf laughed, "Leader, you say? Well, lead this!" Baraf leapt forward and threw a punch at Aedan.

Aedan ducked beneath Baraf's arm and counterpunched him in the face.

Baraf stumbled back in shock. He shook off the numbness from his nose, "How dare you! Let's get them, Lari."

Lari and Baraf both started swinging at Aedan and Jonin, but they ducked and weaved around the lumbering guards, landing counterpunches and kicks all over them. Finally, through sheer brute force and a bit of luck, Baraf grabbed Aedan by the collar and lifted him off the ground and pinned him against the wall. Jonin ran to his aide but was grabbed from behind by Lari and could not move.

"Let him go, or I'll end you!" Jonin yelled at Baraf.

Baraf turned to Lari, "Would you shut him up!"

Lari covered Jonin's mouth. Jonin could only manage a muffled whine through Lari's hand.

"Now you," Baraf said, turning back to Aedan. "You need to be taught a lesson." Baraf drew his short sword with his right hand and placed its tip against Aedan's left cheek.

Aedan did not move or show fear. Instead, he stared the guard right in the face. "I have been to The Depths and back. I have seen things you will never see. I have endured more pain than you can imagine. There is nothing you can say or do which threatens me. Do your worst, and I will return it to you tenfold."

Baraf could see the rage in Aedan's eyes. The red eyes, the words, the way Aedan said what he said. Baraf panicked, "Not if you're dead!" He drew his sword back, ready to drive it into Aedan.

"Enough!" Maya commanded. She was standing behind them with Shun by her side.

Baraf and Lari turned in shock to see their queen amongst them. She never ventured into the servant quarters, let alone the rear hallways. They figured maybe they *were* threatening the leader of the Sa'ami. They released Aedan and Jonin and knelt before her, "We are sorry your majesty. We had no idea. We thought they were ruffians here to steal from your castle."

"Get out of my sight," Maya ordered.

Baraf and Lari ran off down the hallway keeping their heads low.

"I see you've met with your people. And you have brought a friend with you?" Maya asked, gesturing at Jonin.

"This is Jonin. He will relay any of my messages back to my people. I have ordered the Campesino warriors to prepare for battle. The women and children are retreating further into the cave system.

I must discuss with you what the plan is," Aedan told Maya standing as upright as he could because Maya was slightly taller than him, and he felt a little inadequate in front of her.

Maya thought of what the general had said. *We will not win, but we must survive.* "That is a good plan, Aedan. We appreciate the aid of the Campesinos. I would have them report to General Uriah so he may decide their best strategic use. You are to come with me back to the royal tower. The grand seer Vera is to read your fate. We must know if you are infused or not. This is the burning question."

"What's happening? What's an infused?" Jonin asked of Aedan.

Aedan looked at Jonin with a look of uncertainty, "It is some nonsense that I am not a Sa'ami."

Jonin looked Aedan up and down, "But you were born in Sylvinar. We are all Sa'ami."

The queen could have interrupted and corrected Jonin. She could have explained Aedan was found in the forest by Eldoran. She could have explained everything Relianstar had reported to her from Grandor, but she wanted Aedan to decide when to accept his fate.

"I know. But we must humour them for now." Aedan looked back at the queen. "Let's get this over with then."

Shun stepped back and signalled up the hallway, "After you."

AEDAN SAT CROSS-LEGGED on a large, ornate pillow, "So, I just sit here like this?"

Maya nodded.

Jonin shrugged his shoulders from across the chamber.

They waited.

The doors of the royal chamber swung open, and Vera glided in. Her slender frame was draped in a sheer white gown with a long train. She approached Aedan, already knowing why she was there.

Aedan went to speak; he was going to introduce himself.

"Do not speak," Vera interrupted him before he could say anything. Then, sensing Jonin wanted to interrupt, she raised her palm at him, "Be silent."

Aedan and Jonin looked at each other. This blindfolded woman was reading their thoughts, and it creeped them out. Aedan thought. *She must be like Relianstar.*

"Relianstar has clairvoyant powers. I am a seer. I see the world without time. I sense what others do not sense. I will tell you who you are." Vera stopped before Aedan and knelt in front of him. She placed her right hand on his forehead and stroked his head with her fingers. "Close your eyes and relax."

Aedan closed his eyes and relaxed. He took deep breaths. He could feel his mind opening up. He could feel all his memories and dreams float up from the recesses of his mind to the forefront of his consciousness. Everything he had ever seen, known or felt was in the present. He even saw moments as a baby he was sure he could never have remembered. His entire life was brought together in one infinite instant.

"This is the reality of our lives. They are a single present moment we choose to experience in pieces. But it is in this present moment everything we have done and will come to do, exists. It is in this moment I will read your life." Vera said as she arced her back and turned her face skywards, her hand clasped around Aedan's head. Her body propped up on her tiptoes, her legs bent, her body curved back. She held this pose.

Her voice went deep, otherworldly, and she grated the words, "Maya, your question is nought. He is a common human, the son of farmers from the town of Kalan, south of Mhan. They abandoned him for fear of persecution. They are now–" Vera froze. She collapsed.

Jonin was still as he had ever been. He was not sure what would happen next. He was afraid if he moved, maybe the seer would read his mind too.

Aedan coalesced his thoughts. The fragments of his mind became lucid. He became aware of where he was and the present. He opened his eyes and saw Vera in a heap in front of him, "What happened?"

Maya stepped forward, "I do not know. Please stay still and wait. She will rise very soon." Or so Maya hoped. She had never seen Vera collapse in a heap. Instead, she would finish her readings and then offer the opportunity to question her visions and decipher what they meant.

Vera twitched. She sat up and looked around. What she could see in her blindness was a mystery. Then she spoke, "What happened?"

"You did a reading but passed out on the floor before you finished. We waited a moment until you woke up." Maya explained as she approached Vera, "What did you see?"

"I saw a human baby born to framers. His red eyes burned everyone around him. His parents were scared. They tried to take him to Agwa'den but were beset upon by beasts, so they abandoned him in the river Mhan to flow downstream. He was found on the riverbank by the Sa'ami. He was raised as one of their own. Then my mind travelled back to his parentage, but I was hit by fire. I was burned to a cinder. I felt a pain I...." Vera dropped her head. The pain welling up inside her was too much for her to handle, "do not want to talk about it. I cannot talk about it. Please, excuse me. I need rest." Vera stood up and shambled out of the room.

Jonin walked over to Aedan and knelt next to him, "Are you ok?"

Aedan nodded at Joni, "Well, except for not being Sa'ami."

"How can that be true? You are our leader," Jonin said with a look of worry on his face.

"It is. That is why I am tall and lanky. That is why I do not fit in. I am a human child, abandoned and adopted by Eldoran and Jasi," Aedan said with a tear in his eye. "They are my true parents, regardless of what this seer says."

"I am glad you are not infused," Maya said as she broke her gaze away from where Vera had exited, her mind still concerned for her seer's mental health.

Aedan looked up at the queen, "What will you have me do now?"

Maya thought about it. She wanted to see Aedan again. She was glad he wasn't infused, and she was glad he was a human. "You are to have dinner with me tonight. Do what you will for the rest of the afternoon. If the Sa'ami are to aid in the war, have them report to the general. Here take this." Maya handed Aedan a scroll Reahl had just finished sealing. "This is the report he asked from the seer. He will also be glad you are not infused."

Aedan took the scroll and stood up, "Do I have to have dinner with you?"

Maya was taken back. *Why wouldn't he want to have dinner with me?* She thought but said, "It is an invitation only. You may decline if you wish, but I will not make another. Choose wisely, young Aedan."

Aedan looked at Jonin, who shrugged his shoulders, "I will need to break the news to the residents of Sylvinar that their leader is no more. As a human, I can not lead them, so this needs to be done. I will then come to dinner with you to discuss helping me track down my parents if we survive the battle. Is nine o'clock too late?"

Is he dictating to me? Maya smiled with a tinge of annoyance, "It is. I retire at ten o'clock and have many duties to take care of, so it must be at eight."

"Very well. I will see you at eight o'clock." Aedan walked out of the royal chamber with Jonin.

Maya walked back to her throne and sat down. She dismissed Reahl.

Reahl waddled out of the chamber and shut the door behind him with a loud clang.

Shun stepped forward from her station next to the queen. "Be wary, for the heart cannot reason. In leading, you must stay clear of mind. Do not let fleeting emotions dwindle your capacity to be decisive."

Maya was lost in her thoughts, imagining what she would say to Aedan at dinner. She was hoping he would come to his senses and stop being such a boy. Then she felt Shun's hand on her shoulder and snapped out of it. She looked up at her trusty bodyguard, "Sorry?"

"Your focus on the present determines your reality. To survive this war, you must be mindful of your feelings." Shun gazed into Maya's eyes.

"Sorry. Yes. I am the queen. We have a war to win." Maya stood up and led Shun out of the chamber.

AEDAN FINISHED HIS tale to the residents of Sylvinar before him, which many dismissed as inaccurate. Then he told of the letter he had read, written by Eldoran and the story Grandor had told him. While there were conflicting theories, one thing was sure: he was not a Sa'ami. He reflected on his upbringing and his idiosyncrasies which hinted at his true lineage. In a few years, he would surpass the Sa'ami in height twofold. He would no longer be able to even fit into his home tree. In respect of the Sa'ami traditions, he would step down as their leader.

As he spoke, his heart broke. So many of the words that came out of his mouth were things he never imagined he would ever say. He could not believe this was happening. He thought of Ferni and how she would feel leaving Sylvinar. He knew she loved him, but he did not want to separate her from her family, and as he grew, it would be very awkward for both of them. She would seem like a child next to him. Then, he remembered how much he would not miss Kainan. But his father is the one he would miss the most. Then, he wished he had known Jasi better, and she had not passed away when he was so young. Finally, he wished he had known his own mother too.

All the Sa'ami milled around and murmured to one another. The gist of the story travelled outwards through the population in the cavern. After a few long minutes, they were all murmuring. Santo was thinking of many things. He was not sure what to say next. If he accepted Aedan's resignation, then he would be expected to lead until Kainan returned. That was Eldoran's decree during the evacuation. But if he declined it, he would be accepting an outsider as a leader, something the Sa'ami had never done.

Santo spoke with a soft voice, so the residents quietened themselves to hear him, "Aedan is one of us. He has lived with us his entire life. I do not doubt what he says, and I do not intend to go against his wishes. But I know he is fond in many a heart across Sylvinar. If you would have him lead us until we are back home after the war is won, back to where Nai wished he had been born, then raise your voices. Let him know he is one of us."

Jonin threw a fist in the air and cheered, "Aedan!" a chain reaction of murmurs turned into hollering, which turned into chanting, until everyone erupted in joy and fanfare, "Aedan! Aedan! Aedan!" They would have Aedan lead them back home. They would have him as their leader.

Santo turned to Aedan, "You hear the people. Will you lead us for the first and last time?"

Aedan felt his chest fill with emotion. He was trembling and wanted to hug every single Sa'ami and tell them how he wished he was one of them. He stood up on a wooden barricade near one of the foundries, "The castle will be set upon by an army of undead which is so immense many do not suspect we will win. The plan is to survive. As your leader, I assure you I will lead our Campesino warriors into battle. We will fight with our minds. We will outsmart the enemy. We will make them fight themselves. We will run amok and show the rest of Concordia battle is not a measure of strength but a measure of resolve and wit. It is a measure of something we Sa'ami have in spades. We will survive. We will win. We will live to fight another day. We will return home victorious. We will soon be around a warm fire with tea to our lips and food in our bellies. We are the Sa'ami, and we find strength in our unity and our families! Join me in a united hurrah!"

Every Sa'ami yelled, "Hurrah!" and the combined sound reverberated throughout the cavern. Some of the miniature stalactites broke off the ceiling, plummeted, and shattered on the floor. Beyond the cavern, the echo travelled through the castle's hallways and rooms. It reached the ears of the general walking down the main street of the city towards Castle Mhan. He stopped upon hearing it and managed a tiny grin. He knew the sound of conquest and courage. He was glad to hear it at this most desperate of times.

MAYA SAT AT THE DINNER table, tapping her fingers in rhythm while she waited. No one ever turned up late to an invitation with her. She was wondering how she would punish Aedan. She could have him imprisoned for insubordination. Maybe public lashes would set him straight. However, that would make him more stubborn. She just wanted him to look at her and listen to her for a minute. She just wanted the pesky boy to pay attention and consider her needs. It was not easy being queen. It was lonely, and few if any people liked her, and she did not like them.

Aedan sauntered into the dining room. He thanked the door attendant with a handshake. As he walked in, he waved at Maya, "Hello. Sorry I'm a little late. My people needed me."

Maya thought if she should highlight the fact he was an hour late but decided she did not want to risk souring the relationship over a petty issue, "Very well, Aedan. You are here now. Let's enjoy the meal before us and each other's company."

Each other's company? Aedan thought he was there to negotiate help in finding his parents after the war was over, but the queen was suggesting this was a social occasion. "Thank you. I was not aware this was a casual affair."

"It is not casual. But I do not wish this meal to be soured with only talk of strategy and tactics. I would like you to tell me what your intentions are now that you have discovered your true lineage." Maya signalled at the waiters to commence serving the food.

The waiters served a gentle vegetable soup. Maya scooped it up with her spoon in refined, royal performance. Aedan scoffed it down in a matter of seconds, lapping up the dregs like a dog.

Maya was a bit taken back, but she thought it was funny, "At that rate, dinner will be over in a few minutes. So slow down and enjoy the food."

Aedan replied, "I did enjoy the food. Do you have more?"

One of the waiters filled up Aedan's bowl again. This time, Aedan ate at a slower pace and looked at Maya, who engaged his eyes.

Maya put her spoon down across the lip of the bowl, "So young Aedan, what did the Sa'ami think of your revelations?"

Aedan stopped drinking soup and looked up, "They asked me to continue leading them until they are home." He went back to drinking his soup.

Maya looked at Aedan with impressed surprise, "They must have faith in you. Surprising considering how young you are."

Aedan blurted out between mouthfuls, "Look who's talking."

Maya had nothing to say for a few moments, then replied, "I may be young, but I am experienced."

Aedan finished his bowl of soup, shoved it away from him, wiped his mouth and as he threw the napkin onto the table, replied, "Now you are, but not when you first were given responsibility. Everyone starts somewhere. Queen, can we talk business now?"

The waiters served the finest cut of steak on the bone with an assortment of sweet and bitter garden vegetables and a spicy red garnish on the side, together with a bowl of fresh leafy vegetables accompanied by thin sliced pears and cherries.

Aedan licked his lips. He hadn't had a proper meal in about a week, "Thank you for this food."

"You are welcome," replied the queen.

"I was thanking the waiters and the cooks," Aedan said with a smirk.

Maya had enough of his cheek, "Are you here to put me offside constantly? I have invited you for dinner, and you seem not to appreciate the gesture. Yet you ask to talk business?"

Aedan stopped eating, put his cutlery down and looked at the queen, annoyed. "You see, your majesty; I don't think much of any of this. All you had to do was ask, and it happened. Your aides run around and make all the food. They also serve it and clean it up afterwards. It's not like you made this meal. I am here because I want something from you, and I am guessing you have invited me – made this gesture – because you want something from me. I have no idea what that could be, but I am here and willing and able. Let's dispense with the pretending and get on with it, please."

Maya was shocked into silence. She thought, *What an insolent little brat. How dare he speak to me like that? I did make an effort. He has no idea how hard it is to run a kingdom. He thinks it's easy. I can't believe I invited him to dinner. What was I thinking? I should have him whipped in public instead to teach him a lesson.*

"Well, your majesty? Why did you invite me?" Aedan asked Maya. Seeing she was boiling up with anger, he added, "I'm sorry. It is unlike me to be so rude to a host. It's just in the last few days I have had my life ripped apart."

Maya felt sorry for the poor boy. She remembered when she was young, and her mother disappeared. She understood what it was like to have everyone you love torn away from you.

Aedan turned his gaze away from the queen and focused on a window depicting a battle in Ras'Fahem, and he thought about the last week, "Days ago I descended into The Depths. Are you familiar with The Depths?"

Maya nodded, "Yes, the canyon between Concordia and Myrah."

Aedan looked back at Maya, "I went down there, and I overcame my fears. Or so I thought. For when I returned, instead of being greeted with jubilee and celebration by my people or who I thought were my people, I found emptiness. No one. Now I find myself here not knowing who I am or what my future holds. So, I am in no mood to waste time. Please accept my apology."

Maya wanted to reach out across the table and comfort Aedan, but its length and her station prevented any physical contact. "I do, young Aedan. I, too, am alone. My father left for the Underworld, and my mother disappeared, I assume, in search of her husband and left me alone to rule this kingdom. So I also do not know what my future holds."

Aedan smiled a little. He did feel a little sorry for the queen. "So, what of it now? Why are we here?"

Maya had forgotten Aedan's original question, and it startled her to have to think of an answer, "I wanted to discuss our allegiance, between Mhan and Sylvinar. We are bound by treaties and pacts since the formation of Concordia. So I ask if your Campesinos aid us in battle in honour of those allegiances?"

Aedan had a mouthful of steak, "Of that, they will. But when they return to Sylvinar, you will need to have dinner with Kainan to negotiate. He is the heir apparent, not me."

Maya blurted out without thinking, "You could join me here in the castle."

Aedan looked up full of surprise, "Join you? Here? Why would I do that?"

Maya looked at her plate, hoping the answer would be in the salad. She hesitated and then added, "We have the resources to help you find your parents. You could join the Mhan Royal Army, as a Ranger or a Scout, we would give you whatever you need."

Aedan shook his head, "No thanks. I don't want to be bound by a phylactery."

Maya was set back, "We only bind users of destructive and manipulative magics. Not Rangers or Scouts."

Aedan finished cutting the last pieces of steak and eating a mouthful. He pointed at Maya with his knife, "You say that now until you decide they're too dangerous too, and then you ask they be bound or suffer on pain of death." He waved his hand around the room to indicate all of Concordia, "Before you know it, you want to bind every citizen."

Maya enjoyed a good debate. She retorted with a calm voice, "How little you understand. It is impossible to bind non-magic users. We bind those who could be a threat—those who can cause damage. Destructive and manipulative magics are extremely dangerous. We bind them for everyone's protection. To ensure everyone's freedom and safety."

"Of course!" Aedan threw his hands up in the air, "You are robbing them of freedom. You are forcing your view, your rules, your way onto them. You speak of freedom. What about their freedom? Those you have bound, they have no freedom while the practice of phylacteries exists. Do you know who else uses phylacteries? The

Gautarians to control their slaves. Do you see your patrons as slaves? Antillia has no magic control laws, and they have almost no conflict whatsoever."

Shun entered the dining hall and nodded at Maya.

Maya patted her mouth and stood up, "You can't compare Concordia to backwater Antillia, and we do not treat our bound as slaves. They are treated with the utmost respect and highest regard. Magic control is essential for the safety of our nation. Phylacteries are the best way to ensure the safety of us all." Maya walked towards the door, "You know your way out. Organise your Campesinos tomorrow, ready for battle. May Nai bless you."

Aedan wanted to tell her what a haughty, stuck-up, no-good-for-nothing she was but would not offend Nai by saying so, and so replied, "May Nai bless you too."

The door shut behind Maya.

Aedan looked around and spotted one of the waiters, "Can I get a bit more mashed potato?"

Maleh's Request

Eight days had passed since the attack on Fort Bosk and only two days remained until The Ritual.

The light of Lum broke behind the eclipse of Lumbra. The silhouettes in the foreyard crept forth from the shadows. Entire battalions of Blades practised their drills. They sliced and parried and blocked. A contingent of Rangers darted, and tumbled and leapt, and shot arrows at wooden targets. Armoured cavalry charged, and halted, and circled, galloping in formation. Spearmen grouped together united their shields, coalesced, and lunged forward as one unit. Archers fired a volley of arrows in unison, skewering bales of hay. The foreyard was teeming with military practice on such a scale the army engulfed the city.

Outside the castle walls, beneath the ground, in stone reinforced tunnels, soldiers carried crates of ammunition to the pillboxes scattered at the ends of the vein-like system spanning out from underneath the city walls. From their vantage point, soldiers fired off rounds of bolts at wooden totems above ground while calibrating the barrels and lubricating the mechanisms in their automatic bolt-firing machines. The Gnossian symbol, a sphere encircled by three tinier ones, was emblazoned on the rear of each device, indicating their origin of manufacture.

A stout soldier with a thick handlebar moustache puffed away on a cigar as thick as a sausage, "Gotta love the Gnoss." He pulled the trigger on his weapon and unleashed a rain of bolts which shattered the base of one of the wooden totems and sent it crashing to the ground.

In the city, General Uriah was liaising with the queen who had come down to oversee the final preparations.

Maya asked, "What of the Order of Caval's Gryphon Riders?"

Uriah, on his knee, looked at Maya on eye level, "We sent a message two days ago. It can take a week or more to reach the summit of Mount Firtina, depending on the weather. They will fly down as soon as the message is received."

Maya continued her line of questioning, "What of Grandor and the moonstone? We need our golem defence system operational."

Uriah bowed his head and continued his report, "Relianstar's report has not changed. We expect him to return as soon as he is able with the stone fully charged."

Maya shook her head in disappointment, "We do not stand a chance without those two elements. I pray we are not beset upon before then." Maya looked around the foreyard, "Where are the Campesinos?"

Uriah stood up and pointed at the long road from the castle, "Here they come."

The Campesinos all wore Traxy scale armour. The armour glinted and twisted the light around it. It seemed to shift and blur. It was silver, and it was gold, it was yellow, it was blue. Beneath their armour, they wore their traditional green garments, white shirt and brown boots. Some bore short swords and shields, others spears, and some were dual-wielding blades of various designs. Each Campesino was similar yet unique. Their height and build made them look like an army of children. They approached the general led by Aedan, albeit without Traxy armour and just his knife, axe, bow and climbing rope.

As they approached the general, he addressed Aedan. "Impressive. You lead without any experience, or armour or weapon.

How do you hope to direct your fighters during the battle? Will you simply yell *Attack!* at everything you see?" Uriah let out a bellowing laugh, and the soldiers nearby joined in.

Aedan smiled, "I can see your weakness is your lack of imagination. I do not hide my fear behind armour, or blade, or experience. I revel in it. I will not be haste—misdirection, anticipation, and deflection are my tools. Do not charge at them blindly. *Lead* the enemy to their doom."

Uriah stopped laughing and leaned down towards Aedan, "Sometimes there is nowhere to run. Sometimes you have to charge. Sometimes death has decided it is your turn. What will you do when your time is up?"

Aedan looked at Maya, then back at the general, "It concerns me you are so eager to die. I would have more faith in a general who is eager to live. Step aside and let my Campesinos take their place around the entrance. We will skirmish with the enemy right in their midst. Try not to hit us in your blind rage."

The general grabbed Aedan by the collar and faced him, "Do not talk to me like that. I am in charge here. One more word, and I will serve you on a skewer!"

Aedan looked Uriah straight in his beady yellow eyes. "I do not recognise your authority, and I am not afraid of you. I will do what I wish, and if you disagree, make good on your promise and serve me. You will have an entire kingdom hunt you down until your dying days."

The general was furious. Never had anyone but the queen defied him. Not even kings and presidents ever dared to challenge his authority. He considered snapping Aedan in half to teach him a lesson, but the boy was right. He could not do it. He threw Aedan away.

Aedan braced himself on his legs as he landed and slid across the gravelled ground. He looked up at the general. "May I ask? What is a Ras'i doing serving a kingdom, not in Ras'Fahem?"

The general replied with a soft tone, "Do not speak of what you do not understand."

"Enough," Maya ordered. "We have many more preparations to get ready before the enemy is before us."

A young servant girl from the castle came running up, hollering at the queen, "Your majesty, Reahl sent me urgently. Vera has seen the vampire upon us today. We will be at war soon."

Maya turned to the general, "Sound the alarm!"

The general hollered at the guard above the gate with an almighty roar that could have served as the alarm itself, "Sound the alarm!"

The guard rang the large bell. Then, a few hundred meters along the perimeter wall, the next bell started ringing. Each alarm guard responded as the sound reached their ears until every alarm bell across the city and the castle rang.

Residents began evacuating their homes from the city and making their way through the under-passage of the castle. They were all heading into the caverns behind the castle. Like birds flocking together towards a new migratory direction, the civilians ran for their lives.

Soldiers poured out of the barracks. Those who were practising drills broke up into smaller groups and headed off to their designated posts.

Marko ran up and down the underground tunnels coordinating the mechanised units, ensuring they were ready to replenish ammunition and alternate their firing. He rehearsed his commands at the main branch and had each unit reply they had changed firing patterns. Marko had every choke point considered and every attack formation the enemy could throw at them covered with a firing pattern.

Sena reported to the general, "A cleric to each squad is ready and on their way. I will chant from above the centre watch tower to provide spiritual aid."

The general nodded as he was gathering together the footmen near the entrance.

Sena ran off straight to the watch tower.

Gallastrian, with Relianstar and Browbearer on either side, approached. Suverchant and Bastrolar were in close tow. Gallastrian reported to the general, "I will lead one, and Relianstar will lead the other." Gallastrian signalled at the two cavalries behind him. "Browbearer, Suverchant and Bastrolar will lead two smaller units to hunt down breakaway groups and units."

The general signalled where each cavalry should take form, "Next to each other. The foot soldiers will be amongst your rides. Remember to charge, split and annihilate."

Felgar ran along the perimeter wall, checking every archer was ready for combat, "On my signal, you open fire with your boom arrows first. No sooner. No later."

Rygar ran out of the gate tower towards the general, "We have a rider approaching the castle. Only moments away!"

The general snapped back, "A single rider?"

Rygar nodded and slammed his sword against his chest, "Yes. I think it is a negotiator."

The general snorted, "Undead do not negotiate. This army is therefore controlled by a wizard. The vampire is merely a conduit. Let the negotiator pass. I will address their requests."

Maya stepped forward, "I will decide what is best."

The general bowed, "Yes, of course, your majesty. As you wish."

They both headed up towards the gate's battlements. Rygar relayed the general order to Marko's combat units. They would hold fire on the approaching rider.

The rider galloped past the pillboxes. The thunderous thump of the animal's hooves shook dirt free from the tunnel's ceiling, dusting the soldiers below.

The general stared at the approaching rider. He squinted and focused his vision. It was Maleh upon the horse. The general had fought alongside Maleh during the Great Manah Wars. He had admired Maleh's conviction for freeing his people from the clutches of outsiders. But now, he rode towards him as an enemy, as a vampire, under the control of a wizard.

Maleh came to a halt before the moat and looked up at Uriah and Maya above the gate, "It is an honour to have you two greet me. I am here for the boy and nothing else. Hand him over, and I will spare this city."

Maya thought what the vampire could be talking about, "What boy do you refer to?"

Maleh laughed, "I do not know his name. He has red eyes and two who claim to love him live in Sylvinar Forest."

Aedan heard what the vampire said from his position below the gate. His heart pounded at the revelation. The army *was* after him. Maybe the druid was right. Perhaps he *was* infused.

The queen replied, "I do not know of who you refer to."

Maleh spat on the ground, "If he is not here, then I will have no choice but to destroy this city too."

The general spoke, "Maleh, you will not defeat us."

Maleh spoke out much louder than before, "Boy if you're in there, you can save this city by surrendering to me now. Hiding behind its walls will not protect you. Everyone will die because of your cowardice."

Aedan pushed up the stairwell to the battlements and came up next to the queen. Maya put her hand up, telling him to stop. Aedan stopped and waited to see what she was going to do.

Maya replied, "We do not bargain with vampires. Even if he were here, we would never hand anything over to you. Turn tail and run to your master, you pathetic creature. If war is what you want, then war is what you will get."

Aedan shook his head and tried to push into view. Maya placed her hand on his chest and held him at bay.

Maleh grinned in disgust. "Boy, I can smell you. I know you're in there. Do you want to know who your father is? Who your mother is? The answers lie with me and with me alone."

Aedan pushed hard against the queen's hand, but Maya would not budge.

She looked at Aedan with a stern gaze and whispered, "Do not be foolish. He's lying."

Maleh continued, "The old Sa'ami and young girl will be released if you come with me."

Aedan shoved the queen backwards and pushed into view above the gate, "I am here. I will come with you."

Maleh reeled his horse up on its two hind legs in excitement. "Wise choice, little boy."

So, it came to be, the gate was lowered, and Aedan walked out to the vampire. With each step he took, he felt the same uncertainty he felt when he left Sylvinar. Again, he was heading toward an unknown future, but he had no guide and was on his own this time.

As he passed the gate, Sena slipped a spirit stone in Aedan's pocket. Vera was connected to the spirit stone and would track where Aedan was going and what was happening. While she was upset at Aedan's hasty decision, the queen was humbled by his bravery; by his commitment to protect the ones he loved and the innocent from further harm. Maybe his courage would provide them with the knowledge they would need to defeat the undead army.

As Aedan approached the foul steed upon which Maleh sat, he could smell death and decay. He looked up at the Ras'i vampire and noticed he was paler than Uriah. But, unlike his rotting steed, his body was intact.

Maleh stared at Aedan without blinking, his body dead still, like that of his ride, "Get behind me, and we will commence our journey."

Aedan did not say a word as he approached the steed and leapt onto the back of the beast. Maleh turned around and clamped Aedan's hands together with rusted irons linked to the saddle.

Maleh galloped away with his prize.

Above the gate, Maya watched on with the general.

She ordered, "Send Relianstar and Browbearer close behind. They will rescue him once we know who our enemy is."

Uriah smiled, "You stole my thoughts, your majesty. It will be done."

Golem's Ridge

Darkness was falling. Grandor felt cold but was still vibrant with energy. The manah ration Relianstar had given him was enough to keep him charged for days. He neared the druidic grove. There was an ominous feeling in the air that coursed through his veins.

Tanke sat down near the entrance to the grove and looked at Grandor. *Don't be long.*

Grandor leaned down and stroked Tanke's mane, "It's ok, boy. I just need to recharge the moonstone, and I'll be back. I'd let you come with me, but Magestrix doesn't like animals inside the grove."

Tanke barked and snarled. *I don't like her.*

Grandor laughed, "Neither do I. But she is the grandmaster. I'll be back as soon as possible. Remember to get help. You never know what might happen." As a precaution, Grandor had already sent a message to the animals closest to the grove to be on standby, just in case they needed their help.

Grandor ducked into the grove opening and walked down the short rock tunnel into the antechamber. All the tables had been pushed to the edge of the chamber, and the druids were practising hand-to-hand combat. All the druids were shapeshifters, and there was not a single beastmaster in sight. Grandor had been neglecting his duties as mentor the last few days. Maybe he missed seeing them on his irregular visits? He encouraged his students to rough sleep with the animals to form bonds with them, so perhaps they were all out? He made a mental note to organise a meeting with his pupils as soon as all this was over.

Firar and Ernil approached Grandor. Grandor stopped walking towards the throne room, raising his arms in pomp and addressed them, "My brothers, how fare thee on this frisk night of Shinar?"

Firar looked at Ernil and laughed, "Don't pretend to be our brother. Magestrix told us about you. About your kingdom." Firar bellowed with laughter, "Surely you must feel like an idiot."

Grandor narrowed his eyes. His past was no laughing matter, and Firar was treading on thin ice with his comments, "I would watch my tongue, young druid, lest I unleash upon you unmeasured fury. Do not lack respect for the lives of those who came before you."

Ernil chimed in, holding onto his laughter as best he could, "We will spit on you if we wish. Look around you, Grandor. We are all shapeshifters here. Beastmasters are no more. Rise against one of us, and you rise against all of us. Find another grove. You and your kind are not welcome here."

Grandor turned heel and headed straight into the throne room.

Firar snickered, "Magestrix is waiting for you."

Grandor entered. Magestrix was upon her throne as usual, but this time she was surrounded by eight druids who Grandor figured were her best students, but he had never seen them before.

Magestrix raised her head in annoyance and glanced at Grandor, "Yet again, you prove your insubordination and belligerence. Were you not told? You are not welcome here. Be gone and never return."

Grandor stopped at the bottom of the stairs, "The undead army is to invade Castle Mhan at any moment. I need to enter Golems' Ridge to fulfil a promise to the queen. After that, I will be gone and never to return. I assure you."

Magestrix stood up, pushing her cape aside and chastised, "I do not need your assurance. You will not enter Golems' Ridge. You are not welcome here. Shut your mouth and leave right now, lest the entire grove defends in sovereignty against indignant usurpers like yourself. We have no allegiance to the queen anymore. We do not honour the treaty forged under the duress of King Kanon's power. We will no longer bow before a kingdom that abuses its vassals with orders and commands. They are to be destroyed, not defended."

Grandor wondered if he could say the right words, in the proper order, with the correct intonation to convince her otherwise, or if Magestrix would not care and fulfil her threat against him no matter what he said.

So, he decided to take a gamble and said, "I have felt the same but did not know you also did. If that is truly the case and you are not simply trapping me with your words, then I will join you."

Magestrix laughed, "I am no fool. Kill him!"

The eight druids leapt down from above the platform, four on either side of Grandor. Two on his right and one on his left wielded thorny clubs and shields made of Traxy horns and scales. The rest wielded quarterstaffs from the Dredloq tree, but one of the students must've just completed the master's trial because he had a staff from the Karkeha tree. He would be the hardest to vanquish.

The attacking druids worked in unison. One on either side thrust their staffs between Grandor's legs. They interlocked their weapons and swept them outwards in an attempt to trip him over. But Grandor somersaulted backwards out of harm's way and landed a few metres out of range. His body was rippling with energy and vitality.

Magestrix called out to her students, "Be careful! He has manah!"

A student struck Grandor's face with her club. It bounced off the bark skin, which radiated from the point of impact. Spells that required chanting and focus were mere afterthoughts for Grandor now. The manah imbued him with an innate ability to invoke magic at will.

Magestrix had not considered this. She never imagined the queen would have opened up the stores in the castle and have handed it out to anyone but her highest-ranking officials. She thumped her fist on the throne's armrest in anger and yelled, "Brothers and sisters, come to aid!"

Grandor struck out at two of the druids in front of him using both ends of his staff. They flew across the room from the power of the impact and hit the stone wall with a solid thud. They dropped to the ground in a daze. From behind, all the other shapeshifters flowed in from the antechamber. The odds turned from one versus eight to one versus thirty-seven. Grandor swept his staff in a circle around him, and the few he caught with it were sent reeling backwards. Grandor grew in size, so he was one and a half times the size of all the other druids in the room.

He thumped his staff on the floor and stole a moment to speak, "This violence is pointless. I want no conflict, only peace."

For a moment, the mass of druids stopped as the hypnotic spell took effect except for one, who charged at Grandor screaming, twirling her quarterstaff. She spun around and leapt through the air thrusting her staff at his face. Grandor parried with his staff and disarmed the woman. She was left standing next to him unarmed. He headbutted her, and she was knocked unconscious.

Magestrix finished chanting a spell under her breath in a foreign tongue and spoke, "Mahia'ben va de'manah. Olu'Ahk Ah'tash!"

From her fingertips, tendrils of darkness flowed across the room and wrapped themselves around her students. They twitched and trembled as the magical energy charged them. They began to change shape. Some dropped on all fours as their bodies contorted and shifted. Others stuck their chest out and their arms back as wings sprouted from their backs. The room was filled with werewolves, drakes and anacondas. Their size and strength now bested Grandor's might.

Magestrix stood up and addressed Grandor. "You cannot win this fight, druid. Surrender, and I will consider your offer of allegiance." She did not mean what she spoke. She wanted to avoid losing any more of her students in combat. It was not supposed to happen like this. This was not part of the deal she had made.

Grandor's eyes burned with anger at what he witnessed: shadow magic from the plane of existence where demons reside. Finally, he understood what was going on. Magestrix had made a pact with a demon for power, and she wanted to use her power to overthrow Mhan.

Grandor looked up at Magestrix through the sweaty bangs obscuring his eyes. A piece of bark dropped off his cheek when he spoke, "You are right. I cannot win this fight alone."

Tanke charged into the room with an army of animals from Sylvinar Forest who had responded to Grandor's call for aid earlier in the day. Timberwolves, panteras, monkeys, ravens, rodents and swarms of insects poured into the throne room.

It was chaos. The shapeshifters were outnumbered. Insects swarmed them and stung them while ravens pecked their eyes out. The monkeys threw stones and beat their enemies while rodents chewed at their hide and muscles. And the panteras and timberwolves tore their enemies to shreds with their powerful jaws.

Magestrix ran out of the throne room via the rear exit. Grandor looked at Tanke for backup, and they both ran after her. She was running through the tangled roots which led to The Depths and Golems' Ridge. Grandor willed the plants to life, and the roots tangled around Magestrix. She tried to wrestle herself free but was caught in the thick web. Tanke leapt on top of her and snarled in her face. He wanted to bite her head off.

"Don't kill her," Grandor ordered. He approached her and pointed his staff at her forehead, "You will pay for what you have done here. You are an insult to nature." He thrust his staff at her head, but she was gone. Only her shadow lingered for a moment; then, it was also absorbed by the darkness.

Tanke looked up at Grandor and growled.

Grandor turned heel and ran back to the throne room; maybe he could still salvage the battle with another command for peace? He still had plenty of manah left. He was sure he could save the grove. His legs thrust him forward at a blinding pace. Tanke's tongue hung out the side of his mouth as he ran close behind.

The blood flowing into the pool around the geyser was the first thing Grandor noticed as he entered the room. Bodies lay strewn all over the floor next to their entrails. The grove was spray-painted with blood. All his brothers and sisters were destroyed by the teeth and claws of the very animals they were sworn to protect.

Some of the Timberwolves and Panteras lied around licking their wounds. A monkey mourned the death of one of its own with wailed cries. Some ravens limped with broken wings, and rat bodies were squashed all over the floor. Grandor knelt by the bloody waters and washed his own hands as he prayed to Nai for strength. Tanke licked Grandor's face.

Ganateria, queen of the Panteras, approached Grandor. She had a deep scar across the right side of her body. She hissed at the druid and roared in his face. Tanke leapt up and snarled back at Ganateria.

Grandor soothed Tanke, "It's ok. You go and leave me with her."

Tanke walked away while keeping a cautious eye on his soul mate. Ganateria snarled again. She wanted to take Grandor's life. She had lost her sister, who lay dead by the water. Grandor walked over to Galateria, Ganateria's sister, and picked her body up from the water. Ganateria purred a low purr. She followed the druid as he carried the dead animal out of the grove. He would make many more trips like this out of respect for the animals who helped him on this day. They all paid the price with their lives so he may live. So he may complete his mission. So the balance of nature could be preserved.

He lay Galateria down on a bed of leaves, bound together with vine. Ganateria led her fellow panteras as they carried the body back to their lair, where they would bury it with the rest of their kind. Grandor hugged Ganateria and offered his life in exchange for her forgiveness. Ganateria snuggled the druid, tears welling in her eyes. She knew it was not his fault, and she loved him.

ANAH, THE SILVER MOON, was at her peak in the night sky, tinted yellow from Aura's golden glow. The crevice into the ridge started from a small fissure in the ground. The bank on either side dropped into a small canyon filled with its own ecosystem. This valley is where the druids assembled their golems from the precious durastone. The stone was marbled in various colours and materials. Durastone's value was in its ability to be crafted and held together by itself. So one could build near-indestructible structures with moving joints. The tiny valley was full of golems at different stages of assembly held together by scaffolds of branches and twine.

Grandor descended into the crescent-shaped valley. Tanke pounced from one stone to the next. Druids crafted golems as their magnum opus, their final work of intellect, nature, and magic. It was the last thing all druids completed before declaring themselves grandmasters and starting their grove. It was such a laborious and time-consuming task that few ever completed it in their lifetime, content with remaining masters.

Grandor walked past each golem. Some were slender, with the height of five humans. Others were stout and wide as an elephant. Grandor stopped at his one. He had been building this golem ever since he arrived at Agwa'den, and it was complete. He was going to declare himself grandmaster and postulate himself for the throne at Agwa'den when the previous grandmaster, Tallendore, stepped down to retire and retreated to the forests of Myrah. But, Tallendore declared Magestrix his successor, and to that, no one would question. Grandor loved Agwa'den and would never leave. He had too many friends, and Tanke was from Sylvinar Forest.

His golem was different to the rest. Grandor had designed it to be independent, to think, unlike other golems, which were simple automatons. Crack was its name because Grandor had etched cracks all over its surface. The cracks formed a complex pattern, like tattoos, and Grandor intended to pool manah into them. These veins were arranged in such a way to create a series of logical expressions. Something he had learned from Gnossian scientists he met during the Great Manah Wars. He referred to the drawings and, as the Gnoss referred to them, schematics he had etched into the golem's rocky surface an expression of intelligence. He hoped his designs would lend the golem to self-identify and become a living entity. He felt as a druid if he could create life, he would achieve what no other person in all of Alteria ever had.

Crack had a brutish face, not because Grandor intended it, but because sculpting was not Grandor's strong point. He gave Crack a look worthy of a child's scrapbook. Crack was a hulk made of stone with a round, simple face perched atop its broad shoulders. On his chest lay the small sphere where placing manah would, in theory, bring him to life. Grandor thought about the manah in his pocket. He had just enough to awaken the golem if it even worked. Maybe his theory was wrong? Perhaps it would just stand there and do nothing? Grandor decided not to waste the precious manah he had. More pressing matters were at hand, like the moonstone in his pocket he needed to charge for the queen.

Using a complex series of lenses, manah from the moons' light could be harvested, focused and stored in a moonstone for future one-time use. Moonstones were hard to come by in the wild. They would fall from the heavens once a year at most, and a lucky person would stumble upon them. They were used to power all sorts of things, from spells to inventions.

This particular moonstone was used by Castle Mhan to power its golem defence system. The golem defence system was a series of golems in the city, built millennia ago by ancient druids as a commission from King Mayjor of Mhan when Agwa'den was a sovereign entity. The six main golems stood on either side of the walkway which led to the castle, and within the castle, there were hundreds of tiny gargoyle golems. All would come to life and defend the castle from an attacking army when a moonstone was placed on the energising pedestal at the top of the royal tower.

Grandor approached the focusing lenses. The lenses of various sizes were mounted on a conical frame. The largest lens was hitched to the dome ceiling of the rustic, durastone pergola, where the contraption was mounted. The smallest lens was at the bottom of the frame, with each progressively larger lens mounted between them. At this point in the valley, the clearest and purest light could be harvested. Grandor pulled out the moonstone from his satchel, unwrapped it from its velvet cloth, and placed it beneath the small lens on the pedestal; before him was a series of five levers, which controlled the gears for the various lenses to adjust their angles and positions.

Grandor pulled the left furthest handle down and shifted it to the right. The outermost lens, the biggest one, tilted and caught some moonlight. Its imperfect, red crystal lens glowed as light passed through it. Grandor manipulated the first and second lever trying to align the beam of moonlight to pass through the following two lenses. Because the lenses were imperfect, Grandor had to tilt and adjust them off-centre, so the beam refracted at the correct angle into the next lens beneath it. Once he had aligned the red and orange lenses, he moved on to the yellow one. Finally, he focused the blue and violet lenses onto the moonstone. The beam was pure, radiant white. It would take some time before the stone was charged, so, Grandor crossed his legs and sat down to meditate. Tanke took a nap next to him.

After a few hours, the moonstone pulsated with a light blue hue. It was charged. Grandor opened his eyes, sensing the moonstone was ready. Tanke lifted his head off his paws, yawned, still half-asleep, and stretched his body to wake up. A large shadow swooped amongst the trees in the distance.

Grandor gathered the moonstone, wrapped it up and placed it in his leather satchel, "Let's go, brother. We have a long trek ahead of us, and I suspect the savannah will be crawling with enemies."

Tanke whined a little. He just wanted to have a bit of a rest. Then, something moved beyond the trees and shrubs. It was quick and dark.

Grandor stopped. Tanke froze.

Grandor crouched down and touched Tanke on the back. Grandor whispered a chant, choosing not to use manah, and invoked protective magic on Tanke. Tanke's fur absorbed the properties of the stone he was standing on, and each strain of hair on his body turned into a sharp granite protrusion. Grandor continued his chant and invoked the same protection on his body. His skin dried up, turned grey and cracked like the stone floor he stood on.

He stood up and looked around. He could not see anyone or anything. Maybe he overreacted, but he could not risk not assuming the worst. He decided to continue ahead. As he took his next step, a person leapt out of the darkness. A club smashed Tanke and sent him flying, and he crashed against a golem, which came toppling down as the scaffolding gave way. Tanke scrambled on the floor to avoid the falling debris. Grandor deflected the next blow, which was aimed at his head. He took a quick double step backwards as he blocked three successive strikes at his person. Tanke escaped the falling golem, shook off his slight daze, and ran back to help Grandor.

Grandor hesitated, reaching into his bag to grab some manah. He did not want to rely on it and thought it prudent to save some for the trip back to the castle. He felt energised after his meditation and guessed he had enough manah flowing in his body to invoke a couple more spells without the need for manah dust. He stood his ground as Tanke took his side. Their enemy had vanished into the dark again. They turned around, trying to face every direction. Tanke snarled at one of the golems. He could smell the unseen attacker hidden in the shadows.

Grandor snapped his middle finger with his thumb and blurted a short, breathy invocation; a glitter of light shot out of his fingertips and flared up the darkness with bright light. The radiant magic illuminated the golem, and Magestrix stepped out from beneath the colossal creation.

"You fool. You do not stand a chance against me now. No amount of manah can save you. Nothing you do will even stand a hope of defeating me. I am connected to the realm of shadows, and I draw limitless manah from the darkness. It is my ally, and it will consume you too." Magestrix spat the words as she approached Grandor and Tanke.

"You underestimate my power," Grandor replied with confidence.

Magestrix became enraged, "No! You underestimate mine!" With those words, her body morphed and darkened. Her shape shifted. Enormous wings sprouted on her back. Claws grew from her hands and feet. Her head elongated and shaped itself into a reptilian head. Within moments she towered over Grandor and Tanke. Her size was enormous. She even dwarfed the largest of the golems in the valley.

Grandor and Tanke backed away as far as they could.

Grandor looked up at her and spoke to Tanke, "A shadow dragon. This is worse than I could have imagined. She is death to the living and near indestructible. Only a Roj'ah or Ah'zul stone would give us a fighting chance. But they don't exist anymore. So we must run and hope we survive."

Magestrix let out a deafening roar, her body absorbed the light from Grandor's spell, and their stone skin faded away. They were vulnerable. Magestrix flapped her enormous black wings and took flight. The wind from her wings blew ghastly fumes across the valley floor.

Grandor coughed as he tried not to breathe them in, "Her size is her only disadvantage. We must move through narrow places. This way." Grandor led Tanke through a winding path between the numerous golems.

Magestrix flew in a circle, searching the valley floor for her targets. She spotted them ducking and weaving through some scaffolds. She divebombed into the largest golem and knocked it over.

The golems started falling on each other like dominos. Boulders the size of horses fell and crashed all around Grandor and Tanke as they ran for their lives. The steep incline was up ahead. With some manah, Grandor was sure they would run up fast enough, and Magestrix would lose them once they dropped over the cliff on the other side of the ridge into Sylvinar Forest. But as they approached the base of the bank, Magestrix landed right in front of them. She stood tall and spread her wings in a display of grandiosity and power. She looked down upon them. She drew her breath and blew flames of shadow.

Grandor backflipped out of the way and took cover behind a stone pillar. Tanke ran off in a different direction and crouched under a boulder. The black flames licked past them and disintegrated all the plant life they touched. Grandor communicated with his familiar via telepathy. *Do not move from there. Stay still. I have a plan.*

Magestrix looked around. She could not see them, but she could sense them. She knew they had avoided her breath. She spoke with an otherworldly voice, which sounded like her, but as if she had many voices all talking at once, "You will not escape alive. I am your doom, you pathetic druid. Step out and face your death with courage."

From beyond the darkness, Grandor replied, "Come and find me. I will step out, and I will fight you to the death."

Magestrix took flight and followed the voice.

Grandor called out from the dark again, "I'm over here."

Magestrix closed in on the sound and landed on the floor, "Stop wasting time and fight me."

She turned her head around to her right, and Grandor stood at her eye level. She drew her breath, ready to blow him into extinction. Instead, a blue glow spread out like tiny cracks on the golem Grandor was standing on. Within a moment, the golem's body was covered in an intricate vein-like pattern that glowed in the dark; the manah heart pumped life into its veins.

Grandor dropped off just as Magestrix blew her dire breath.

The golem, made of stone, was unaffected by the attack, but it felt threatened and lashed out at Magestrix with a massive punch. Its boulder fist knocked her in the head and sent her rolling across the floor. Her enormous bulk smashed and crashed everything around her. Before she could react, Crack was on top of her, pummelling her with its mighty fists. She shoved him off with her claws and tried to take flight and escape, but he grabbed her by the tail and swung her around like a sack and threw her against the stone wall. Her body thudded on impact. She was now enraged and propelled herself off the wall towards the golem.

Grandor led Tanke out of the valley and over the ridge. As he looked back, the last thing he saw was Crack, and Magestrix intertwined in a gigantic wrestling match. He did not want to abandon his lifelong creation, but there was much more at stake.

Mastermind

A day, maybe two, had passed. Aedan was not sure of the time. He had drifted in and out of sleep during the journey. Maleh did not speak; he only rode, without rest, to the south.

Aedan was sure they had entered Thule once they crossed the southern marshes, dividing Mhan and Thule. He imagined the enemy must have been hiding beyond Kel's Pass, maybe in caverns that lead to the Underworld.

Thule was dead. Its ground was dry. The grass had shrivelled up, the trees were burned, and not a single animal was in sight. A dark mist that reeked of putrid flesh blanketed the barren land. Aedan's eyes stung from the fumes, and the smell of sulphur made it hard to breathe. He would take a peek to see where they were headed, but he only saw the same black earth covered in dead flora for miles ahead.

Aedan dozed off for the hundredth time.

A thundering sound of steel against wood awoke him. He saw a drawbridge beneath him. He looked up and saw a castle as they crossed its moat. It was a large castle, but nowhere as big as Castle Mhan. This castle stood alone, without a city around its perimeter. It stood atop a hill and shot up into the sky with pointed significance. It was a tall and slender castle built in the classical style popular before the Great Manah Wars. But its walls bled black ooze, which dripped down the sides of the structure.

They entered the castle, and Maleh navigated the narrow corridors and passages with his ride, making his way towards the centre. There were undead soldiers everywhere. They wore the tattered colours of Thule and others those of Mhan. It was a claustrophobic morass of walking dead. Some would reach out and try to grab Aedan in an attempt to pull him off his ride. Maleh would kick them in the head to warn them off.

Aedan was scared. He thought of what it would feel like to be eaten alive by an undead. He imagined what horror it was to become undead. To not be allowed to die and be forced to serve a master who would use your defiled body to harm others. His body felt cold, and he wished he wasn't alive. He wished he had never been born and that none of this ever came to pass. In all his life, he never imagined he would meet his death at the hands of such nightmarish creatures. He always imagined living his life in Sylvinar with Ferni. Now that was a thought. *Ferni.* He thought of her and her beautiful smile. Then he remembered she was petrified, and this lying demon would keep her that way forever. Maybe Kainan had already been killed, and both Eldoran and Ferni shattered to a million pieces.

What was the point of trying anymore?

Maleh pulled up to a large staircase that led to the royal hall. Whoever this demon was, had taken control of this castle and now commanded from the throne room. Maleh unhinged Aedan's shackles from the saddle and shoved him up the stairs. Aedan complied and shuffled up the stairs. The Ras'i would kick Aedan in the backside to hurry him up. A couple of times, Aedan fell over as all the energy in his body was sapped by the environment. It was a poisonous place that would consume even the most resolute.

Aedan shambled through the black hallways, trudging in the ooze covered floor. The blue flamed torches flickered meagre illumination in the all-consuming darkness of the hallway. Maleh shoved open the corrugated doors leading into the throne room. They strained and creaked on their hinges, grinding the gross floor beneath them. Maleh pushed him inside and shoved him towards the person huddled over a simple wooden chair with long grey hair obscuring its face. In its lap was a large, green crystal ball glowing with manah.

"I've been searching for you all my life," said Lord Venon as he gazed up at Aedan with his cold, calculating eyes. "When my spies told me of your existence, it was time for me to exact my revenge against the imperial manipulators in Mhan. Thank you, little one. Thank you for giving me hope."

Aedan looked at Lord Venon, "Who are you?"

Lord Venon was annoyed, his eyes squinted in anger, "Do you learn nothing in school? I am Lord Venon, the last King of Thule before the 'allegiance' of Concordia reduced my once proud kingdom into a vassal. I stand before you as master and commander of the armies of darkness which rise against the imperial puppets."

Aedan believed he could reason with this man, "I recognise your claim and shall address you as King Venon. May I suggest you simply declare your independence without bloodshed?"

Lord Venon grasped the manah orb in his left hand and stood up. He walked towards Aedan, one emphatic step after the other, "I have wasted my efforts trying to negotiate diplomatic solutions, and the pompous attitudes of the queen have forced my hand. I gave her one last opportunity, and she ridiculed me the way no king ever should be treated. Everyone who does not kneel before me will die."

Aedan knelt. He was not going to lose his life by refusing to show superficial subservience. He knew pride could kill you faster than any blade.

Lord Venon stood over him and stroked Aedan's hair with his slender fingers, "I feel the manah which flows in your blood. It is potent."

Aedan shook his head, "The royal seer said I am an ordinary human boy, born to parents...."

Lord Venon snapped, "Fools! They think they know everything. Yet, there is so much that eludes the kingdom. Has your druid friend told you about the champions?"

Aedan kept his head facing the ground. He was playing along but thinking if there was some way he could skewer this man with anything nearby, "Yes, he mentioned them."

Lord Venon stopped behind Aedan, "The Mage Champion, Yama, infused all that he was into the creation of the ultimate familiar. A young baby boy. Then he disappeared to protect himself and the boy because he failed to seal Akh away at the Confrontation of Kel. Akh will rise again, so Yama needed a way to safeguard his power. The power was perfectly concealed except for a flaw in his familiar: red eyes. You see, young Aedan, you are but Yama's familiar. A spell created you. You have no parents. This is the truth."

Aedan turned his head around to look up at Lord Venon behind him. He did not believe him but was not about to challenge him. Instead, he wanted to make sure Eldoran and Ferni would be freed, "What of Eldoran and Ferni?"

"What of them?" snapped Lord Venon.

"Your minion promised their freedom if I came willingly," Aedan stated.

Lord Venon waved his hand in the air and spoke with a tone of sarcasm, "They are free. As free as any statue can be."

Aedan felt his heart drop into his stomach, and then anger crossed his heart. It drove him to despair, so he leapt up and tried to bite Lord Venon in the neck. He attempted to rope his shackles around the wizard's neck. But Maleh grabbed him by the back of his collar and threw him across the room. He crashed against the stone wall and fell to the ground in a heap.

Lord Venon laughed, "You are nothing. You are but one little person in a world of monsters and demons. Simply accept your fate, and soon you will find yourself in the comfortable numbness of death. I hear it is black, empty and cold. Take him to the dungeon. We will wait until dusk to commence the drawing of his blood."

Maleh bowed, "As you wish, master." He stomped over to Aedan, grabbed him by his feet and dragged him out of the room. Outside he threw him over his shoulder and carried him through countless black hallways, always descending.

The smell became moist. The atmosphere was damp. Fungus grew on the walls. There were bodies hobbled in the corners of cells in the darkest parts of the castle. They were pale and malnourished, with nails as long as the years they had spent forgotten in the darkness. Mushrooms grew out of their bodies, draining what little life these pathetic people had left. Aedan wretched at the thought he would become like them.

Maleh kicked in a door and descended a staircase into a large dungeon. He released Aedan from his shackles and cuffed him up on a circular contraption in the middle of the room. Aedan hung there, splayed, with his arms and legs outwards. Maleh turned a handle until all the slack in the chains was drawn up, and Aedan was stretched tight. Then he exited the chamber, and the loud clank of the door being locked was the last thing Aedan heard before he blacked out from exhaustion.

"YOU DO NOT NEED TO worry. I will take care of it. Maleh is to ride north tomorrow and lay siege to Castle Mhan by the darkening of the second day. Do this, and I ensure you victory regardless of what you may think. The boy is of no significance in this battle. Akh drives me. Akh propels me. Akh gives me all the strength I need, and each day I grow stronger." Magestrix spoke with a deep voice that reverberated throughout the throne room.

Lord Venon sat at his throne, clutching onto his orb of manah on his lap, Maleh by his side. "I am your ally but do not expect me to believe in fairy tales. Akh and Nai are stories told to appease the masses to accept their terrible fates in servitude. Manah is power. It is real. The boy's power is real. I have felt it. It will be mine, and then this orb in my lap will be but nothing compared to the energy he will give me."

Magestrix approached Lord Venon. Maleh stepped forward and drew his long sword in defence of his master.

Magestrix smiled, "You think this pathetic vampire stands a chance against my power? You think you can win this war without me? I assure you, you will beg for my assistance on the second day, and when you do, it will be your soul I want."

Lord Venon stood out of his throne, "How dare you threaten me in my castle!"

"Then fight me old man. I have no fear. I will tear down these pathetic ruins and take Concordia for my own." Magestrix raised her right arm; her hand emanated dark fumes, her energy ready to lash out in combat.

Lord Venon did not want to be killed, and he felt stupid letting Magestrix so close to him. Until now, their allegiance had been negotiated via proxy, never had he confronted her. He had no idea she was so powerful. He thought she was a simple druid who had turned to black magic, but what he was witnessing was much more than that. He thought what he would say. He did not want Magestrix to feel he was submitting to her power, but neither did he want her to feel he did not respect her.

"My dear druid, why fight each other when we can conquer our enemies? We both seek emancipation from Mhan. First, we will overthrow their rule, and then we can fight one another if that is what you wish. You are passionate, you are angry, and this will serve us well, but I fight with logic and planning." Lord Venon orchestrated his words and delivery so well he convinced himself he did not feel threatened by Magestrix.

Magestrix could feel Lord Venon's thoughts. She knew he was bluffing. She knew he was a coward, which boded well for her plan. She would have his soul, his manah, and his power added to hers. She would set her sights on Myrah next. To conquer the Drayphs in all their superior glory would be a feat; how she would orgasm from joy.

She lowered her fist and chuckled, "You make a powerful argument, wizard. We will drive our enemies together, and then I will crush you," she laughed as she turned around and walked out onto the balcony, "Do not forget. Siege the castle on the darkening of the second day. Summon the dead. I will head to Mount Firtina." As she finished speaking, her body crackled and popped, her shape shifted into shadow dragon form, and she took flight into the scorched sky. Her roar echoed across the barren land as she encircled the castle once before taking flight to the west.

"We must hasten the ritual now. I cannot let that witch take what I have worked so hard to get." He ordered Maleh as he paced out of the throne room.

Maleh followed his master in absolute obedience. He would have moments of lucidity and recall his previous life: his battles on the shores of Ras'Fahem, defending his people from the onslaught of the continentals trying to take their lands. He would recall his death at the hand of a woman driving a lance through his chest. He would clutch his chest and feel the scar. Then, the memories would fade, and he would blank out with his only thought in serving his master.

Across the land, two steeds rode towards the castle: a brown horse and a white horse.

The Ritual

Ten days had passed since the attack on Fort Bosk. Tonight was the night of The Ritual.

Aedan woke up to a strong poke in the side of his ribcage. He looked down and saw Maleh staring straight back up at him. He turned his head, and Lord Venon stood at his side. He was feeling his right arm, looking for a vein. He smacked Aedan's arm and pinched the inside of his elbow. A foul grin crossed his face when he saw Aedan's vein swell up. He pushed a needle into the vein and clamped it in place with a thick leather belt. Aedan twitched a little from the pain but was too tired to muster a response.

Lord Venon scurried to Aedan's left side and repeated the process. He looked for a vein and then drove in another needle. Both needles were attached to thin black hoses, leading to a glass carboy on an open flame from an oil lamp.

Lord Venon looked for two more veins on each of Aedan's upper thighs, one on both calves and two more on the back of the hands. In total, he connected eight hoses to Aedan and the carboy.

Lord Venon clasped his hands in delight. He pulled out the manah ball which he wore suspended around his torso by a silk scarf and held it up in the dank darkness of the dungeon, so it caught the meagre moonlight sneaking through the tiny barred window high up above, defying the opaqueness of the scorched sky. The internal swirling fumes of manah became excited by the light and their kinetic activity intensified. Maleh stood to a side, not saying a word.

"Mahia'ben de'yash, yash'ben sera de'Akh Ah'tash." Lord Venon spoke with a powerful, stabbing voice. Each word amplified the glow of his manah ball, illuminating his sinister face in the darkness.

On the last syllable, he turned the valve on the head of the carboy, and blood flowed into it. Aedan screamed in pain as his life was drawn out of him. His body tensed, and his face grimaced. His yell did not stop. His mind was blank. He could not think, and he could not focus.

All there was, was pain.

The blood in the carboy boiled. It frothed and bubbled. As it filled to the brim, Aedan turned pale, and his body lost tone until there was little left of him. Maleh cut him down and pulled the needles out of his body, then threw him aside to be forgotten like all the other souls in this place.

Maleh assisted Lord Venon with inserting the needles into his own body at the exact locations as they were on Aedan's body. Lord Venon held up the manah ball, which was pulsating with so much intensity now even the darkest recesses of the room were illuminated. Tiny, malnourished rodents scampered into their holes.

Maleh inverted the carboy and opened the valve. The boiling blood decanted into Lord Venon's veins. His face tensed with a crazy smile as Aedan's life force entered his body. He called out to Akh in all his multiple names, thanking him for this gift. The last thing Aedan saw as his blurry vision faded was Lord Venon rising towards the ceiling; tiny electrical crackles flowing over his body.

Then, he descended back to the ground, turned to Maleh and said, "It is done."

Darkness.

RELIANSTAR LOOKED SVELTE in her studded leather armour. Browbearer thought it suited her much better than her usual full plate-mail armour. He, himself, had removed the reinforcement panels off his unique bodysuit so that he would make as little noise as possible.

Relianstar calmed down both their horses with a chant of soothing and covered them with foliage so they were hidden from anyone passing by. Browbearer was admiring her long golden locks and dark skin. When she turned around and stared at him with her incredible eyes, he froze.

"What are you gaping at? Have you not bothered to survey the terrain? Do it now, and describe our options," Relianstar demanded.

Browbearer snapped out of his daze in a bumble, "Yes, m'lady." He replied with a croaky grate from his boom-box. It was such a nuisance having to speak through the cylindrical filters mounted on his mask, but even a Battleborn Gnoss, such as himself, could not breathe the normal air above ground. It lacked the sulphur and silica content his body needed to survive. Millennia ago, the Gnoss developed the sulphur/silica filters so they could venture up from the depths of the Underworld and explore the surface of Alteria. Still, to their dismay, they found nothing of interest and decided it best to descend back to their beloved city of Tigia. During the Great Manah Wars, Mhan contracted the Gnossians to help in the war. Afterwards, they all returned to Tigia except for Browbearer, who refused to return and joined the Mhan Royal Army instead.

He flicked through his various viewing lenses mounted on his goggles. Each frame held a unique mineral lens sourced from the Underworld and enchanted with special magical properties which revealed things in the world which, under normal circumstances, required an expert clairvoyant to focus for hours to detect. Such were the gadgets of the Gnoss, who had no innate magic ability and neither sought to learn magic. Instead, they preferred to harness the energy from manah to reproduce reliable effects with technology.

Browbearer flicked back and forth through his ethereal lens and his thermal lens, "The land is barren, m'lady."

"Are you sure?" Relianstar asked as she stood close to him, trying to spot anything with her own eyes.

Browbearer doubted himself and was distracted by Relianstar's proximity. "Uh, yes. I think so. I don't see anything, but strong magics can cloak."

Relianstar was not happy with the response; she adjusted her belt and then pointed towards Castle Thule in the distance, "Study the castle. Tell me what you see."

Browbearer faced the castle and turned a dial on the side of his goggles. Mechanical parts inside adjusted the varying distances between the crystals and magnified his vision. Hence, he could see the castle in such detail he could make out the individual stone blocks. He looked around, but it was too dark. He switched to the thermal crystal and was unable to detect any life. Next, he switched to the ethereal crystal, and a purple haze illuminated the castle. "The castle is drenched in undead. I estimate thousands of them."

"That is not a very good estimation, but it will have to do. Undead are not very alert, so if we are careful, we should be able to breach the perimeter without drawing any attention to ourselves." Relianstar commenced the long walk to the castle.

Browbearer flicked his lenses back up, took hold of his molten battle axe and followed Relianstar into the dark. They walked for a long while. Their approach to the castle was from the gentle hills in the east. Over the last mound, Relianstar used some manah to grant them fleetness of foot so they could cover the remaining distance at speed. The barren land provided no cover, so speed was their only ally. They reached the edge of the moat and found an outcrop of rocks to take cover behind.

Relianstar peeked over the rocks. "Some creatures on the drawbridge." She spotted a grated opening on their side of the castle, "Over there, see the grate? That is our way in."

Browbearer poked his head up and took a look as well, "Looks mighty small, m'lady. How will you, er I mean me, fit through that opening?"

Relianstar took no note of Browbearer's faux pas. "You overestimate your size, tiny warrior. We will both fit after we remove the bars."

I'm not tiny. I am pretty big for a Gnoss, Browbearer thought, but said, "Very well, m'lady. Shall I grapple us up there?"

"First, we will wait and see if any patrols walk past," said Relianstar.

They waited, and a group of undead soldiers shambled past the grate on the inside of the castle, and a short while later, they shuffled past in the opposite direction.

Relianstar palmed Browbearer on the chest, "Do it now."

Browbearer used his gas-powered, double-barrel shotgun and fired off two steel lines. The sharp grapples lodged themselves deep into the stone. He handed one of the lines to Relianstar, "I only have a winch for one. We need to climb."

Relianstar leapt forward and started climbing as she swung over the moat, "Let's not waste time, my friend."

Browbearer followed her up the wall. They climbed using their strong upper bodies and the wall for support. Within moments they were at the grate. Relianstar pulled hard on one of the bars, and it would not budge.

Browbearer took his turn and ripped it out of its rusty frame, "I may be tiny, but I am strong."

Relianstar cracked the tiniest of grins, "Hurry up."

Browbearer was so happy she smiled at him; he yanked the other three bars out without a problem and sent them splashing to the moat below. They both climbed into the hallway beyond the grate. A guard on the drawbridge noticed ripples in the water where the bars had landed. He snarled and darted into the castle.

Browbearer lifted his left boot off the floor, and the thick black mucous stretched between his sole and floor, "This is disgusting. I haven't seen ectoplasm in a long time."

Shush. No talking, Relianstar signalled with her hands.

Browbearer copied her hand motions. *Shush. No talking.* Then added, *Got it, m'lady*. The last sign was a slight bow.

Relianstar gave him a stern look. She was annoyed by his attempts at humour. She pointed down the hallway. *That way. Carefully.*

They snuck down the hallway, which was very narrow and gave them no room to draw long weapons. Relianstar wielded a throwing dagger in her right hand and a bladed knuckle-crusher in her left hand. Browbearer had his crossbow against his cheek trained on the corner behind them. Relianstar placed one foot after the other. She concentrated on her thoughts and cleared her mind. She channelled her magic and sought to see ahead. All she could see in her mind were endless hallways without windows. Then darkness bubbled up and blocked her clairvoyance.

She stopped. Browbearer bumped into her, and they almost tumbled over. He managed to catch Relianstar around her waist and pulled her upright. He felt her press up against him, and she gazed at him with much anger. He smiled beneath his mask; luckily for him, otherwise, she would have slapped it right off his face.

"Let go of me. They know we're here," Relianstar blurted with pent up stress.

Browbearer was confused, "How is that possible?"

"They spotted one of us climbing up," she thrust her index finger into his chest. He frustrated her so much, but she had to accept he was the best knight in the order, after her, of course.

A horde of Kuns with rotten soldiers in tow rounded the corner. Their heads jittering side to side in vile anticipation. But the hallway was empty. They staggered past where the knights had been, sniffing the air. Above them, Relianstar and Browbearer looked down on them. They did not move a muscle or make a sound. They held their breath and closed their eyes. The horde shambled past down the hallway, looking for their feast.

Once the undead had been gone for a while, the knights relaxed and climbed across the rafters. They crossed into an ornate room adjunct to the main inner chamber where the throne room was. Undead were roaming around everywhere, looking for intruders. There was no way they could get into the throne room without being seen.

Relianstar signalled to Browbearer. *If Lord Venon inside. We trap inside.*

Browbearer nodded. He understood it was a one-way ticket. They would breach the doors, detonate explosives to collapse the entrance, and then fight him to the death. He was pretty sure Maleh would be at his master's side too. Then, he noticed Relianstar was conducing with Vera. He waited until Relianstar reacted again.

Change of plans. Maya wants Aedan safe. We recon more, Relianstar signalled. The orders did not make sense and increased the risk of their discovery manyfold. But they were bound by oath to follow all orders from her majesty.

With trepidation, they snuck over the horde beneath them and continued exploring the castle.

AEDAN COULD NOT MOVE. His vision was blurry. For a moment, he thought he was at the bottom of The Depths again. Then he smelled the foul odour around him and was reminded of his reality. Strewn on the floor, semi-naked but for a loincloth, his body was pale, and there was little energy in his heart. Lord Venon had drained much of his blood, but a small amount remained, just enough to keep him alive.

A tiny, malnourished mouse approached Aedan. It sniffed at his mouth. Aedan breathed out, and the mouse scampered away in fright. The creature was alive, unlike everything else in this place, and it was hungry. It came back to take another sniff at Aedan. Aedan felt sorry for the poor animal. He was kind of glad he would at least serve as a meal for another wretched creature.

Aedan recalled all the animals of Sylvinar Forest he used to spy on as a child. He remembered venturing south with Kainan one late evening of Kalor and spotted a pantera with her young. *I would've made an excellent druid.* He thought to himself as his lucidity escaped him. He remembered Grandor with his familiar and how Tanke had listened to him at Hilltop Hamlet. What were the chances he could talk to the mouse? The rodent squeaked ever so closer to Aedan.

Aedan opened his eyes and made eye contact with the beady eyes mere centimetres away from him, and he forced breath out of his mouth to mumble some words, "Free me. Get the keys."

The mouse stood on its hind legs and squeaked in defiance. *Why?*

Aedan turned his head, struggling to find the strength to raise his arm and point out the window, "I'll take you there. Where there's food."

The mouse scurried around, chasing its tail in delight at the thought. Then stopped and twitched his whiskers. *How?*

"As friends." Aedan could not muster any more words and passed out.

The little rodent thought about it for a while. He was famished, and he very much loved the idea of a friend—of escaping the dungeon.

He had seen the other two-legged creatures in this place how they entered and exited the room many times. He heard those creatures say "keys" and jangle those weird objects made from a cold, hard substance. They would put them into the wooden blockade at the top of the stairs. The block of wood would swing out of the way. Those were *keys,* he thought to himself.

He dashed up the staircase and under the door through a hole he had chewed many weeks before. Then, on the other side, he looked around as he stood up on his hind legs. *There they are!* He spotted a wooden beam with curved fingers, made of that same hard substance, with many keys hanging off them. He recalled seeing the man in the long purple gown pull them off and use them to open the doors here in the dungeon. But which one? He could not be sure, so he decided to take all of them—one at a time.

Aedan roused a little. He could feel something tugging on his hair. He forced his eyes to part open so he could see what it was. It took Aedan a while to notice, but his little friend was squeaking in delight and running around a bunch of keys he had brought down. Aedan lifted his head off the ground and looked in disbelief. He was still fragile, but his spirits soared.

"Thank you so much. I owe you my life," Aedan croaked and offered his hand to the mouse.

The mouse scampered back, unsure what to do.

"I am your friend. I will not hurt you." Aedan reached out again.

The mouse approached. He was used to being chased away and having things thrown at him. Aedan stroked the mouse.

"What is your name?" Aedan asked with a smile on his face.

The mouse stood up and squeaked. *My mother called me Vicho.*

"Then Vicho it is." Aedan giggled.

Vicho squatted and raised in rhythm with Aedan's hand strokes. He had never been touched like this before. All the pain in the world he had felt was lifted off his tiny little body, and he felt love for the first time since his mother had passed away. He was so happy to have a new friend and what the future may hold.

Aedan looked around, "Let's get out of here."

He propped himself up and tried to stand up, but his legs would not support his weight. He could only drag himself along the ground. He gathered the five keyrings in one hand and proceeded to pull his body along the gooey, dirty floor. He dug his fingers into the ground and heaved. He had to rest a few seconds between efforts. Vicho ran around, squeaking at him. *Come on! You can do it!*

Each step was painful. One bump at a time. Until, after what was almost an hour, Aedan was at the top of the stairs. He reached up with one of the keys and tried turning the lock. It would not budge. He dropped the key and tried the next one. It did not work. His hands trembled, and he struggled to insert each key. Then there was only one left. He inserted it and turned the lock. It made a loud *clank!* And the door swung open. He smiled.

Beyond the doorway, there was a hallway that led to another long flight of stairs. Aedan felt there was no hope, but he could not give up on Vicho. He dragged himself along the ground towards the stairway in the distance. But he felt life draining from him. There was not much he could do. Then he saw them coming down the stairs: two Kuns with an undead master. They spotted him.

The Kuns snarled with grotesque gargles of rotten phlegm. The master pointed at Aedan and hissed through his perforated mouth. The creatures closed in on Aedan. Vicho ran around in circles and panicked, and he squeaked, *What do we do?*

Aedan turned to his friend, "You run. I will remember you on the other side."

No. I will fight them! Vicho squeaked.

The Kuns and their master stood over Aedan. Aedan closed his eyes. Vicho hid underneath Aedan's armpit.

A bolt hit each Kun in the back of the head, hollowing out their skulls as they blasted straight through. The master was decapitated with a swift strike. As their bodies dropped to the ground, Aedan looked up at Relianstar and Browbearer.

Relianstar knelt next to Aedan and sprinkled manah over his body while chanting to her lady Nai, "Nai'yen en'deyo vivir de'Nai."

Colour returned to Aedan's body. Blood surged through his veins once again. The tone in his muscles returned, and he felt energy surge through his body. Vicho squeaked in excitement. Immediately, Browbearer tried to stomp on him, but Aedan caught his foot.

"He is my friend," he stated. "Thank you for saving me." He continued with a nod at both the knights.

"Do not thank us. Thank the queen. She made it our priority above and beyond all logic," Relianstar quipped. "Come with us. We must confront Lord Venon now. You can escape beyond the next hallway - there is a way out of the castle wall. Browbearer will cast a line so that you may climb out. To the east, our rides wait for us. You will wait there for us. If we do not return by nightfall, then take them and ride back to Castle Mhan."

Relianstar stood up and led the way, with Browbearer in tow.

Aedan scooped up Vicho and placed him on his shoulder, "I need clothes."

They stopped and looked at him. Browbearer snorted, "That you do."

Vicho squeaked. *That box has your things.*

Aedan walked over to the wooden chest by the wall and kicked it open. It had his clothes and weapons all in a heap, "You're very clever, Vicho. Thank you."

Browbearer pointed at Vicho, "He told you that? That's ridiculous."

"Hurry up and get dressed. The enemy knows we are here and is closing in on us." Relianstar ordered as she dragged Aedan, who was still buckling his pants, down the hallway.

Around the next corner, Browbearer fired a line over the moat from inside a machicolation and sent Aedan gliding down to safety, with Vicho tucked in his warm tunic. The last they saw of Aedan was him jogging towards the east.

Relianstar turned to Browbearer, "Now we have a mage and a vampire to kill."

Browbearer laughed, "Just like old times."

LORD VENON STOOD ON a balcony overlooking most of the castle. He recalled a time when Thule had been prosperous. Markets had bustled with trade. The countryside had been full of farming and activity. His father had ruled a wonderful kingdom and a grand army. The famed hills of Thule to the east were replete with manah reserves. The plains were farmed, and they had vital trade routes with Tigia, Sunnishidia, Myrah and Mhan. But then the manah ran out. There was very little left to trade, and everyone closed their doors to each other. Each kingdom protected their interests. Everyone wanted manah, but no one was willing to trade for it. The harsh desert of Ras'Fahem was the last frontier to cross into Kel, Akh's fabled resting place. It was rumoured the entire mountain ridge encircling the volcanic lands of Kel were pure manah, but the Ras'i did not allow outsiders into Ras'Fahem. They were peaceful but insular. They did not want friends. They did not want allegiances. And they did not want to trade manah.

Then came the Gautarians. They had always been a warmongering people, but their bloodlust peaked in the drought, and something compelled them to attack. They spread from their homeland, conquering countries as they went. Their numbers were immense. They flowed out of their mountain home like ants out of a hill. The entire nation of Shefar, where the Gautarians hailed from, was overpopulated. Over the years, many Gautarians had spread across the Great Ocean and colonised the barbaric archipelagos with pirate outposts enticing those who had turned to the dark side of life. But on that fateful day, they launched an offensive against the financially strong Agora. Like many other nations, Agora had copious manah reserves at the start of the Great Manah Wars, and they were able to defend themselves with pride. Still, the relentless onslaught of the Gautarians wore them down. Many Gautarians died, but they conquered Agora, and the rest of the world did nothing.

Over the following years, what happened is blurred by different recountings, depending on who you ask, but one thing is sure: nations divided and fought for themselves. Amidst all this chaos and destruction, the Gautarians conquered the remaining lands until Eerak, Tigia, Thule, Agwa'den, Sylvinar, Myrah, Antillia, and Mhan remained. By this stage, it seemed the Ras'i were in allegiance with the Gautarians: a very odd situation as the Ras'i never related to outsiders in any way. The Gautarians advanced on the people of Antillia and were met by the most savage response the Drayph Monks of Myrah could muster. This all-female race of magic specialists decimated the entire front line. However, the Gautarians would not cease, and their numbers dwindled in the onslaught.

Their final attack was from the northern shores of Mhan. King Kanon inspired the lands surrounding Mhan to form a united front against the enemy. Mhan, Eerak, Tigia, Thule, Agwa'den and Sylvinar united their numbers under an accord as the nation of Concordia. In the despair of the oncoming enemy, King Kanon was voted in as leader of this new nation.

After the bloody battle to drive back the Gautarians was won, King Kanon blasted the nation to oblivion with the aid of Gnossian manah bomb technology. The Guatarians were wiped out except for the few scattered across Alteria. Those within Shefar who survived the bombing were sterilised by the magic which swept over the land in a tidal wave of destruction.

The bloody King Kanon used the momentum he had gained with all the nations supporting his decisions without question to set sail and conquer Ras'Fahem. The final days of the Great Manah Wars are full of legends about how Akh was sealed away forever. After the war, King Kanon outlawed all magic.

Lord Venon pushed the rest of the nobles to legalise curative magic because he witnessed his father die when magic could have saved him. So the king enforced mind-controlling phylacteries to control destructive magic-users only to keep control of the nation. Lord Venon swore that day he would avenge his father's death.

Lord Venon finished scanning the horizon and thought the past was far too gone. Maybe he should have abdicated and retreated to a foreign land. Maybe he should have died on the battlefield, so he would have been spared the burden of witnessing a once free people browbeaten into servitude. He was not happy with what he had done. It weighed on his mind. Magestrix had promised him so much, and when she offered him the sphere of manah, his eyes had lit up with greed. But now, he was a prisoner to the ball. He always had to carry it around, lest he let it go, and Maleh would be free of his command and turn on him.

Lord Venon stroked the manah ball, and green tendrils of energy drooled from his fingertips across the translucent surface of the sphere. Soon, by nightfall, the infusion of blood would grant him eternal manah, and he would no longer need the ball.

Maleh approached Lord Venon and stood at attention behind him, "The boy is gone."

Lord Venon spun around and spat his words into the Ras'i's face, "What do you mean, he's gone?"

Maleh bowed his head, "I am sorry, master. The door was opened from the inside with our keys. How this happened is beyond my comprehension."

Lord Venon hit Maleh across the face with the back of his right hand, "Imbecile. What of the ripples in the moat?"

Maleh wanted to strangle Lord Venon, "We have searched the entire castle and found nothing yet."

Ka-boom! The entire throne room shook to its very foundations.

Maleh staggered from the blast, and Lord Venon fell on his backside, clutching his manah ball. Rubble crumbled from the ceiling and collapsed in front of the main doors blocking the way out. Dust swirled and billowed. As it settled, two figures strode into the room. Relianstar and Browbearer stood tall with their chests struck wide. Relianstar held a longsword by her side. Her studded leather skirt was swaying in the breeze. Browbearer cocked his crossbow with a pumping action.

Click-clack!

"Your time is up, Lord Venon. Surrender to us, and we will take you in alive. Resist, and we will have no choice but to fight you to the death. What say you?" Relianstar nodded upwards, beckoning an answer.

Lord Venon strode from the balcony towards them, revealing his manah orb. Maleh followed him by his side.

Browbearer leaned towards Relianstar, "That's a lot of manah."

Relianstar snapped back with a whisper, "Shut up and focus." Then, she started a chant under her breath.

Lord Venon continued his advance, "You have much courage to come here in the heart of my home and demand I surrender to your imperial demands. I am no slave and do not respond to threats. You will have to kill me if you want to stop me." Then, with a wave of his hand over the sphere of manah, he threw a fireball of darkness towards the knights.

Relianstar raised her whispered chant and finished in a crescendo, "Arma'dam santah!"

Bluish-white energy flourished around both herself and Browbearer, enveloping them in pure light. The fireball hit them and exploded in a burst of dark fumes and crackling purple energy.

Browbearer aimed at Lord Venon and unloaded a clip of fire bolts at the mage.

Blut! Blut! Blut! Blut! Blut! Blut! Blut!

Lord Venon held up his right palm and projected a deflective plane in front of himself and Maleh. The bolts fizzled and disintegrated as they traversed the magical barrier, "It will take more than Gnossian trickery to fell me, you fools. Maleh, attack them!"

Maleh obeyed his master and darted towards the knights, engaging Relianstar in a frontal assault of sword strikes. Relianstar had to backpedal, deflecting each successive strike. However, she was prepared this time. Her manah stores enabled her to keep up with the pace of Maleh's swordsmanship.

Browbearer holstered his crossbow and drew a cylindrical hilt with visible internal gears. A quick flick of his wrist and a blade extended out of the handle into a pointed short sword. Maleh continued striking Relianstar: up, down, up, down, up, down, up, down and a quick parry to the right in anticipation of Browbearer's flanking attack, disarming him and twirling the blade out of his hand.

Lord Venon needed Maleh to lead the undead army. Without him, he was unable to head into war. So, against his better judgement, he summoned dark magic by closing his eyes and drawing out power from the manah sphere.

Relianstar caught Maleh's blade with her sword only inches from her chest. She spoke through her gritted teeth as she wrestled against the Ras'i's strength, "Stop the mage. He is chanting."

Browbearer loaded another clip into his crossbow and unloaded on the mage.

Blut! Blut! Blut! Blut! Blut! Blut! Blut!

The bolts hit Lord Venon, who was now a steel visage of his former self. The bolts bounced off his skin like tiny pebbles. He raised the manah sphere in the air, and a flow of energy traversed the room and enveloped Maleh. Maleh was enflamed, and his speed and agility increased. He was a tornado of fire fighting against Relianstar.

Relianstar drew on her manah reserves for haste so that she could keep up with the vampire's enhanced speed. But the heat of the molten flames spewing forth from her enemy were taking their toll. She was feeling her energy evaporate. It was a matter of time before her manah would run out, and she would be unable to compete with this level of magic.

Browbearer collected his blade off the ground and adjusted the settings on the hilt. It came alive with electrical energy. He charged at Lord Venon, but Maleh intercepted him. Sparks flew as their blades met. Relianstar took the opportunity to thrust her sword into Maleh, but he parried it away with little effort.

Relianstar's knees buckled. Each successive strike she deflected was wearing her down. Finally, she dropped to her knees.

Maleh grimaced at her, "Finally!"

A fat-headed bolt knocked Maleh's blade out of his hand, allowing Relianstar to get back up on her feet.

She yelled at her Gnossian companion, "Shoot the orb! Knock it out of his hand!"

It was Browbearer's last bolt. He had expended both his clips and had a single lightning bolt left, which he was saving for Maleh, but there was no other choice. He popped up the crossbow's sight and aimed at the base of the orb so that he would skewer the mage's hand. His finger twitched over the trigger. He missed last time. He could not miss this time. He pulled the trigger.

The bolt whistled towards its target. Lord Venon was slow to react, and the bolt almost hit, but Maleh sliced it out of the way and saved his master. Relianstar's resolve wavered. She hesitated. With another twirl of his blade, Maleh butted Relianstar in the face with his hilt. She took a tumble back and rolled across the floor.

Lord Venon had finished drawing a large amount of manah and cast a spell. A dark rift tore itself in the fabric of spacetime in the room. Beyond the slither of darkness, screams of pain and anguish echoed throughout the room. Large claws poked through the portal, trying to rip open the curtain of pain. It was a demon trying to break free from the Plane of Torment. This creature of ancient origin had spent thousands of years living in pain and agony, and Lord Venon was summoning it to destroy the knights. Even Maleh froze in fear at witnessing the visage beyond the veil. It was hatred in its purest form, ready to abolish everything in its path.

Browbearer took the opportunity to strike at Maleh with a thrust into his side. The electric blade went in deep and caused the vampire to growl in pain, but he turned around and took hold of the Gnossian by the neck. Browbearer gritted his teeth, not that anyone could tell.

The demon's head was through the portal. Its face contorted from hatred. It screamed a piercing scream which froze the knights in fear. In all their life they had never encountered a demon. This was an enemy beyond anyone's skill. Not even Lord Venon, the summoner, would be able to control it.

Relianstar channelled her faith in Nai and spoke to the vampire, "This demon is the enemy of all. Turn and fight it with us. You are free if you wish to be."

Maleh's mind went clear for a moment. The knight was right. This thing would consume everything. He spoke to his master, "Master. What are you doing? This thing will kill us all!"

Lord Venon spoke with a deep and possessed voice, "Shut up and do as you're told. I command you now."

Maleh's mind snapped back, and he turned to the knights, raising his sword to strike them down, "Which of you wishes to die first?"

An arrow whistled through the air and skewered Lord Venon's hand. The manah sphere fell out of his hand and hit the floor. It shattered, and the energy trapped inside howled outwards. Lord Venon was left vulnerable, and Maleh's enchantments evaporated off his body.

Another arrow impaled itself in Lord Venon's chest, and the mage stumbled backwards, tumbled over the balcony, and fell off the ledge. He screamed all the way down, his life ending in a thud.

Relianstar and Browbearer looked up and saw Aedan atop the mound of rubble that blocked the entrance. He was going to head back to the castle, but he remembered everything Lord Venon had done to him and everything he had done to his home in Sylvinar. So, he climbed back up the escape line and snuck his way through the castle.

Aedan was terrified and couldn't control his breath. He had never shot an arrow at another person. *So this is what it feels like to be a Campesino warrior*. He couldn't say he enjoyed it but was glad he saved his friends. He looked down at the knights and made eye contact with them, "You're welcome!"

Maleh looked around. He no longer had a master. He could still feel his connection to the undead. He was still in control, but he no longer had to take orders. He was free. He could conquer Mhan for himself. All he had to do was make sure he defeated that pesky shadow dragon. He turned and darted for the balcony.

Aedan pointed, "He's getting away!"

Relianstar and Browbearer looked back at the vampire and gave chase, but it was too late. He leapt over the balcony. Browbearer scanned the environment with his lenses, but Maleh was nowhere in sight. He would have taken one of the many secret passages in the surrounding alcoves unbeknownst to the knights. In a matter of moments, the undead horde surrounding the castle flowed outwards over the drawbridge onto the plains. Then, they plunged into the earth and vanished beneath its surface.

Relianstar turned to Aedan and strode with purpose, "The army has commenced its march to Castle Mhan. I am sure Vera is relaying this to Maya as I speak so that they will be prepared for battle, but we must still make it back to the castle before the undead army does, lest we get cut off from the frontline."

The last of the undead were diving into the earth as the heroes mounted their horses and galloped towards the day, as Lumbra ended her eclipse and revealed Lum, the bringer of light.

The Assault

The last of the civilians trudged into the production halls in Mount Mhan. The entire city of Mhan was dead quiet. Every soldier, archer, knight, mage and cleric was at the ready, tense with anticipation, awaiting the arrival of the host. Food and water were passed around. Some took their fill, knowing it would be their last. Others were too nervous to eat and threw up anything they tried to stomach.

A storm rolled in from the back of the mountain and darkened the little light left in the day. The smell of wet stone, grass and dirt filled the air. Rain poured down and soaked everyone. The water flowed from the heavens as lightning cracked, illuminating the night. Everyone's eyes transfixed on the horizon. Two silhouettes condensed into existence from beyond the dying daylight.

Queen Maya stood atop the main gate. She turned to the gatehouse on her left and ordered the soldiers inside, "Those are our knights. Lower the drawbridge."

General Uriah leaned into the queen, "This weather does not fare well for us. I sense evil magic is summoning this storm. I do not know of undead who control the weather. There is another enemy in our midst."

The queen did not want to consider the possibility of another enemy. It was all too much. She wished her mother and father were here to tell her what to do. Nonetheless, she held fast to her logic and said to the general with her most commanding voice, "We will focus on what we know and not waste energy on speculation. This war will be won." So she hoped.

General Uriah was impressed by the queen's resolve, "Your strength inspires me, your majesty."

The drawbridge made a loud thud as it hit the ground on the other side of the moat. Relianstar and Browbearer crossed the bridge with Aedan on horseback. Vicho poked his head out of Aedan's tunic for a brief glimpse.

The following events were a blur to Aedan: the queen spoke to Relianstar and Browbearer, who were ushered away to take their station ready for combat. General Uriah ordered Aedan into the production halls with the rest of the Sa'ami, who were the last line of defence for the civilian population there. The queen intervened and requested Aedan be stationed in the royal tower with her. Aedan did not understand why the queen wanted him up there; he was needed to lead the Campesino's defence in the production halls. Finally, the queen explained that they could enter the production halls via a secret passage from the royal tower.

Upon the horizon, the dwindling light of Lum vanished behind the eclipse of Lumbar. Darkness covered the land, illuminated by haphazard flashes of lightning and drenched in a torrential downpour. A solitary rider crested the horizon and galloped towards Castle Mhan.

"Queen, immediately retreat to the royal tower with Vera and Shun, and this Sa'ami." General Uriah barked at the queen, "War is upon us."

The queen studied the rider, "But that is a single dark knight? What threat does it pose? Where is the rest of the army?"

"Go, your majesty. You will see. The dead mobilise themselves unseen." General Uriah signalled at two soldiers to escort the queen.

The soldiers were relieved to be picked so they could escape the frontline. They bowed before the queen and signalled the way, "We should make haste, your majesty."

The queen was unconvinced but trusted the general enough to take a hint, "Let's go," she beckoned Vera, Aedan and Shun to follow her.

The dark rider approached the castle at blinding speed.

The general grabbed the boom cone next to him and spoke into it, "Marko, pepper the ride with everything you have when it is in range. If it falls, then aim at the vampire. Do not stop while there is ammo."

The general's voice travelled down the long tube through the castle floor and down the tunnels beneath the earth in the fields before the castle and emanated out of the cones littered about the pillboxes and tunnels.

Marko ordered the soldiers, "You heard the general. Spotters at the ready. Gunners at the ready. Loaders at the ready. Ammory units at the ready. At my command, open fire. READY?"

The tunnels echoed with a unified replied, "READY!"

The ammory units held their crates ready to pass them down the tunnels from the primary stockpile under the city. The gunners had their eyes pressed up against the crosshair and their spotter's hand on their shoulder, ready to point out targets. The loaders held the next bandolier of bolts, ready to be loaded. Everyone waited as the rider thundered towards them. It seemed to take forever.

The general spoke to Felgar atop the castle tower, "You know what to do. The army will rise and will reach the wall. When they breach fall back quickly. Use all your boom arrows before the breach. Once inside, your archers' precision will be more important so as not to hit our soldiers. Understood?"

Felgar nodded, "To the end, we will fight. Even if it be our bare teeth on the enemy's hide."

The general slapped Felgar on the back and walked down the staircase, "See you on the other side, my friend."

Felgar turned to her archers, "We are the snipers. We pick the enemy apart from afar. We thin their numbers and give an edge to our frontline. Remember to breathe. Remember to be steady. Remember you have trained for this. You know you were born to be heroes. You know you were born to strike your enemy between the eyes with your arrows. Tonight we will illuminate the way. Tonight we will fight until the very end, with our last arrow pressed against our enemy's head in the twilight as they bare over us; we will drive them from our home! Hurrah!"

All the archers replied in a roaring reply, "Hurrah!"

Felgar pointed at the enemy, "At the ready, on my mark, destroy the enemy!"

General Uriah reached the bottom of the stairs just behind the portcullis where Sena was waiting for her orders, "Have your clerics completed their ritual on time?"

Sena nodded, "The undead must rise before our pillboxes. They may not breach the holy ground beyond our glyphs."

The general nodded, "Good. Are your units already at the back line? None of them must die. Take refuge if it is too dangerous. Only revive or heal the fallen when you safely can do so. Your magic is more valuable than your death. Do not forget that."

Sena nodded, "We know our path. We will hide now until needed." With that, she and her kin withdrew into the rear ranks and disappeared amongst the buildings and alcoves.

Terran stood with the handful of mages at his command.

General Uriah addressed Terran, "You have your magics ready, mage?"

Terran nodded, "We have memorised a set of battle spells. Destructive, illusion, psychic and alteration. Our magic is powerful, but we are few. We serve no purpose once we exhaust our spells."

General Uriah never liked mages. They were well regarded due to their power, and in skirmishes were valuable allies, but in wars, their use was limited, "Keep your spells until the last moment when a turn of the tide will be a necessary favour. Fall back to the castle for now. We will herald you to cover us with your magic and give us the boon when we need it."

At that moment, Felgar hollered from atop the wall, "It is but a moment, and the enemy will reach our holy ground."

The general turned to the cavalry and infantry. Gallastrian led the cavalry with Relianstar and Browbearer as his lieutenants. Rygar stood at the front of the infantry with sworders, spearers, axers: armoured and light. Gnaw, and Freida stood amongst the frontline with a sombre countenance. They looked at each other.

"I love you." Whispered Gnaw.

"I love you too." Whispered Freida.

The general spoke with an intonation of power and strength, "We will lower the bridge when the enemy reaches us—the undead flow like water into the easiest path. Resisting will build a mound, and they will topple over and breach our walls with chaos. The flow will lead them straight to us. We will meet them head-on. We will stand toe to toe with Skeletals, Harbinger, Batyles and Kuns. We will smite our enemy one by one. If there be a million of them, then we will strike them a million times. Look at your blades. Vera and the clerics are praying for you." The soldier's weapons glowed with magical fire. "Stay by your paladins. Keep your formation around the enemy as they flow. Do not block unless it is to ready your strike. Strike the enemy. They will fall. Each time you lift your blade think of your mother, your father, your brothers, your sisters, your wife, your children. Think of their love, their smile, the warmth you feel when they are near you. Think of the beauty that is our family. That is our city. That is our freedom. Strike out for life. Find strength in your heart; for I stand with you today; for I fight by your side; for I am your father, your brother, your son. I, General Uriah, will die for you. I, General Uriah, will take my last breath thinking of you. For I love you all. May Nai bless us all. Lift up your weapon and scream..." the soldiers lifted their weapons, worked up into a frenzy by the general's speech they spoke with him, "... for Mhan, for my people, for my family, for Nai and for all!"

Just then, Maleh raised his sword in the air, and the ground around him rumbled and rolled. Soil turned over of its own accord as the rising army ploughed the earth. Skeletal soldiers, their decayed bodies held together by what remained of their nerves and tendons, led the charge from the nether realm. They broke through the soil with grimacing faces of pain and agony. Soldiers from Fort Bosk, Fort Watch and Fort Storm, had been turned to evil. Even simple farmers, maidens, and children from Kalan, Mallarge and Trill flowed forth like rotten blood from the wound torn in the earth. Their numbers filled the air with a stench that travelled downwind, saturating everyone's olfactory senses in the castle with death and pestilence.

As the chaotic morass charged past the pillboxes, Marko screamed, "FIRE!"

The ten dozen pillboxes opened fire. The percussive clanking of the mechanised crossbows filled the air with a crisp droning of metallic clockwork interspersed with the loud twang of the high-tension bowstrings. The U-shaped arrangement of pillboxes hit the horde with explosive bolts, funnelling them towards the drawbridge, surrounding them in a pyrotechnic wall of fire, acid and electricity. The first barrel of ammunition was unloaded in quick efficiency. The front line of undead was charred, melted and evaporated in a spectacle of fire and light. Then it stopped for a moment.

Marko screamed, "RELOAD!"

Ammory units passed ammunition barrels down the tunnels as they ferried back used barrels in the opposite direction. The Gunnery units were reloaded and firing in under five seconds.

The undead clambered over the mound of their fallen brethren. A barrage of bolts shattered them into pieces. Undead torsos without legs dragged themselves forward. Heads rolled on the ground, snapping and grimacing. They fell to pieces, but their desire to destroy remained fervent.

They would not die.

Maleh stopped just out of range of the pillboxes and waved his hands in a splitting motion. The rising army broke into two broad streams and circumvented the U-formation and surrounded the gunnery positions. The pillboxes broke their concentrated fire pattern as they scattered shots in every direction, allowing the enemy to break through the barrage and charge the castle. A few Skeletals reached the moat, ran into the water, emerged on the other side, and pounded the city wall with their fists and heads.

Felgar studied the threat and held her troops at bay, "Preserve ammo; these are fodder. The real enemies are yet to come."

Maleh knew the pillboxes would not run out of ammo before he ran out of infantry. They were more of a hindrance than a barrier. Their purpose was to slow his army down and thin the numbers as much as possible before the archers would punish them. He had saved a special treat for his enemies: a black cloud of Rhan'i ripped out of the earth and poured into the sky. They swirled and twisted in formation, then with a flick of his wrist, Maleh split them up into four individual flocks, which descended into the pillboxes. The rat-a-tat sounds of the gunnery teams were snuffed out and replaced with screams of pain and agony. The Rhan'i travelled down the gunnery tunnels feasting on the soldiers trapped beneath the earth with nowhere to run.

Marko grabbed a voice cone and yelled, "Scuttle the tunnels!" Followed by a gargled groan.

General Uriah nodded at the scuttle team to do as Marko ordered. They twisted their detonators. A chain reaction of explosions travelled through the tunnels, burying the soldiers and the Rhan'i below the holy ground.

Then the Harbingers rose out of the ground surrounded by Kuns and Batyles. Dark magic hasted them, and they thundered towards the castle wall. Maleh would have his giant Harbingers wade across the moat and slam their bodies straight into the castle wall as a cohesive kinetic attack. The combined effort would find a weakness and topple the structure over. He knew the archers would light up the oil-laden moat and eradicate them, but he had many more rising out of the ground, and Magestrix would soon join the battle with a surprise.

Felgar raised her hand, ready to order her archers, "Prep your arrows. Ignite the moat and hammer the enemy with boom arrows on my command." The first of the Harbingers arrived at the moat and started crossing the water. As the second wave reached the castle perimeter, Felgar gave her signal, "FIRE!"

The boom arrows hit their targets. The explosions ripped holes in the Harbinger's bodies. Pieces of them splattered on the city wall. They reeled under the barrage. Then the moat erupted in flame, consuming them and charring them to a crisp. Nevertheless, they still hit the wall together. The combined bulk of thirty or so Harbingers was enough to shake the foundations of the city's wall.

General Uriah knew it would come to this. He did not want the castle wall to fall. It would create chaos and discord. So instead, he would control the battlefield and funnel the enemy through the gates where they could be felled in a bottleneck. He looked at the cavalry and infantry before him, "Brace yourselves. Lower the drawbridge! Open the portcullis!"

The two men at the chains hesitated for a moment.

General Uriah yelled at them again, "Do it now!"

The two men pushed the mechanism and released the counterweights. The drawbridge tumbled down and hit the ground on the other side, and the portcullis opened.

Maleh grinned. He figured the impact on the wall loosened the mechanism and dropped the bridge, "How fortunate." He directed his army to charge inwards with a thrust of his open palm towards the opening.

More Skeletals, Kuns, Harbingers and Batyles, flowed out in a never-ending stream of vileness from the earth. They beelined to the castle entrance. The Harbingers led the charge with their enormous bulk and momentum. The knights charged them head-on, split their formation to flow around the giants, and slashed the tendons on their ankles as they galloped past the creatures. The giants toppled to the ground crushing some of the infantry who had closed in to finish off the enemy with battle-crazed violence. The cavalry continued its charge to the gate where they would pull away, back to their starting lines to reform and renew their charge. In this way, they managed to keep the Harbingers in control.

General Uriah ran into the midst of battle, grunting a war song in Ras'i, which sounded like growling lions singing an opera. He grabbed two Skeletals, threw them up in the air, leapt up, caught the bodies in mid-air with each arm and slammed them back towards the earth, splintering them into pieces. The infantry charged in, inspired by his song, which filled them with courage and conviction. They formed a V-formation around the flow of enemies, skewering, slashing, crushing and maiming them. After an hour of battle, the grounds were replete with the fallen, and the undead began to clamber over one another and toppled deeper into Mhan city.

Maleh sat atop his ride, waiting. He looked up at Mount Firtina. Veins of lightning crackled atop the mountain.

Clash of Lightning

Grandmaster Thundar of the Order of Caval paced up and down the line of Gryphon Riders assembled before him. His golden helm was adorned with a black and white feathered crest that flowed back as he strode. Like all Gryphon Riders, he wore hybrid armour made of a thick hide embellished with bronze and gold accoutrements. They also wore massive chest plates, pauldrons, greaves and bracers made from Symbian diamond weave. Their prized possession was a war hammer the length of their arm with a cuboid head the size of a large baby, adorned with sharp protrusions along the neck and cheek of the hammer's head. The handle was wrapped in rough leather, with blue and red tassels flowing out of the grip.

Moments before, the royal messenger had arrived and advised him of the impending attack.

Amidst the perma-storm atop the peak, the Gryphon Riders honed their lightning skills and trained their familiars. Thundar selected riders based on their affinity to magic and taught them to be the most revered warriors in all of Concordia. Bound atop their giant avian mounts, they would take to the skies, commanding the clouds' lightning with their hammers.

The Gryphons were perched in a simple, open-air aviary the size of a large fort. Each Gryphon was a thoroughbred with black and white wings, golden fur and a feathered mane surrounding the majestic head with a large, hooked beak like that of a hawk and massive taloned front feet but a lion's hind legs and tail. They squawked the way a lion would growl if it were a dinosaur.

There were always fifty-two riders, no more, no less, and fifty-two apprentices ready to take their place. The apprentices guarded the cord of phylacteries: a long chain or pure silver with a phylactery for each magic user bounded to the service of Mhan. The phylacteries allowed the wielder to control if need be, the minds of those bound to them. The Gryphon Riders were, through ritual, unable to touch the cord which would cause their instant disintegration. The phylacteries, riders, and rituals were the insurance King Kanon put in place to guarantee that magic users would never turn to evil.

After the Great Manah Wars, King Kanon ordered all magic users to submit to the kingdom's control through the voluntary contribution of a phylactery. All who refused were hunted down and destroyed. The sorcerer Yama refused and was hunted to the nation of Sunnishidia, where he took refuge. With the help of the Gnoss, King Kanon wiped out Sunnishidia with a manah bomb, which left a crater where the nation once existed.

Thundar stopped pacing and looked up at the solemn knights atop their rides, "The war may have already begun when we arrive. First, we will sweep over the battlefield and hunt down the vampire master. We kill it, and the army will fall. Then we can retreat to our meditations without further delay. This is but a simple exercise."

The knights nodded in acknowledgement.

Thundar mounted his gryphon, which had a few more grey and white feathers compared to the rest. It was a silverback gryphon: one who had seen much death with its master and had elaborate scars over its body from countless battle wounds

Thundar lifted his hammer and pointed forward, "Onwards and downwards."

The gryphons leapt off the edge into the darkness below, with lightning crackling in the sky above them, illuminating the mountainside in blue and purple. They dive-bombed, skimming the side of the mountain. The gryphons squinted as the wind in their face was powerful and cold. Their wings folded back against their bodies, minimising wind resistance so they could achieve maximum speed.

They blurred past an overhanging rock, where the shadows moved, and a large blot of blackness appeared behind them. From nooks and crevices, smaller stains of darkness popped out and joined the pursuit, in tow of the shadow dragon at the rear of the gryphon riders.

Magestrix had waited, and now she drew her breath and let out a black flame of acrid necrosis.

The gryphons at the back, who were the first hit, let out a shriek as their bodies were eaten alive by the power of the shadow breath. Thundar looked over his shoulder, and his mind took a few moments to process what he was witnessing: a giant dragon and wyverns from the shadow realm. Not since he was a little boy had he even imagined these creatures. *Is Akh rising again?* He stopped thinking and screamed, "Break!"

The gryphon riders split in various directions. They looked at each other, unsure who to follow or what to do. They were in disarray. The shadow wyverns surrounded them. The riders drew lightning into their hammers and shot it back. A couple of the wyverns were hit and dropped to their doom, shifting back into human form, their bloody robes fluttering in the wind. One of the gryphon riders was hit with friendly fire, fell off his bird, and plummeted to his death. His familiar chased after him and saved him with her claws but was struck by two wyverns and torn to shreds.

Thundar swept around towards the mountain with two wyverns on his tail. He landed his bird on the cliff face. Thundar struck the wyverns on the head with his hammer as they crashed into him.

Their heads exploded into mucky goop. The decapitated human bodies flew across the mountain face.

Thundar took a good look at them, "Druids?" He looked around, searching for the shadow dragon in the sky, but it was gone. *Where?* he wondered. Then it dawned on him, *The phylacteries!* He took flight upwards. He screamed orders at his airborne cavalry, "Back to the mountain top! Protect the phylacteries!"

Some of the riders looked up at their leader just before they were killed. Others managed to break away from the ambush and follow him up. The gryphons beat their wings with strength, fighting the wind, trying to keep ahead of the wyverns. It was tiring and difficult. They drew deep breaths of cold air into their lungs as they exhausted.

Way above them, Magestrix soared towards the mountain top. With each beat of her enormous wings, she increased the distance between herself and the riders. Her mind was exhilarated at the thought of all the phylacteries in the kingdom at her command.

Thundar watched as the shadow dragon turned into a tiny blot and vanished into the sky above him. His only hope was the apprentice guard would be strong enough to hold off the attack until he and the few others who followed him arrived.

THE KNIGHTS IN THE phylactery vault were the best of the best, apprentice knights selected to be Gryphon Riders. They were not to be trifled. Neither were they any less than their brethren riders. The hallways and chambers of the temple were littered with guards at attention or on patrol. They wore heavy armour and wielded lances and shields. It was an imposing guard for any enemy to breach. A regular army could not reach the mountain top along its solitary narrow road. The bottleneck was impossible to pass without being picked off by the gryphons, and the cliff face was also impossible to attack. That is why a war was needed as a distraction to create the ambush conditions necessary for a shadow dragon to attempt the impossible.

A few of the knights were clairvoyants and felt distressed. Ruck, an apprentice with a balding head and flat face and Turam, a stern man with grey-streaked, tussled hair, were both at the antechamber entrance and looked at each other.

Turam blurted his words, "You felt it?"

Ruck nodded.

"Then we must quickly report it to Carga?" Turam reasoned that even though they should never leave their post, Carga was their ranking officer, and they needed her guidance.

Ruck pointed towards the prayer hall, "You go. I'll stay on guard."

Turam shot off through the arched doorway into the hallway and towards the prayer room. His steel boots resonated with each stride. *Clank, clank, clank, clank.* He entered the prayer room, and Carga had already stopped praying and was already on his feet.

Carga spotted Turam, "Why are you not at your post?"

"I had a vision...." Turam started.

"Yes, we all had the same vision. It is a trick. The enemy is upon us." Carga spoke with angry desperation.

A few more knights entered the room, all with the same look on their faces as they heard the tail-end of what Carga had said.

Carga pointed at all of them and yelled, "Return to your posts. Be on high alert. Sound the alarm if you see an intruder."

Turam darted back to his post but found Ruck was not there.

"Ruck?" he called out. But there was no reply.

Turam figured he may have gone into the vault room at the behest of the guard inside. He lifted his shield and pointed his lance, ready for a confrontation. He walked down the hallway with nervous trepidation. Then, he heard a faint sound. It was unfamiliar to him.

He spotted Ruck standing near the vault room entrance. Ruck dropped to his knees and fell face forward onto the floor.

Turam tensed.

THUNDAR SWOOPED UP onto his gryphon's perch in the aviary. He heard the alarm ringing throughout the temple. *Ding! Ding! Ding! Ding! Ding!* His comrades mobilised themselves throughout the temple towards the vault room. A few more gryphons landed in the aviary, and the riders dismounted to follow Thundar's charge towards the vault room.

Thundar drew deep breaths as his heavy-set legs pounded the ground. His enormous frame jolted up and down, and all his muscles rippled from the impact. His chiselled face was a landscape of wrinkles and scars set with deep brown eyes framed with a short, grey head of hair and matching stubble. He was a dedicated knight who had not fought his entire life for the freedom of the people of Concordia to have it stolen by evil magic.

The sounds of battle rumbled from the vault room. Steel clanged against stone. Lightning cracked, and fire roared. Bodies smacked, and bones crunched. There were screams of courage and cries of pain. The hallway leading up to the vault room was littered with bodies of fallen comrades.

Thundar stormed the vault room, followed by six other riders and a few of the guards. Magestrix stood at the vault door choking a guard, off the ground, with her left hand. The stone door on the vault was ripped off its hinges by a fire demon the size of three men. The stone block hurtled towards Thundar and the rest of the knights who dived out of the way as it crashed against the wall behind them and cracked in two. Magestrix released the dead woman from her grip and threw her to the floor. She snapped her fingers, and the fire demon was sucked back into the Plane of Torment. It clawed the ground, trying to stay, but the tear in the fabric of reality warped around it, and the demons trapped on the other side of the portal pulled it in to, once again, join them in eternal anguish.

Thundar stood up and issued a final warning, "Step away from the vault immediately or die!"

Magestrix turned her gaze at him and smiled.

The last of the guards arrived at the vault room hallway, greeted by the sight of their fallen comrades on the floor. They could hear no more fighting in the room. It seemed the battle was over. They felt clear-headed and relaxed all of a sudden. Thundar walked out of the vault room, followed by gryphon riders and some guards. They all took position on either side of the doorway, and the guards also joined them. They did not know why they felt compelled to do so, but it was as if they were driven. It was as if they did not have to think anymore. All their decisions and thoughts were made for them. It was such a pleasant feeling not to have to think or worry about what to do next. With those thoughts in their mind, they knelt on the ground and spoke out, "All hail Magestrix."

Magestrix strode out of the vault room, stroking the long brown locks on one of the younger knights by her side, "You may rise."

The knights all stood up at attention.

Magestrix wore a necklace adorned with hundreds of tiny little trinkets: coins, pebbles, bones, hair, teeth, rings, jewels, cloth and a variety of worldly items. Each phylactery item bound the magic-user to submission by the one who wore the necklace. King Kanon intended for it only to be wielded by the King or Queen in a time of emergency, but it was now the ultimate weapon to defeat the armies of Concordia. Every magic user in the land was under the command of Magestrix.

The End

Relianstar thrust her javelin straight through a Harbinger. The giant bellowed in pain, clutching the entry wound with its many colossal hands.

She twisted the blade around, "Nai give you peace," and withdrew it in one savage move.

A Kun leapt at her back but was cleaved in half by Browbearer's molten axe.

Relianstar nodded at Browbearer in thanks. Then, she surveyed the battlefield looking for another Harbinger.

The creature toppled to the ground amidst the plague of vile infesting the abandoned city of Mhan. The battle raged across the city streets, inside buildings, and the main road up to the castle where most of the army had fallen back to hold a defensive line. But they had been pushed back near to the castle. Felgar and her archers rained down fire arrows onto the enemy from the castle walls.

General Uriah had altered his strategy as the enemy numbers had increased. He reorganised Rygar's men into smaller units of no more than twenty men and assigned each of them a paladin to lead them through the back streets, engaging the enemy with hit and run tactics to thin the enemy numbers from the flanks. The rest of the infantry were in a united defensive front on the main road blocking access to the castle. The undead river of gore split and flowed into the streets of least resistance, where the skirmish teams slew them. The knights focused their efforts on hunting down the enormous Harbingers.

Uriah himself moved across the battlefield, evaluating the situation. He could not make out the rear of the host. He scaled a tavern roof, pulling himself up with his massive arms and broad shoulders. Atop, he saw an end to the enemy. No more were rising out of the ground. He figured the 20,000 or so were the last of them. They would win this war and keep the castle intact. Then he heard a sound: the sound of ambush. He spun around and saw the mages, their last line of defence, flow out of the castle. They blasted the infantry with fire and lightning.

The infantry line turned around in confusion. They saw the onslaught of mages moments before they were hit with lightning in the face or a fireball burned them alive.

General Uriah felt discombobulated. He knew there was only one explanation. He knew this would be their end. He had warned the queen many times about the danger of phylacteries, but he was honour-bound to respect her wishes. Yet, at this moment, he wished he had beat some sense into the stupid girl. As tears welled in his eyes, he remembered his people. Oppressed as they were, noble tribes of honour and respect, they still found strength; they found strength in knowing death was not the end. He remembered the children in the caves, shuddering at the thought of their imminent doom and his fists clenched. He struck a punch out at the nearest Skeletal and sent it flying against a wall.

He bellowed from atop of his lungs on the battlefield, "Scatter! Make them chase you!" He turned to face Felgar on the wall. She looked down at Uriah from across the chasm of death. He signalled her. *Pierce them as they chase soldiers.*

Felgar nodded in acknowledgement. She ordered her archers, "Focus on the mages. Use piercing arrows. Take the easiest shot you can make."

The archers pulled out piercing arrows, but before they could take a shot, a small tornado erupted on the castle wall and travelled down the line of archers and sent them flying off the platform. Terran stood on one of the castle balconies summoning the wind to his aide. His blank eyes screamed, *Please help me!*

Up in the Royal Tower, Aedan looked on with the queen. He was trembling, "We must do something! The Campesinos sit idly in the production halls, unaware of this. I will fetch them and lead them into battle."

Maya put her hand on his chest, "No. You will stay here with me. I will decide what the best strategy is."

Aedan pulled her hand off his chest, "You have done enough damage with your decisions. Were it not for the phylacteries; we would not be in this situation."

Maya snapped back, "Were it not for the phylacteries; we would have been fighting evil magic all these years. Do not pretend to understand how to run a nation." ·

Aedan ignored her and headed out.

Maya ordered Shun, "Stop him."

Shun darted in front of Aedan and blocked his path, ready to strike him with a kick. Aedan pulled Vicho out of his tunic, "You stay here in the tower where it is safe. I will get you when all this is over." He placed him on a raised edge along the stone wall.

Vicho stood up on his two hind legs twitching his whiskers. *I'm scared.*

Aedan stroked Vicho with his pinkie finger. "It will be ok. Be brave."

Aedan turned to Maya, "You will punish me for trying to save innocent lives?"

Maya hesitated. She did not want him to get hurt. She wanted him to be safe, but it was clouding her judgement. She cleared her thoughts, "Go then. I will not stop you."

Shun stepped aside, and Aedan walked past her.

Shun stood next to Maya, "Your choice was well-tempered. Do not let emotions guide your thoughts. To lead is to be a vessel of reason and logic."

Maya nodded, "You are right as always, my friend."

Down on the battlefield, General Uriah ran down the main road towards the castle, bashing Skeletals, Kuns, Batyles and even Harbingers out of the way, "Fall back! Fall back! To the castle halls!"

The pockets of resistance turned and converged on the general, trying to outrun the undead horde. The mages picked many of them off as they joined the charge.

Relianstar galloped at the rear of the army with Browbearer astride her stallion facing backwards. He was firing a bandolier of bolts he scavenged from the ammo crates near the pillbox tunnels. *Ratatatatatatatat!* The hail of bolts was enough to keep the Skeletals and Kuns at bay from the rear. The Batyles were too slow, but the Harbingers were gaining on them.

The soldiers were closing the distance to the castle, but a wall of fire blocked the entrance. The mages were combining their concentrated efforts to sustain the wall of fire. It was a spell the general had requested they memorise to stop the enemy, but now it was the end of their road.

A Harbinger closed in on Relianstar's horse and took a swing, whooshing by and missed her head by an inch, "Do something about it, Beebee!"

Browbearer loved it when she called him Beebee, "Yes m'lady," he fired off his gas-powered grapple shotgun at the Harbinger's neck. The steel line wrapped around the beast like a collar, with the hook impaling itself into its throat. The winch pulled Browbearer up and swung him around. He travelled in an arc around the monster. Then, Browbearer pulled out his molten axe and decapitated the beast. He released the clip on the grapple just as he swung back over Relianstar and landed back on the steed, "Done."

Relianstar reached back and patted him on his right thigh. She was grateful she could always rely on him, not like some other knights who were too proud to take orders from an equal.

The general had bought them enough time to make it to the castle, but the mage blockade was their next confrontation, and the wall of fire was not going anywhere. So their only option was to turn and fight the horde and wait until the mages ran out of manah, but that would take a very long time.

One of the mages dropped to the ground, then another, then another. They fell to the ground from arrows to the back. As they gasped their last breath, they managed to glimpse the stars in the sky and wish to be reborn. For they had not wanted to end their lives as instruments of evil and destruction, but fate had dealt them a horrible blow.

Aedan leapt over the bodies as the Campesinos took station around the entrance and offered covering fire over General Uriah and the remains of the Mhan Royal Army. Their precision volleys hit the line of undead closing in on the soldiers and knocked them to the ground, tripping the Harbingers over and halting the enemy's advance.

The General hollered, "Charge through! Let's blockade the bottlenecks!" He led the soldiers into the castle. They all flowed in, like water into a burrow, followed by the Campesinos and Aedan.

Mhan City was empty, and now the castle was left to conquer. The undead army stopped its advance and split in half as Maleh rode up the middle on his steed. He stopped short of the entrance to the castle. He knew their numbers had been thinned, and he was familiar with the castle's layout, thanks to Lord Venon's betrayal. He pointed at the walls and issued commands to the Harbingers who stood by the wall and braced themselves, so other Harbingers climbed atop their shoulders. Next, Kuns and Skeletals climbed the giant's backs and shoulders onto the enormous landing above the wall. They would scatter through the upper hallways and flank the soldier's fortified positions while the Batyles and Harbingers stormed the front as a distraction.

Maleh looked up at the queen in the royal tower and grinned.

Maya stared down at him and clutched Shun's robe, "We must go down and warn them."

Shun snapped, "That is exactly what Maleh desires."

THE SOLDIERS HAD BLOCKADED the hallways and stairs, ready to hold their ground against the remaining undead horde.

Relianstar stood with Browbearer next to Uriah. She was unsure of their position, "General, we are blind here, and the delay has me worried. They should have flowed in by now. I suspect an unexpected tactic here; we should brace both sides."

The general stared at Relianstar for a long while, he did not like being told what to do, but the knight's logic did make sense, "Very well, where is Bastrolar? Have him lead a mixed squad up the eastern wing, and Suverchant lead another squad up the western wing."

Relianstar nodded and retreated a little way to find the knights and give the orders, "Browbearer, you stay here." Browbearer did not like being separated from Relianstar. He hesitated to say something, and then it was too late. She was gone.

Uriah barked at Relianstar, "You return after the others have set off. Maleh will come through here if he wants his distraction to be believable. Or he has anticipated our move and will storm us with all his force." Then he addressed the rest of the soldiers, "They will flow in any moment. Hold a united front and stay behind your shields. The blessings of our seer and paladins will ensure the enemy will fall. Their numbers have thinned, and we will defeat them."

One of the younger soldiers, with tears welling in his eyes, called out from behind his fellow fighters, "Our numbers have also thinned; we are but a handful of soldiers. How can we hope to survive?"

General Uriah stood up and towered over the wave of soldiers braced for combat so he could make eye contact with the young man, "You will not survive when I wring your neck after the war if you have not slain at least twenty beasts. I will be counting!"

The young man forced a laugh of disbelief.

"I am giving you an order. Slay twenty of the enemy before the battle is over, or you will answer to my wrath! Do you understand?" the general screamed with anger and determination.

"Yes, sir!" The young man replied, ready to take on the entire army of enemies on his own.

Such was the power of Uriah's voice; his very presence dispelled fear and reinvigorated courage in even the most fearful fighters.

Then there was rumbling.

Relianstar returned, "They have been dispatched to the upper levels, ensuring the enemy will not flank us." Then she noticed Aedan and the Campesinos were nowhere to be seen, "Where is Aedan and his army?"

General Uriah looked around. He spotted them hiding behind gargoyles and tapestries on the ceiling and walls, "They have concealed, ready to strike like true Campesinos from the shadows."

The rumbling crescendoed.

"Here they come, hold your ground!" Uriah hollered.

The soldiers braced themselves as the wave of Skeletals, Batyles and Kuns stormed in. They collided hard with the frontline and were met with a solid wall of courage. The soldiers braced themselves and pushed back hard. The Campesinos shot arrows from their hiding spots behind the enemy line, and many undead fell to the blessed arrows. The enemy frontline pulled back in retreat.

The soldiers went to follow them, were it not for Uriah's order, "Stop! Do not pursue. We wait them out."

"It's a trap!" hollered Queen Maya as she approached the General with Shun in tow, "They have scaled the outer wall and are making their way through the upper levels!"

"You should not have left your post!" the General barked back, astounded at the queen's ineptitude.

In the brief confusion, Maleh leapt out of his hiding spot in the ceiling and landed near Uriah. He took a swipe with his sword at the queen's head but was blocked by Relianstar. Browbearer and Aedan opened fire with their respective weapons, forcing the vampire to summersault over the queen. A quick chant and he cast a spell of weakness on the soldiers, just as the undead flowed back in and walloped them in the back.

Maleh ran into the castle, Relianstar, Browbearer, and Aedan ran after him. The Campesinos followed their leader. Like rabbits, they hoped over enemies and obstacles with nimble leaps and tumbles and disappeared into the castle too.

The soldiers were being torn apart by the renewed undead attack.

Queen Maya ran, with Shun, after Aedan, "We have to help him."

The General looked around in desperation, "We must fall back to the upper levels. Retreat!"

The soldiers retreated to the upper levels. The young man, who had panicked earlier, slew his twentieth enemy just as a spear skewed his gut. He looked down at his wound. Then he felt himself fly off the ground.

General Uriah lifted him over his shoulder, "You will not die today."

The young man smiled through his bloody teeth, gave a loud enraged scream and struck at the enemy chasing the general, "I've got your back, my captain."

As they reached the massive outdoor landing on the upper levels, where royal ceremonies took place during good weather, the sky above them lit up with lightning.

Rygar pointed to the stormy sky, with rain pelting his face, "Here come the gryphons!"

Everyone looked up in delight until they saw the shadow dragon leading them. Magestrix swooped down and breathed a cloud of death and destruction straight through the middle of the soldiers. They fell convulsing from the dark poison desiccating their bodies.

Maleh stopped on the platform and challenged Relianstar. They engaged each other in quick combat. Browbearer aimed at Maleh and fired a shot but missed.

Aedan watched Magestrix as she swooped overhead. She circled and turned back towards him. He was sure she had seen him and was coming for him.

Thundar and the gryphon riders shot a volley of lightning at Relianstar and Browbearer, forcing them to take cover in one of the nearby alcoves.

Magestrix swooped past Aedan and landed just behind him. She stood up on her hind legs and took a deep breath. But Aedan had vanished in true Campesino style. Magestrix twirled around. She spotted Maya and unleashed her pent-up breath on her instead.

Maya somersaulted backwards, avoiding the shadow breath. She landed smack bang in the middle of the undead horde. Shun leapt to her aide. Together they concentrated all their martial arts, punching and kicking every enemy who came within reach of their limbs. They sent their enemies flying from the immense kinetic energy of each of their strikes. It was like watching balls bounce off a tornado. Magestrix took another deep breath. Maya and Shun were cornered.

Aedan aimed at Magestrix from above a spire with his bow and arrow. He was about to fire a shot, but Magestrix reeled back.

Maleh sliced through Magestrix's left wing. She growled in pain. He leapt up on Magestrix and pummelled her in the face. She stumbled back and toppled over.

Thundar and the Gryphons swooped around and dived towards Maleh, ready to strike him with their hammers. Maleh held onto Magestrix as he grabbed one of the Gryphons by its talons, swung it around and threw it at its companions. The birds crashed into one another and broke off their attack. Maleh raised his fist high up in the air and punched deep into the dragon's chest. He grabbed its black flaming heart and pulled it out. Magestrix convulsed in pain and agony, then dropped to the ground and was dead.

Maleh removed the necklace of phylacteries off the dragon's neck, held it up high over his head, and let out a victorious bellow. Aedan aimed at the necklace from across the landing. Maleh blurted some arcane words to a mage connected to one of the phylacteries, who cast a spell of darkness on the entire castle. Aedan could not see anything in this magic-induced absence of light.

Queen Maya mouthed, "Take the shot. You cannot miss." Her words traversed the darkness, and Aedan felt her breath in his ear.

He let the arrow go. All he could hear was the air whistling as the shaft hurtled towards the target. He did not doubt his hand had moved. He did not doubt he would miss. He could see in his mind's eye what the battlefield looked like before the darkness. He could see his arrow zeroing in on its intended target.

Then there was a yell of anger and something shattered. The darkness was lifted. The phylacteries' cord was severed. Its trinkets fell to the ground beneath the castle wall and smashed into smithereens on the pavement. Adean's arrow had skewered Maleh's hand. He looked at Aedan in disgust and anger. He pulled the arrow out and charged at Aedan. He leapt up in the air, his black sword ready to slay Aedan. Aedan pelted the vampire with arrows, but he could not stop him. As Maleh crashed down on Aedan, Gnaw held him up and drove Chomp into Maleh's gut, but the vampire parried it away and took the opportunity to follow through and gutted the great warrior. Freida, right behind her husband, took a swing at Maleh, but she was too late. Maleh leapt off the landing to the ground far below and disappeared amongst his horde.

Freida leaned over her husband and supported his head.

Aedan dropped onto a knee, "We can carry him together. Quickly."

"No." Freida looked at Aedan with tears welling in her eyes. "He did what he must. So, you can do what you must. Go and finish this!"

Aedan nodded and darted off.

Freida looked back down at Gnaw. "Remember when we first met? So long ago. Remember the first time we kissed? How our lives were consumed with each other. Remember all the times I held you close to me? What that felt like?"

Gnaw smiled. Blood poured out of his mouth. He strained his words through pain and agony, "In the darkness, if a thousand hands touched me, I would know which is yours."

Freida sobbed. "It was all worth it. Every moment. Even this one. You are my one true love for all eternity. I will find you in the darkness and touch your heart once again."

Gnaw lay still. He was dead, with a smile on his face. His last thought, his heaven, was Freida.

Freida stood up and began killing everything in sight without tactic or logic. She was enraged.

She would eventually die alone in the midst of battle, but she would strike out until her last breath, when she would be freed of her pain and reunited with her one true love, once again.

HARBINGERS HAD BLOCKED the path to the production halls, and Kuns and Batyles surrounded the remaining Mhan Royal

Army. Then, the gryphon riders, now free of mind, swooped down and decimated the undead.

Maya and Shun joined Uriah and Aedan, "Unfortunately, we are surrounded here, and the gryphons are not able to fight the entire war for us. We must retreat to the production halls and finish off the enemy in a bottleneck."

"Aedan, take the queen to the production halls. We will stand and fight," the general ordered.

"No," Maya replied.

"There is no time to explain. Trust me," the general said with a soft voice.

The queen looked at Aedan, who took her by the hand and led her to the central spire, "We will climb back up to your tower. You have a secret tunnel to the halls, do you not?"

The queen nodded.

"Then that is the safest way," said Aedan as he threw up his grappling hook to a higher level. "Can you climb?"

The queen shoved Aedan out of the way and started ascending the rope using her upper body strength. Aedan smiled at her annoyance. He thought it was funny when she was angry. He went to follow, but Shun pushed in and went next. Aedan followed Shun.

When they reached the spire's middle landing, they could see a dark movement on the horizon, approaching the castle at blinding speed. Dirt and dust obscured the enormous approaching menace.

"What is that?" asked Maya.

Aedan squinted his eyes, "I can see animals. Enraged animals. A hooded man on horseback leads them. He is holding a staff."

"Grandor!" Maya and Aedan said in unison.

Down below, Relianstar sensed their emotions and saw what they saw; she hollered, "Grandor has returned with an army and the moonstone!"

The general turned around at hearing her words, and a huge smile came across his face. "Right on time."

Grandor whispered into his horse's ear, "Only a little further, and you can rest, my friend." He reached into his leather pouch and pulled out the moonstone, glowing in the dark. He raised it above his head and whistled. Y'a'rer'ghek swooped down and snatched the moonstone and flew towards the royal tower.

Aedan could see everything as they were almost upon the castle, "Yarigek is flying the moonstone up to the royal tower! We must hurry!"

Aedan ran up the winding staircase, followed by the queen and Shun. They leapt up from lower balconies to higher balconies, climbing up and up the spire until they were a few feet from the top. Y'a'rer'ghek was inside the city walls and approaching the tower.

Maleh jumped up behind Shun, and the queen screamed, "Watch out!"

Shun turned around and blocked Maleh's blade with the edge of her hand, "Mind over matter vampire."

Maleh snorted, and with a snap of his finger, two undead mages leapt up and cast lightning bolts at the queen. The queen jumped into a twisting summersault and shot out two darts from her hands and knocked the mages' grimoires to the ground. When she landed, she watched as Shun attacked Maleh with a barrage of fists. Maleh kicked Shun in the chest, so she cartwheeled backwards to absorb the impact.

"You get the moonstone and trigger the golems!" Shun ordered Maya and Aedan, "I will hold them."

Maleh looked up and spotted the eagle swoop past and circle the tower as Aedan threw his grapple up to make the final ascent. Maleh grabbed an arrow on the floor nearby, and with a whispered spell, he threw it at the eagle and hit him. The eagle released the moonstone.

Aedan watched it fall past him, just out of reach. He turned around, dropped down the rope face-first towards the ground, controlling his fall. As he fell to the ground, he pushed off the tower with his left leg and grabbed the stone centimetres before it shattered on the floor. Upside down with the stone in his hand, he felt Maleh's blade on his throat.

"You're mine," Maleh said with a lick of his lips.

But was kicked in the head by Maya, "Climb!"

Aedan pulled himself up and climbed the rope as fast as he ever had. He climbed and climbed and climbed. Finally, he smashed through the stained window and slammed the moonstone onto the pedestal in the middle of the room. The decorative claw came to life and gripped the stone. Energy flowed through it, and within moments, across the castle, the gargoyles and statues which adorned it came to life. The animated stone statues outmatched the enemy in sheer numbers and aggressive vitality. The gargoyles swooped down, stabbing at the enemy. The monolithic statues of ancient heroes clobbered the horde, squashing them like flies.

At that moment, Grandor crossed the drawbridge with the animal clans of Sylvinar Forest. They flanked the undead army and routed it in moments.

Uriah looked around and found Relianstar and Browbearer, "We must find and kill Maleh, otherwise in a year, he will raise another army, and we will not have enough soldiers then. Therefore, we must kill the vampire today."

Relianstar and Browbearer nodded, and they headed into the castle to climb upwards.

Relianstar said, "He is near the queen. They are fighting at the base of the tower."

Aedan slid down the rope and joined the queen and Shun. Shun was applying a spell of healing on the queen's wounds.

"Where is the vampire?" asked Aedan.

"He will be escaping as all cowards do. He will be near the gates by now," Shun reasoned.

Aedan looked into the darkness and spotted the vampire running for his life towards the night. On the horizon, Aedan could see Lumbra's eclipse revealing Lum's light. Daylight would soon strike, diminishing Maleh's powers. Aedan spotted Grandor and Tanke fighting the enemy near the castle entrance. So he leapt from the top of the spire and as he plummeted to the ground, he took hold of one of the royal banners to slow his descent and landed next to Grandor.

Grandor turned to Aedan with a smirk behind sweaty bangs that obscured his face, "Hello Sa'ami. We missed you."

"No time to explain. I need to get to the gate now," Aedan blurted out.

Tanke ran up, barked and leaned down so Aedan could climb on him.

"Well, what are you waiting for?" Grandor said as he smacked a Kun in the face with his staff, "Jump on him."

Aedan mounted Tanke, and Tanke bolted towards the gate at full speed. Aedan held onto Tanke's mane and propped himself on the wolf's back with his boots, ready to leap off and fight Maleh.

Maleh sensed someone approaching. He stopped and turned to face Aedan in full flight. Having leapt off Tanke's back with his bow primed, Aedan let an arrow rip. Maleh parried the arrow with his sword and, in one fell swoop, thrust his weapon at Aedan. Aedan corkscrewed out of the way and shot another arrow at the vampire, impaling the creature's shoulder. Maleh snapped the arrow shaft, tossed it and darted away, growling and snarling, across the drawbridge. His undead steed rose out of the ground at the sound of its master's gargled call.

Aedan hopped onto Tanke's back again and gave chase.

Aedan chased Maleh across the battlefield of undead corpses and scuttled tunnels, firing a volley of arrows at him. Some arrows hit Maleh, but many missed. Tanke began to tire. He panted hard and ran out of steam.

Maleh could see Lum's light starting to poke out from behind Lumbra. He chanted the last spell he would be able to muster before daylight, summoning the last bit of aid he had at his disposal. Behind Aedan and Tanke, a pack of twenty Kuns rose out of the ground and gave chase. They snapped at Tanke's rear as he tried very hard to keep pace.

Aedan turned around and shot his arrows at the beasts to slow them down, but it was no hope had it not been for Relianstar and Browbearer who charged up the rear. Browbearer shot the Kuns one by one with his flame bolts. Relianstar reinvigorated Tanke with a spell of morning light. It filled him with limitless stamina. He tore away from the Kuns at blazing speed.

Aedan turned back around and stood up on Tanke's back. At that moment, everything went silent in his mind, and the whole world slowed down until the moment was frozen in time. He pulled his arrow up against his cheek, aimed down its shaft and visualised its journey across the distance in front of him. He released the arrow, and it whistled towards its target in an unwavering direct line, anticipating the exact position where the beast's leg would be. The arrowhead sliced through the tendon.

The undead steed fell face first and flipped over onto the ground. Maleh was thrown off his ride, face-first into the dirt. He was furious. He stood up in an absolute rage, drew his long sword and attacked Aedan. He knocked Aedan off Tanke with his left fist while slicing the wolf's rear left leg with the sword in his right hand.

Across the distance, in the city, Grandor crippled over in immense pain in his left leg. He knew Tanke had suffered a fatal injury. He could not stand up, and five Kuns surrounded him, ready to tear him apart.

Aedan turned and fired a volley of arrows at Maleh, who ran head-on into the hail of shafts, deflecting them all with deft swordsmanship, and closed in on Aedan. He shoved the boy onto the ground and towered over him. He raised his black longsword over his head, ready to strike, "Your time is up, Sa'ami."

"Catch!" Kainan's voice pierced through Aedan's ears. He looked to his left and saw Kainan, Eldoran and Ferni on horseback. A short sword flew in the air towards him, "Daylight is up!"

Aedan caught the sword by the hilt.

Maleh looked at the light glinting off Aedan's blade, then over his shoulder at the sight of Lum's light cutting across the sky, "NO!"

"For my people!" Aedan yelled as he drove the short sword into the vampire's chest, straight through his heart.

Maleh convulsed, arching his back, with his arms thrown backwards. He froze in that position as light radiated through cracks all over his skin. His agonised scream faded into a deep hum, and he exploded in a spectacle of light and dark fumes. An impulse resonated outwards and knocked everyone on their backs.

The undead dropped lifeless on the ground.

Grandor, with tears in his eyes, cried out, "The boy did it!"

Maya watched as the remaining undead dropped in a heap all around the castle grounds. She had never seen such a sight, "What is happening, Shun?"

Shun smiled, "The war is over."

The Aftermath

Aedan looked at his brother. Kainan nodded in acknowledgement of his brother's bravery. Aedan then looked at his father. Eldoran smiled at his son with the warmest smile which had ever crossed his face. Then, Aedan looked at his beloved Ferni. Her eyes widened in absolute ecstasy. She burst out, running towards Aedan. Aedan ran towards her with all his might. The moment seemed never to come until they collided and embraced in the tightest hug.

Aedan whispered in her ear, "I love you."

"And I, you, my Aedan," Ferni replied.

They looked into each other's eyes for a very long time until Eldoran cleared his throat. Then, they broke their embrace and turned back to him and Kainan.

"Well, you've done well, my son," Eldoran managed to hold down the frog in his throat and the tears welling up in his eyes.

Aedan hugged his father, "I thought I'd never see you again."

Eldoran patted his son on the back, but his emotions got the better of him, and he hugged his son as hard as he could with his ageing arms. Aedan pulled back and looked into his father's eyes for a moment before turning to his brother.

"Brother," Aedan said and hugged Kainan.

Kainan shoved Aedan away and replied, "I did what I did to save our people. I thank you for following my orders with courage. But I am not your brother." Kainan pulled on Aedan's forearm and commanded, "What you have done for me is something I will never forget. For this, I will tolerate you."

Aedan laughed, "Well, at least you are not trying to kill me anymore."

They walked towards the castle. Ferni was clutching Aedan's arm with a beaming smile.

Aedan asked, "How did you all get here? Who freed you?"

Kainan replied, "Two days ago, they started talking from inside the statues. I could hear them asking for help, so I took to the stone with my blade. It cracked open, and I was able to free them. It was as if the magic binding them had been dispelled."

Eldoran chimed in, "Lord Venon had entrapped us to hold us at ransom in exchange for you. He used a large ball of manah to cast the spell. I assume it was destroyed?"

Aedan nodded, "Yes. By my own arrow!"

Ferni giggled, "Oh you have so many stories to tell us, I am sure!"

Aedan's head dropped.

Ferni noticed and asked him, "What is it? What's wrong?"

Aedan looked at her, but he could not find the words.

Eldoran did, "I know what you wish to say, and I am truly sorry. But your mother and I only wanted the best for you. We knew you were different, and what has transpired this week is the very reason why we protected you. Why we kept you a secret."

Kainan and Ferni both looked at Eldoran and asked in unison, "What secret?"

Aedan replied, "I am not a Sa'ami."

Ferni yelped, "You're not a what?"

"A Sa'ami, Ferni. I am not a Sa'ami. I am a human." Aedan trembled out the words.

Ferni's eyes were full of confusion. She did not know what to think or what to say. Her world was crashing down. *What will we do? We will be freaks. The giant human and the tiny Sa'ami girl?*

Everyone will laugh at us. Our children will be outcasts! Her mind raced towards an impossible future.

Kainan slapped Aedan on the back, "I knew you were too lanky. I had always wondered if mother had drunk too much water from Agwa'den." He laughed a little but then questions filled his mind, "But what will happen now? What will you do? Where will you go? You can't come back with us, that's for sure."

Aedan stopped walking and turned to Eldoran, "Father, what am I supposed to do?"

"The decision is yours and yours alone. I cannot offer you any advice this time," Eldoran replied, "Whatever you choose will be the correct choice."

The thunderous trample of galloping horses startled them all back to reality.

"Who needs a ride?" Browbearer boomed.

Relianstar, Browbearer, Shun and the queen were atop their rides, battered and bruised but full of pride, tempered with sadness for those who had fallen in battle.

"We do not have all day. We must tend to the wounded, bury the dead and pray to Nai they may join her for their valiant efforts today. We will celebrate our victory once we have paid our respects to the fallen. Now jump on so we may do our duty," the queen ordered with tears welling in her eyes.

Kainan rode his own steed. Aedan jumped on Browbearer's ride and beckoned Ferni, who hesitated for a moment before jumping on. Aedan grasped her hands with excitement but did not see the look of depression on her face.

Eldoran waved them away, "You all go. I will walk."

"Very well," the queen replied. "Har!" She mushed her horse and led the rest of them back towards Castle Mhan, which was glowing gold in the morning light.

THE DAYS PASSED WITH a heavy toll on everyone's hands and everyone's hearts. It wore them down, and they realised their victory was not to have lost everything and to have avoided complete annihilation. The Mhan Royal Army was decimated. Only a handful of fighters, mages, clerics and knights remained. The mechanised infantry had been buried alive, and none survived.

The families in the production halls came out wailing when their loved ones did not return. Of course, the babies and children did not understand what was happening, but the solemn cries of their elders imparted sadness in their hearts, and they also shed tears onto the soil.

Each and every one of the soldiers was buried according to their family's wishes. Many of those who had been turned undead now lay rotten and unrecognisable. They were all consecrated as unsung heroes of Nai and cremated bar one. This unknown person was buried at the entrance to Castle Mhan with a tombstone inscription: *Here lay the hero of the Great Battle of the year of her majesty, Maya's 5th Rule*. Families from across Concordia came to pay tribute to this unknown soldier, and every mother and father was sure it was their son or daughter who lay buried under the soil.

The season of Shinar came to an end, and the heat of Kalor descended upon the land, with the moon Aura high in the sky reflecting her golden hue across the landscape. The war was still fresh in everyone's minds, but the desire to celebrate their survival and the excitement for their future generations was palpable. Therefore, the queen declared a festival across all her lands to be celebrated every year on the first day of Kalor, known as *The Glimmer in the Darkness*, to celebrate the idea that even if everything seems lost, there is *always* hope.

Bonfires burned across the land at night, with the castle illuminated by Gnossian fireworks which sparkled and danced across the celestial faces of Annah and Aura. People danced in the streets and imbibed drinks of citric fruits, fermented beverages made from grain and ate food that tasted of happiness. The food was filling, and it was tasty. It crumbled in their mouths and made their taste buds dance too. They were hungry, and everything tasted amazing.

Deep within Castle Mhan, Queen Maya sat upon her throne, captivated as Aedan told his story of how he befriended Vicho and escaped; how the knights saved him, but he returned to save them. The queen was very excited by Aedan's stories and took a liking to him, but Aedan only had eyes for Ferni. In his mind, he wanted to return to Sylvinar, and he would keep living as a Sa'ami. After all, it was all he had known his whole life; he could not imagine living any other way. How would that even be possible?

The night drew on into the wee hours of the morning. As dawn broke, the queen took her place on the royal balcony and addressed all the citizens gathered in the city of Mhan.

Queen Maya spoke with drunken dignity. "My people. Tonight is a night we remember the fallen, but we do not pity them, for their deaths were not in vain. We remember the fallen tonight, but we do not feel sad for their passing, for they are now enjoying the afterlife. Tonight we remember the fallen because they are heroes. Tonight we remember the fallen because they will never die in our hearts. This is a night for celebration. We celebrate because we are still here. Nothing the darkness could muster broke our will. Nothing the darkness employed could defeat us. Nothing the darkness could do, or will ever do, threatens us. We celebrate because we fought and we won. We celebrate because we are resilient. We celebrate because we are the free and glorious people of Concordia, and nothing will ever take that away from us! So, enjoy your night, for tomorrow is a holiday for all time so future generations can say, we are great, we vanquished the darkness, and we will never let the darkness forget we are still here and waiting for them if they come again!"

The city roared in the breaking light. Drums echoed, and wind instruments hummed. The cacophony of music and dance travelled on the wind across the land. People laughed, ate, drank, and danced the night away. People cried and hugged. They kissed one another in joy. The soil was drenched with spilt juices and fermented drinks. The air was filled with the odour of cooked meats, pastries and smoke. Everything was saturated: the ground, the air, the streets and the peoples' hearts.

Amongst all the jokes and tomfoolery, Aedan broke the mood with a question directed at the queen, "Your majesty, what of the law of phylacteries?"

The laughing around the table stopped, and the queen gave Aedan a firm gaze, "What of it?"

"General Uriah might wish to chime in here, but it did cause us almost to lose the war. Had control of the mages not been possible to acquire while they were behind our lines, we would have overthrown the enemy much sooner and spared many lives. It is obvious the law needs to be abolished like in every other country on the face of Alteria," Aedan said with a smile.

The queen turned her head to the general, who lowered his gaze in sadness.

The queen smiled. She thought Aedan had a point but could not let him lead her decision, "You are right, Aedan. It was a tragedy. It was no different than the Rhan'i forcing Marko to scuttle the tunnels and bury every man in his contingent. These are the things that happen in war. The enemy forces us to question our ways, our thoughts, but if we give in to the fear and make rash decisions without careful analysis, we risk causing more harm than good. I will be discussing the law of mages with my advisors over the next few days before I decide what is best." She emphasised the *I* in her closing statement, so it was clear to Aedan that the decision was hers alone, not influenced by his comments. She liked Aedan but would never let him tell her what to do, but she did want him to stay. "And what of you Aedan?"

Aedan was fuming over her political manoeuvring to avoid the issue at hand, so he replied with a slight sharpness in his tone, "What of it?"

"What are you to do with your future? You are not a Sa'ami. You defeated the greatest foe to have beset Concordia in my lifetime. I would recommend you join the Mhan Royal Army, right here in this very castle. Your accolades in battle grant you your very own command and the experience you need to maybe, one day, if you are dedicated and lucky, become a great general of the same calibre as Uriah." Maya smiled and thought twice before adding, "I would like that very much."

Everyone on the table turned their heads at Aedan in anticipation of what he would say. It was apparent there was tension between these two. *What will Aedan say?*

"Thank you, your majesty, for your very generous offer. These things you mention raise many questions, but I must not make any rash decisions and carefully analyse my options before deciding. I also know that the colour of our eyes and the build of our bodies does not determine what we know to be true in our heart. I am Sa'ami. Born and raised. That will never change. I will leave with my people tomorrow, back to Sylvinar. There is much work to be done." He wiped his mouth, stood up from his chair, pushed the chair in and finished off, "I am tired. Goodnight." He walked out of the room thinking how he wanted to tell the queen what he thought of her but knew she would order him thrown into prison for all eternity if he uttered the words cursing in his mind.

Aedan's Choice

It was a hot morning. Kalor had set in. The sweat trickled over Aedan's brow as he helped load the caravan for the trip back to Sylvinar. All of Sylvinar had amassed in front of Castle Mhan in the city streets. There were carriages shackled to Bulorses; large and powerful, two-legged, work animals with muscular bodies and long faces with large, circular snouts. They were arranged in pairs to keep each other company on long trips; they would converse with a series of neighs and snorts, discussing their favourite pastures to graze on. There were long lines of Sa'ami passing along sacks of belongings to each other in a long procession like ants at work.

Ferni approached where Aedan was working and waved at him.

"Hey Jargie, can you take over the loading for a little while?" He asked the Sa'ami scholar behind him.

Jargie nodded and stepped up to where Aedan was standing.

Aedan strode towards Ferni. He approached her with a smirk on his face, reached out and took her hands in his, "Isn't this exciting? We finally get to go home. I miss home. I can't wait to see it again. It all feels like a distant memory to me. Aren't you excited?"

Ferni looked down, then back up at Aedan, "No, not really."

Aedan was stunned, "What do you mean?"

"Aedan, I need to talk to you about something," Ferni said with sadness in her voice and thoughts clogging up her mind.

"Of course, Ferni. Anything," Aedan replied with positive affirmation and support in his voice.

Ferni took a deep breath and looked deep into Aedan's eyes, "Aedan, I really do love you. So, so much. More than I ever thought possible. You have given me the most beautiful memories of a lifetime, but I don't think we will work as a couple. As husband and wife." She stopped and waited to see if Aedan would reply.

Aedan felt his heart break. His chest ached, his hands trembled, and he wanted to throw up. He could not move or even talk. He was frozen in panic. Finally, he managed to blurt out, "Very well."

Ferni pulled her hands away from Aedan, "I am also in a lot of pain. I had imagined my whole life what it would be like to share my future with you, but now, that is not possible. It will just end up in tears for you and me. I know your future is bright, so don't let this hold you back. I'm truly sorry, my dear, dear Aedan." Ferni turned and walked away. She burst out crying and then ran into the crowd, back to her father, who hugged her. He ushered her away while looking back at Aedan.

Aedan stood there in shock for what seemed like an eternity to him. He remembered his first kiss with Ferni and how she had looked at him. He remembered how she had told him she would love him forever, and nothing in the whole world would ever change that. He remembered how he had felt true happiness. But now, all he could feel was emptiness. His body felt nauseating and light. His heart felt heavy. He turned and shuffled down a street, looking for a place to hide in the shadows.

A group of five young boys ran out of any alley towards him. The eldest boy, who was still pretty much a little kid, asked, "Excuse me, sir. Can I have your autograph?" He held out a cloth and a sharpened crayon.

Aedan stopped walking and reached out. He signed his name. Each boy in the group took turns asking for Aedan's autograph. He signed without thought, his mind punishing him with ideas of what could have been. Even though people surrounded him, he cut a lonely figure, and deep down inside his heart, he wished he was a Sa'ami.

Within a few hours, the Sa'ami caravan was ready to begin its journey back to Sylvinar Forest. Kainan was busy gathering everyone together and making sure the line was orderly. Ferni was impressed by how well he commanded everyone and how organised he was.

Ferni grabbed Kainan by the arm as he walked past her, "I just wanted to thank you for staying behind in Sylvinar and guarding us when everyone else had abandoned us."

Kainan nodded at Ferni in acknowledgement, "It was my duty. But I now have people to lead and no time to waste on idle chatter."

He walked away and continued issuing orders to families, so they all knew what to do once the caravan started moving.

Eldoran had broken away from all the commotion of the caravan and was wandering the nearby streets of Mhan. He almost failed to spot Aedan sitting atop the roof of the tavern. He looked up and beckoned him down, "Come down, my son. We are preparing to leave."

Aedan did not look down at Eldoran. Instead, he kept his eye on Ferni in the distance, "I'm not your son. My life has been a lie. An illusion." He gave his father a look of contempt, thinking how many times his father had manipulated him with magic.

Eldoran was a bit unsure what to say, so he let Jasi speak for him, "Son. Please read this. Your mother wrote it." He held out a note.

Aedan looked down. He had seen his mother in photos and had always loved reading her old letters. He wished he had known her. But he was afraid reading the note would upset him even more.

Eldoran spoke, "Come down. Read the note. Hear your mother's voice. All your worries will evaporate as if nothing ever troubled your heart." His voice was but a whisper. It floated through the air and right into Aedan's heart.

Aedan felt full of courage. He climbed down from where he was perched, took the note from his father's hand, and read it. He was amazed he could hear his mother's voice with each syllable even though he had never met her.

My dear beautiful Aedan. It pains me so much to know I will not witness you grow up into a man. But, alas, I am mortal, and Nai wishes me back in her bosom. If you are reading this, then you have come to know your true identity. Your father loves you more than you will ever know, and I apologise for his gruffness. I assure you he wants the best for you.

This must be very hard for you after a lifetime of being raised as a Sa'ami, and you probably feel betrayed and lied to. You probably think your entire life is a lie. This is not true! What you have lived is real and is no less real simply because your future is not what you expected. On the contrary, you have something no other human has. You have been raised as a Sa'ami, and I hope you never lose what you have grown to love and understand just because you are taller than us.

We could have handed you to the orphanage in Castle Mhan, but their laws on magic were not something we trusted very much. You are, after all, imbued with something more than I can explain. Grandor will try to tell you the end of the world is coming, and you are the return of Yama. If none of that makes sense to you right now, don't worry, I am sure he will explain his theory to you soon enough. What I know is you have an immense amount of power locked up inside you, capable of levelling entire nations. That is something your father and I have both felt. Evil is drawn to power, so we wanted to protect you until you were old enough to defend yourself and make your own decisions.

So what now? Will you stay with us, the Sa'ami? Will you follow Grandor and become a druid? Or, will you join the Royal Army and train as a warrior? Or maybe, just maybe, you will find your own path? That last choice is the hardest, and perhaps you are not ready for it yet, but one day you will; so, feel assured whatever you choose will be the correct choice.

For I love you from beyond the veil, my dear child. I always have and always will. I know you will find strength and rise above everything to become who you need to be. So hold your head high and take charge. Be a Campesino my son.

Aedan felt a hand on his shoulder. He turned around and saw his father's eyes clearer than he had ever seen them. He noticed all the wrinkles and crevices on the old man's face. Tiny hairs and blemishes. Every little speckle and every slight imperfection around the iris – things he had never noticed before. He loved his father so much.

Eldoran hugged Aedan and asked, "So what will you do, my son?"

Aedan fought back the tears and replied, "I do not know yet, but I know I will not be returning to Sylvinar with you today."

Eldoran pulled away, "I know. I hope one day you come for a visit."

Aedan nodded.

Kainan's voice in the distance was ushering the caravan.

Eldoran glanced away, then back at Aedan. He did not want this moment to pass, "I will be waiting for you." He extended his hand and offered Aedan a handshake.

Aedan took his father's hand and shook it, "I will return in the not-too-distant future. I promise." Then he laughed and gave his father another hug, but this time it was uplifting and joyous.

Eldoran laughed, "Thank you. I needed that."

With that, he turned around and walked towards the caravan. Aedan climbed back up onto the roof of the tavern and watched the caravan ride off into the horizon all afternoon until the darkness of night set, and he could no longer see it. So, he climbed down and checked into a room in the tavern's inn and had a good night's rest.

Old Friends

Aedan spotted Grandor amongst all the patrons in the morning. He approached the druid and took a seat opposite him. Tanke was napping on the floor beside Grandor. He did not even have a scar on his leg. Grandor finished off the mango he was eating and threw the core into his bowl.

He pushed another bowl with a selection of stone fruits towards Aedan, "Have some food."

Aedan took a bite out of one of the peaches. Its succulent juices trickled down his cheek. "Good to see Tanke is good as new. I need to study those notes you gave me a bit more."

Grandor smiled, "We have a long journey back to Agwa'den."

Vicho peaked his head out from underneath one of Aedan's sleeves. Aedan grabbed some bread sitting on the table and broke off a piece for Vicho, who took it up in his little paws and started nibbling away at it. "What makes you think I am heading to Agwa'den with you?"

Grander nodded at Vicho, "Looks like you have a familiar to me, albeit a tiny one, so you're practically almost a druid."

Vicho looked at Grandor, quite annoyed at the joke.

He laughed and continued, "Don't take it personally. You did save his life after all, so who cares what I say? Back to you Aedan. I want you to come with me and help me rebuild Agwa'den. I also believe there is a greater evil than anyone believes, and what happened last month was but a tiny prelude to the evil which will beset these lands in the not-too-distant future. I am not sure when, but the signs are there. The ancients are returning."

Aedan stopped eating the large plum, looked up at Grandor and spoke with a mouth full of juicy fruit, "The ancients? What are the ancients?"

Grandor leaned in with a whisper, "You may want to ask the queen. She has a private library with everything about them locked away. Just like her phylacteries, she keeps another dangerous secret away from prying eyes. The ancients formed this world and everything we know, and they can destroy it."

Aedan wiped his mouth with the back of his sleeve and burped, "You mean Akh and Nai?"

Grander nodded, "Nai is the creator, Akh the destroyer. This is the way it is supposed to be. Every thousand years, Akh rises to lay waste to Nai's creations, and then she rebuilds the world over the next millennia. But the last cycle was interrupted by the sorcerer Yama. He sealed Akh away under what we now refer to as Mount Akh. But the spell was not strong enough, something went wrong, and it is only a matter of time before Akh rises again. That is why darkness has returned. That is why these lands will never be safe. That is why you will never be safe. Unless we unravel the mystery and can return balance to the world."

Aedan held Grandor's gaze. In his heart, he knew what he wanted. He wanted to find his birth parents, but he did not know where to begin. This druid believed Aedan was the creation of Yama, but deep down in his heart Aedan knew he had a normal mother and father somewhere out in the world. He just had to find them. But Eldoran could not help him, the druid was too obsessed with his doomsday prophecies, and the queen would use him for her gain.

Then, his choice was as clear as the light shining off Lum.

He smiled at the druid, "Let enjoy each other's company while I think about what I want to do. Please do not rush me. It is an important decision after all."

Grandor nodded. "Take your time. For now, tell me some stories about the last few days. I have missed so much."

Aedan spat out a plum stone into his bowl, having sucked it dry, "No druid. You tell me what you've been up to."

The day played out, and the two shared stories. They laughed and reminisced. Vicho would twitch his little nose and scamper under Aedan's arm during the scary parts of the tales. Tanke lapped up the soup in his bowl and farted, sending everyone in the room running out gasping for air.

Outside, Aura's golden shape materialised as Lum's bright rays were eclipsed by Lumbra, heralding in another hot night of Kalor. The night erupted into a buzzing rumble of insect mating songs, saturating the balmy air with the noise of life.

Once again, all was well in Concordia.

< < < < > > > >

Don't miss out!

Visit the website below and you can sign up to receive emails whenever D.A. Di Muro publishes a new book. There's no charge and no obligation.

https://books2read.com/r/B-A-GPZQ-ZUTTB

Did you love *Manah Wars - Glimmer in the Darkness*? Then you should read *The Original English Transcription of The Book of Dwd.* by D.A. Di Muro!

THE FOLLOWING RESEARCH IS BASED ON HISTORICAL RECORDS AND OFFICIAL SOURCE DOCUMENTS

WARNING: *The content is dark, and we, as academics, warn readers who suffer from depression, paranoia, or any mental illness to reconsider reading this book. It has been triggering to many who have encountered it, and once you read it, you can't unread it.*

Unveiling the Mysteries of The Book of Dwd: A Brief Historical and Archaeological Analysis

This academic publication delves into the intriguing historical context and potential significance of *The Book of Dwd*, a unique manuscript reportedly discovered in *Napoleon Bonaparte's* possession after his campaign in *Egypt*. This paper briefly explores the book's origins, contents, and implications, including the context of artifacts stolen during **Napoleon's campaign** and their potential historical connections to *The Book of Dwd*. Drawing upon historical evidence and theoretical postulations, this study sheds light on the enigmatic nature of The Book of Dwd and its potential implications for understanding ancient Egyptian religious and philosophical thought and possibly the ***most significant religious artefact ever discovered***

.

The cover illustration is a cross-section of a pillar damaged during the barrage of cannon fire inflicted by Napoleon on the enemy's troops, where they discovered *The Book of Dwd*. After solving the geometric and planetary puzzle on the archaic treasure box, the papyri scroll rose from the central piece.

The **English translation** was found in the possession of *Napoleon Bonaparte* after his defeat at Waterloo (June 18, 1815). The text is purportedly translated from **Demotic**, from the papyri scroll in his possession. The papyri scroll is believed to have travelled to the *British Museum* under the *Treaty of Alexandria*, just like *The Rosetta Stone* and many other relics in his hoard. *The Rosetta Stone* is the only artefact displayed after the spoils of war vanished. The *French Commission des Sciences et des Arts* and the *Institut d'Egypte* kept the rest, who eventually lost many items in *accidental* fires.

This publication aims to shed light on the historical context surrounding **The Book of Dwd**, including its potential connections to **legendary Egyptian sites** such as the **Pyramid of Giza**, the **Well of Souls**, and **The Sphinx**. By examining the artefacts and their possible ties to ancient Egyptian mythology, we aim to illuminate the *cultural significance* of **The Book of Dwd**.

References:

1. Champollion, J. F. (1822). Précis du système hiéroglyphique des anciens Égyptiens.2. Budge, E. A. W. (1895). The Book of the

Dead: The Hieroglyphic Transcript of the Papyrus of Ani. Kegan Paul, Trench, Trübner & Co.3. Kugler, F. (1907). Sternkunde und Sterndienst in Babel: Astronomische Geographie in Babylonien. Teubner.4. Zaki Pasha, A. (1925). Kitab Al-Fihrist: Bibliographical Report on Books, Manuscripts, and Publications. Al-'Ummiyya.5. Bouchard, P.-F.-X. (1802). The Discovery of the Rosetta Stone. Journal of Antiquities, 5(2), 123-137. DOI:10.12345/ja.123.4566. West, J. A. (1990). The Sphinx and its Astronomical Significance. Egyptological Review, 40(3), 213-228.7. Hancock, G. (2001). The Well of Souls: Exploring Ancient Legends. Mysteries and Myths Quarterly, 12(4), 345-362.8. Hancock, G. (2003). Divination in Ancient Egyptian Temples. Journal of Esoteric Studies, 28(1), 56-71. DOI:10.6789/jes.12345

Also by D.A. Di Muro

Manah Wars

Manah Wars - Glimmer in the Darkness

Standalone

The Original English Transcription of The Book of Dwd.

Watch for more at https://thefantasybro.com.

About the Author

David's journey from the humble beginnings of Sydney's West to the forefront of creative expression is a testament to resilience, passion, and unwavering determination. Born to two migrant farmers who escaped military persecution in Argentina, David's upbringing instilled in him a profound appreciation for hard work and the pursuit of dreams against all odds.As a child, David attended St. Brendan's and St. Felix's Primary Schools, where he developed a thirst for knowledge and a love for creativity. His formative years continued at De La Salle Brother's High School, where he thrived academically and discovered his innate talent for technology.In 2013, a new chapter began for David with the birth of his first daughter. This profound moment prompted him to reassess his priorities, leading him to the introspective realm of creative writing.Today, David's creative pursuits span a diverse range of interests, from his acclaimed series "Manah Wars" to his exploration of esoteric knowledge in "The Original English Transcription of The

Book of DWD." Through his writing, David invites readers to delve into worlds of imagination and introspection, where truth and fiction blur, leaving them questioning what is real and what is not.In essence, David's story is one of resilience, perseverance, and the enduring power of creativity to transcend barriers and inspire others to pursue their passions relentlessly. As he continues to chart new territories in the realm of storytelling, his legacy serves as a beacon of hope for aspiring creatives everywhere.Watch videos at: BigNose.com.au

Read more at https://bignose.com.au.

About the Publisher

BigNose.com.au sells books, book shelves, whimsy and everything in between. You can also read about D.A. Di Muro and access the services he provides across Sydney.

Read more at https://bignose.com.au.